living
a life of
unconditional
love

HOW TO GET IT, GROW IT, KEEP IT, AND SHARE IT

MEGAN LOOSE

Virginia

Published in the United States by WriteLife Publishing

(An imprint of Boutique of Quality Books Publishing Company, Inc.)
www.writelife.com

Printed in the United States of America
978-1-60808-221-6 (p)
978-1-60808-222-3 (e)

Library of Congress Control Number 2019954556

Book design by Robin Krauss, www.bookformatters.com
Cover design by Rebecca Lown, www.rebeccalowndesign.com
First editor: Olivia Swenson
Second editor: Caleb Guard

PRAISE FOR MEGAN LOOSE
and *Living a Life of Unconditional Love*

"Megan Loose has such an extraordinary way of covering the topic of forgiveness that you can almost not help but to forgive. The entirety of the topics she covers to lead you to unconditional love is equally thorough, compelling, and transformative! The book is life changing!"

— Deva DeAngelis - Earth Restoration Scientist, Activist, Collaborator, and Educator

"A beautifully written book that embraces the reader with all of the tenants of *Unconditional Love*. The meditations are powerful and gently guide you to understanding the principles of this book!"

— Claudia M. Baca - Author of seven nonfiction books; Principal, Project Management Consulting Services

"I absolutely loved *Living a Life of Unconditional Love!*" Megan's words are thought provoking and insightful. This is definitely a book that I will reference again and again!"

— Eliza Mendez - Independent Sales Representative

"Reading this book has infused my life with a constant state of joy. Megan Loose offers a brilliant set of concepts and techniques that can certainly change lives. This book has helped me heal my energy and given me the clarity and courage to live a life of unconditional love."

— Conrad J. Boeding M.A.

- Psychotherapist; Author of *The Love Disorder*

"This personal energy work is the hottest new healing trend in self-help!"

— Cynthia Weeks

- Owner of spiritual store Luna's Mandala

TABLE OF CONTENTS

I dedicate this to my Beloved Paul—
my eternal love, support machine, and generous, handsome,
amusing place to fall.
And to my girls—
Alhana, a true beauty and pure soul,
and Clara, magnificence personified.
To my constant furry and divine writing companions.
And to all who have mattered to my ever-growing soul—
far beyond thank you.
I feel overwhelming gratitude for your presence in my life.

"We have to take care of this Earth,
And we have to take care of each other."

—Unknown

ACKNOWLEDGMENTS

To Terri Leidich, you are more than publisher, owner, and author. You are the beacon of light I prayed for to help get my healing out to the world. All these years I looked to spread love to the masses, and you made it possible. Thank you for your vision, your belief in us together as a team, and your generosity in seeing this dream come true.

Thank you to the entire community at BQB and Write Life Publishing, especially my steadfast editor Olivia Swenson. You contoured this book into its present form, and I thank you for shaping my passages with meaningful changes. Your always willing guidance and expertise was invaluable.

Thank you to Lauren Drabble my hard working ingenious and steadying publicist. You have done so much to uplift this endeavor and help in its manifestation. I could not have done this without you.

To Eva Thoemke my web Goddess and computer guru from "The Visual Aide", thank you for all your work, advice, hand holding, and belief in these messages. You make the world a better place.

Thank you to my second editor Caleb Guard for your fine tuning and finishing. Thank you to the design staff, especially Rebecca Lown and Robin Krauss, and to all who help distribute, market, and make this book available to help humanity.

Much thanks to my family, friends, and teacher Paul Miller, and to anyone who in any way helped this entity into being.

I am grateful for every one of you, and I acknowledge your light. Together we are all powerful, and the world is healing with love.

INTRODUCTION

Unconditional love: An abiding affection or devotion, enjoyment of or interest in, not limited or subject to conditions or stipulations; absolute, unlimited, complete. Deeper than acceptance, unconditional love means always, no matter what, constantly, forever, actually, truly, and absolutely. Predominating, pervading, whole, and continual. No questions, no judgments, no criteria. Given without a single demand or desire for any return, given without guilt, obligation, or ego. Not toward an end . . . *just love.*

Unconditional love—what more could anyone need? What more could anyone give? What loftier goal could ever exist for us to study, encompass, and live? What other attribute would so help those we know, all who we encounter, and the world? It costs nothing to find, increase, or give. It takes nothing from us in order to fill others with it; in fact, the more we give, the more we have. We can share unconditional love with family, friends, loved ones, or strangers. It can disarm enemies, heal wounds, and show firsthand how much beauty the Universe holds. It is the best teacher, with the biggest, most valuable, and longest lasting lessons. It contains the magic of teaching us about ourselves while we learn, grow, and share it.

MY STORY

My great-great-grandmother on my mom's side was an Irish famine immigrant, third of four sisters out of five children who made it over by boat, utilizing their cottage industry of making lace and linen from bog flax after farming was over for the day, from which all spoils went to English landlords. They arrived before records were even kept at Ellis Island and headed straight to Morrison, Colorado, during the gold rush and cattle drives, opening a boarding house for the miners until each could make enough money to send for the next sister. Our family has been in Colorado ever since. As a hardy nature-loving mountain girl, I like to say my roots in Colorado go all the way down to the core of the earth. I grew up in a household poorer than most, and remember my parents crying at tax time, calling us boat people.

I found myself through music at age nine. Music was always a part of our household. I joined the orchestra playing cello and soon after joined the drum corps of the bagpipe band my mother played in—a tangibly magical world I would remain in, and even shine in and lead, for almost three decades. The competitive pipe band community was rich in its own valuable life lessons and love—as well as hate.

I came into my consciousness at age nine as well. My writing changed, my awareness keyed in, and I began to understand what was happening around me. When we were young, my parents brilliantly taught me and my older brother, sister, and twin sister about different religions each Sunday. Hearing that souls were born again and again to learn in this school called earth resonated with me. When I learned meditation, I woke up. I was soon creating my own silly meditations with an encouraging mother. I felt deeply and was highly sensitive.

It was my mother who first explained to me that the colors and light I saw around others were their energy, called auras. Later, from books and psychic school, I learned that part of what comprised the aura was the function of main energy meridians in the body, known as chakras (the Sanskrit word for "wheel"). Energy I saw coming out of people seemed to correspond with whether these chakras were open, spinning, and bright, or closed, stuck, and cloudy. Chakra health is important to the quality of life and gives clues to the health of other vital organs running the physical body.

My parents and I talked a great deal about the soul, or the part of Spirit that resides in people. Later I began seeing and hearing those who had passed on, as well as working energy with the spirits of living people. I learned that karma was what we held against ourselves—emotions, experiences, trauma—from life to life until we engaged in the integration of that energy. Angels have taught me, spoken to me, and helped heal me through years of difficulty.

I met my soul mate my junior year in high school. Paul was a drum instructor for the marching band. We married when I was twenty and soon had two magical daughters. One of the few things I knew I wanted at that time was children.

In 1995 I discovered Feng Shui, the ancient Chinese and Indian art science of how energy flows. It described how I had lived through colors, numbers, and elements, and why I moved objects around my bedroom intuitively. I felt its tenants as a sense. When I discovered that Feng Shui paralleled what I had been doing, I needed to learn everything about this divine form of enhancing good energy and shifting negative, and I studied and became certified through The Taoist School of Feng Shui.

In addition to studying spirituality since age nine, in 2007 I embarked on a deepening journey to specifically find more healing. I exhausted every book I could find. Years of classes and chakra balancing/aura cleansings later, my husband and I became certified energy healers and readers. This wisdom from the Berkeley Psychic Institute tradition changed our lives and was a catalyst for creating the life we always dreamed of.

We learned to work our spaces, look at past lives, and heal others. We learned that the point of each life we live is our individual and collective journey toward enlightenment. Enlightenment occurs when all we carry with us is integrated into our soul. Every lesson is learned, every moment is grateful, and we are love. As we feel and then share love, our souls are uplifted, and our spirit remains with our body more often because it feels so good there. This connects us to the light, and fills us purely. Thus we are enlightened.

Suffering several tragedies in my younger years, such as poverty, abuse, trauma, and illness, led me to wonder about love—and its absence—and to search relentlessly for it. And when I found it, *felt* it, unconditional love tied together everything I had learned throughout my spiritual quests of the heart spanning almost four decades. Finding unconditional love answered everything, unveiled everything, and then healed it too.

ABOUT THE BOOK

Before we incarnate here, we all make soul agreements, or contracts with other souls who we love or will need in this lifetime. Everyone we interact with, like it or not, is a teacher we agreed to participate with. I have many pacts with souls in order to approach enlightenment and to do what I agreed to help the Universe with this time around. One of my agreements is to feel and spread unconditional love, and to that purpose, I present *Living a Life of Unconditional Love: How to Get It, Grow It, Keep It, and Share It*.

This book begins by touching on all aspects of love. We begin together to identify love in all its varieties and disguises, both beautiful and profane, so we can grow toward the perfection of the love that brought us here, and to which our lives are spent searching to be brought back to, consciously or unconsciously. Part One speaks to this search, at our cores, for *getting* abiding love, and for recognizing it as it arrives.

In all our relationships and activities, it is this source of being loved for who we are, no matter what, that we reach to embrace. We want to feel loved. Some of us may be desperately seeking love, and in this process attract situations and relationships that leave us emotionally scarred or spiritually wounded. We come to know in Part One what living a life of unconditional love looks like, and how we can heal its opposite through loving ourselves, forgiving, learning through joy over pain, and letting others go who keep us from experiencing our highest love.

Growing unconditional love becomes tangible as this work continues in Part Two with active meditation and energy principles for our everyday life. Learning the power of our focus and perspective leads to the heart of expanding love. This part invites you to cultivate love's presence through observation, nature, manifesting, and practical techniques. By working through this book, you will see and feel unconditional love everywhere.

Part Three invites us to *keep* the love we have found thus far. We learn how to keep our unconditional love despite loss and distraction, and with healing. A level of havingness enters as we awaken our ability to hold on to what we desire in a healthy way, which includes treating our bodies well. If we cannot completely "have" something, we limit its capacity to affect us. Upping our havingness increases what can come to us. Sustaining love's presence in our lives is important to the final piece: sharing it.

I have dedicated the fourth part of this book to helpful methods and regular routines that ensure we are living and *sharing* a life of unconditional love. These are common actions, thought processes, and practices that have profoundly changed life experiences for the masses and have personally increased my ability to love without condition. We instill love in our days with the simplicity of reachable tools like sunlight, water, surrendering, breathing, and nature.

Sanaya Roman in *Spiritual Growth: Being your Higher Self* embodies our best reason and approach for unconditional love: "[Go] beyond the illusions created by living in the density of matter and [remember] the truth of the higher realms." Unconditional love is at the basis of truth and matter.

USING THIS BOOK

This book comes with healing. If you are reading a book such as this, then I suspect you have been searching through many ideas, teachers, and paths toward inner and outer health. Wanting to be loving, lovable, and loved is natural and possible in the pure state of unconditional love. Acceptance in its entirety brings experiential lessons, and ultimately purpose, joy, and peace to our human existence.

This book invites you to absorb its information through various meditations sprinkled throughout its chapters, allowing you to pause, take in, and contemplate so your reading can be felt. I suggest reading each short meditation, centering exercise, or visualization in its entirety as you come across them, and then taking your time to engage it in whatever way feels best to you. Perhaps that means pausing between reading and performing each line, recording yourself reading the lines aloud with pauses for action, or having a trusted friend lead you. Just get into your space, whatever that means for you, and ponder what resonates with you in the moment. Note anything of interest following each meditation, either mentally or in a notebook. No matter how you approach the meditations, take heart—your spirit knows what you need.

None of this information or guidance is meant to

replace your own knowing. This is simply a sharing and an acknowledgment of my process, exhilaration, and journey with Spirit toward the power and healing of love. This is simply an expression of my truth, and we create harmony when we all honor our own truths. Take what resonates with your own lightening vibration. *Feel and listen* from that glowing and beautiful soul that you uniquely possess. Out of unconditional love, leave the rest for another waiting with openness.

BEGIN TO LOVE

Learning unconditional love is moment by moment in our daily lives. As we begin to see patterns of when love was not present, we realize what the world needs. Becoming an arbiter for and most zealous proponent of love is a worthy vocation. Choose more carefully what you accept and put out.

Unconditional love will bring the peace we seek and create around us the world we would *choose* to live in. It amends any trespasses we might feel, including from within, if bestowed internally. It lets us walk with Spirit, allowing us to receive as our highest self. It corrects the eyes with which we perceive pain, hatred, or injustice, and it brings harmony and balance to every action we take, each moment we live. It teaches us valuable lessons about our potential. It guides us to treat others—and want to treat others—with unwavering compassion. Unconditional love will fulfill us, expand our joy, lovingly lead us to feel at one with all, bring purpose to our lives, and enlighten our paths immeasurably.

Here we learn ways of either releasing or relating real love to people or situations we thought might repel it. We better our lives through being aware of what goes on around us, how we let it affect us, and how we affect everything else. We learn where unconditional love starts, and how each of us can get it, grow it, keep it, and share it. We will transcend our actions toward our loving power, and with mystical sources at our side, unconditional love will open doors for us to the life, health, and abundance we have always imagined.

It is all about love. Light and grow yourself. Fresh air and friendship helps; so does nature and nurturing, sunshine and silence, moving water and removing energy blocks. Our entire environment and life is here to grant us wisdom and love. Climb a tree or hug a person to gain some perspective; it will change more than just your afternoon. Be yourself, love yourself, and accept yourself. Once you have felt that, extend it to others. Then nothing else matters, nothing hurts, and everything finds its rightful place and vibration. How to love unconditionally is easy: just begin.

Let love confirm to us our best and greatest way. Love opens our hearts to grand expansion and leads the way to bliss. Love carries with it the seed of hope and faith, and it encircles our lives with the highest and brightest light known to us. Love enraptures our being and creates healing in every cell inside us. When we are by love possessed, anything is possible, and abundantly probable. We can see forever with the clarity of love and can feel peace deep within the pulsing of its potent power. Love compels us to connect our energy toward the Divine and to be the dream we envision. Through the most magical and real gift of love, we come to accept ourselves, allow diversity in others, and know deeply the beauty of our purpose.

Let us then bring in light to our hearts, Divinity to our thoughts, and unconditional love through ourselves, filling, nourishing, and sustaining each other and our planet. It is both greater and easier than we know. It will change not only our lives, but also the lives of all with whom we generously and caringly share its energy. It is an excellent, purposeful, and powerful achievement. Like your angelic spirit and the luscious stuff the stars are made of, unconditional love is an ideal and idyllic accomplishment to which to aspire. May you have great luck and study basking in its supreme glory.

PART ONE

Getting Love in All Conditions

While there are not actually kinds of love, there are limitless forms in which love appears, and we look at some of those here. There is but one all-pervasive light energy of love. Where love is created, it is pure, whole, divine, and beautiful, but it is how we learn to love (or not to love) as humans that determines the sort of relationship we have with it. Part of getting love comes with focus on forgiveness, as well as learning how to love ourselves.

What of our own perverse perceptions have we put in love? What are our beliefs about its access or limits? Are we allowing or resisting the forces of love? And how have the ways in which love exists in our own lives caused us to twist it into our own illusions? Even control or insecurity may be one's best attempts at giving love. Everything is either a degree of love or a degree of going away from love, and we look at gaining love through joy instead of pain. In this first part, we also evaluate relationships that might be unhealthy, and we learn how to release.

Love is shaped by countless factors, and it then shapes us. Society and culture shape love; so do the past, our spirit, our desires, and our families. It can be absent if we block it, it can wait for us if we do not notice it but want it, or it can heal and expand into every space if we but let it. It is the one truth of our Universe but has unbounded guises and features depending upon its use, neglect, or recognition. How has love been shown to or kept from you, and where in our search will you find your answers? We will delve into a few common yet profound faces of love's potential. Understanding these will allow us to reach our own infinite unconditional love.

I am fulfilled
when I am connected with Divinity.
I am satisfied
in nature.
I feel free
when I take a moment,
and loved
in every breath of awareness.
I am light,
able to spread upon the Universe.
And when I have peace,
I manifest dreams.
I embrace
the truth and present.
I follow right action,
finally.
My life
opens with acceptance.
My purposes
are given generously.
With new faith,
love is everywhere,
patiently waiting to walk with my soul.
In all this, revealed
is unconditional love.

CHAPTER 1

Why Unconditional Love?

The phrase "unconditional love" has come to mean so much in my life. In the last few pages of an exciting book, *The Intenders of the Highest Good*, Tony Burroughs inserts those words only in his description of the perfection of humanity living our sacred best together. It is potent to learn how others use this term, and of the impenetrable force it carries within its simplicity. It moved me in a personally powerful confirmation to know that his view of the best feelings that can be felt, the highest vibrations that can be known, and the dearest visions possible for humanity were that of unconditional love.

This chapter explores our purpose on earth. We learn how getting unconditional love and then sharing it is an integral part of fulfilling that purpose. Delve into how love presents itself and learn to feel it expanding as your spirit shows how unconditional love is part of your purpose.

HIGHER PURPOSE

We all are here for a higher purpose. Yes, we are here to learn the land rules of work, play, relationships, career, etc., and to find joy in the earth school while illuminating the human experience. However, it is about what we do despite the earthly obligations, games, and obstacles that magnifies our goodness and fulfills our souls. It is not how well we appear to play these mundane roles, but how we play them as to allow for time and focus on our significant higher work, which adds to humanity and the evolution of the human spirit.

When we focus on our higher purpose for this lifetime, which looks different for each person but involves making the world a better place while also making our heart sing, the Universe applauds our callings and supports our tasks. It then assures our needs are met so we can focus on our true path. In order to reach the height of potential, the Universe needs us to fulfill our best selves and experience living deeply as humans. Spirit rides to our aid within love, making certain that our survival is taken care of and that we are sustained, so we may carry on our greater work. When we choose unconditional love, the Universe stands up and takes notice that we are reaching for purpose. It lights the way with what we require physically, so we may help grow the collective spiritually.

Why we make certain choices and avoid others are important observations into what we really think the purpose of life is. Is life about collecting money, gaining approval, or appearing prestigious? Or is the real higher purpose happiness, love, gratitude, and expansion? No matter what your answer, those who wish to be beacons of light can develop by being servers of love. How could we not then send light, even to another who does not support us? Rise to the challenge of being kind, just because. Because it is better for you, for all souls, and for the planet.

When we are enlisted as servers of love, as finders and givers of love, we begin to manifest what poets and songwriters wax lyrical upon. When we strive for unconditional love, the road rises up to meet and support us. The winds are behind us, pushing us forward with gentle momentum. The sun shines on our path, and the light guides us. The rains of abundance fulfill our every need, and while we are connected to this purpose of spreading love, the Universe embraces us.

No matter our situation in life, we can utilize any avenue at our disposal to accomplish this effortless feat of unconditional love. We may appear to only be teaching music, getting students to learn the notes and embellishments, but we know it is of greater essential consequence to discover the deeper experience within the music or group. Hearts enjoy this line of work because, more than just exploring the feelings of the music, one connects with all the people, their gifts, and the beauty they possess and radiate together.

Depth occurs in any avenue of pursuit when we notice, appreciate, or express love. Hidden behind the labels are profound substances shining light on our truths. It is how we do what we do and with what qualities that makes the difference. Love can be poured forth at any moment, from any place, person, or vocation. No reason is ever needed.

EFFECTS OF UNCONDITIONAL LOVE

We may not understand how our actions can penetrate the life of another until it is too late. It is best to be cautious and caring with each other's souls, even if we choose not to share our lives with them. One gift of unconditional love can save a life. Each moment we consciously choose to ignite goodness makes a difference to the energy we all share.

What we develop around us changes what is spoken to, from, and through us. One wisp of sunlight streaming through a forest lights the whole woodland, changing the scene from dark and scary to beautiful and serene. If you have ever noticed how one flower in a vast field makes it beautiful, happy, and life affirming, so does a single moment of unconditional love add to, change, and make better our consciousness.

What we do has essence and affects the world at large. We know very little of our rippling influence, so trust that the effects of sending love are far greater than expected. If you were a veterinarian and chose not to assist in caring for an old friend's dog because you felt upset by that friend a number of years ago, you might think your decision justified. Pretending to be too busy at the time may seem harmless. The dog then passes away. What if, with your help, that dog would have lived to save a child's life by breaking a fall down the stairs, warn of a fire, or rescue from a near drowning? And what if this child could have been the future leader who brought peace to our planet? What has that inability to act out of unconditional love, even for an innocent animal, then cost everyone, from now to future generations? You never know how your actions might be changing someone else or the future, so act with unconditional love every chance you get.

We are here as physical bodies, but we also bring our spirit with us. We live not just as flesh but can tap into that highest part of ourselves as we go along. This is the part that always loves. We can strive to not be bogged down in our flesh and form. There is so much more to us and available from us than we often see or utilize.

Look into all your actions. Perform them with creativity, grace, and patience instead of force. Connect with your higher self—that part of you who remembers why you chose to be born at this time. Come not from a controlling or manipulative will, but from your higher loving will. We can give with great power that allows and creates instead of destroys. We must keep in mind that we are not in this alone, or in this to win. If we do not each live our highest purpose, figuring out the secrets of Spirit together, then none of us truly wins anything.

"For the higher good of all" is an important mantra to access consistently. All we have to possess is the desire to be in communion with friendly supportive energies, and the doors open for us. We can consciously come back to the center of why we are here by getting quiet and listening to the guidance of Spirit, and by feeling good. We can gather tools that help balance our feelings and thoughts like energy work, journaling, nutrition, and introspection. With the divine aspect of our vibrations, we can remain faithful to our cores through meditation and other practices of stillness and listening, but always we need a higher connection to elevate our living. When you or I condemn or worry about others, or listen to those judgments cast upon us, we lose focus of what truly matters: love. Our guardian angels cheer in concert as we finally get it.

GIVING UNCONDITIONAL LOVE

Unconditional love is a major ingredient in growth and spiritual evolution, but it can also be a necessary tool for sanity. We enter several dichotomies as we investigate the last few incentives to love unconditionally. Although self-gratification is not a pure motive to learn this way of being, there is a first step to all learning, and everything has its benefits. Giving love for any reason primes our pump for giving more unconditionally. Sometimes we get it simply because we create it, and this still increases love.

If we can truly send out the energy of love with no stipulations or requirements, we clear our own aura. Feeling love automatically kicks out lower emotions, so if you can feel it, you can grow it. Love dispels hatred from our energy field, allowing grand and glorious sensations to take their place. It allows us to come into ourselves more fully. Cleansing toxic elements from our thoughts and deeds purifies us, giving us greater connection to the cosmos.

Unconditional love can also be your best defense, a beautifully freeing and harmless protection. When others in your surroundings are not gratifying your desires (and they often will not), unconditional love is the perfect mechanism for bringing all-encompassing sovereignty. Giving this pure, non-dependent love allows them to be who they are, where they are, while also giving you what you are seeking. You can thus fulfill your own desires, detach from their behavior, and retain peace of mind in a way where everybody wins.

If these reasons are not enough to convince you to give love next time you feel negativity, then give it for no other reason than what you put out will come back to you. The Law of Attraction will come up again and again in this book, and it is that simple. If you want love, give it. Again, this is not the pure intention of unconditional love, but it is a start. In the beginning, just wanting unconditional love in your life and giving it in a specific instance is a celebratory milestone. Eventually you will be more aligned with the unconditional reasons to give unconditional love.

"What you put out will come back to you."

ENVIRONMENTS AND LOVE

Do your own experiments on how your environments affect your ability to love. We all know we can feel and give love when all is well, and the Universe is flowing with us. We also know it can be much more difficult in the presence of someone who tries our patience. Pay attention to how you feel love within differing circumstances.

Stand near a busy area. What do you hear, smell, see, and even taste? Do all the loud noises and restless people derail your peace? Suddenly, notice your breath. Are you able to breathe deeply or focus on love while in this madness? Are you pulled into knots and irritation more easily as others around you exhibit stress?

Now place yourself outside in quiet, natural surroundings. Feel the clearer energy of the plants and living creatures. Breathe slowly and deeply, and know that this heals your soul, your mind, and your energy. Sitting in the grass watching birds creating their nest allows us to connect. The stillness of nature helps us be still. In these environments we can more easily choose how we feel because energy from others is not influencing our feelings. Once we get better at holding unconditional love, the places we are in and the people we are around matter less. We will help ourselves immensely by starting in a supportive environment. Our energy and what we fill our spaces with is paramount to our ability to love. Unconditional love cleanses, clears, and heals. It is the most powerful energy we know.

"The stillness of nature helps us be still."

Also pay attention to your internal environment. If you are spreading contaminated emotions then you will receive little else. You will experience what is surrounding you, and the best evidence of what is around you is what comes from within you. We all want and need love, even those who cannot admit it. Find situations in which to interject your little ray of light. Accept and reach out with the joy you now possess in your life. If we heal consciously, we will make a constructive transformation of what evil is possible. You, by yourself, have the authority and ability to make a difference. You will receive unconditional love as you give unconditional love. Every time you open your mouth or sit with your thoughts, that love will change your world toward what we all envision.

HEART AWARENESS

To know unconditional love, we first become conscious of *heart awareness* by feeling what our heart is telling us. Place your attention on your heart and ask what it is telling you. Is it fluttering because something has excited you? Does your chest literally ache because you are enduring pain? Is it beating hard because you are stressed? Do you even feel so disconnected from it that you cannot sense anything? Get quiet and simply feel how your heart feels. Then you can begin to change it to more desired qualities by focusing on moments when you felt love or joy.

Begin to learn how you interact with love and to what extent you have felt it unconditionally by contemplating what love you see in your surroundings. When you interact with others, do you feel good, warm, and happy? Do these interactions expand or contract your love? Are those around you offering love, or asking for love? Are you able to receive their love or give it? Are they denying or accepting your love?

In this present life we can evolve our souls and heal ourselves with heart awareness. Gently noticing what we permit to infiltrate our sensitive heart spaces assists us in balancing love's energies with our strength. We want to be safe but still moving, allowing, and open. Awareness creates not so much boundaries and protection, but personal seniority. This means we are in charge of our lives. With seniority we know we are making choices for ourselves instead of being thrown this way and that anytime we experience another's emotions.

As we recognize how loving happens or doesn't happen in our life and our interactions, we can then live as one of love and heed the calls for the sharing of it. When we develop greater heart awareness, we awaken the love within us. This allows us to surrender pain and take our next step. Feeling love will become a familiar experience, and creating these moments consciously will change your life.

MEDITATION: FEELING LOVE

- Close your eyes and breathe calmly.
- Envision what real love looks like to you.
- When and where did you experience this love?
- Feel it begin in your chest.
- Allow it to embrace your space, both physically and mentally.
- Take slow breaths and focus on love for at least one minute.
- Feel love emanating from your heart, growing and spreading through your body, and all around you as you breathe.

This single wave will expand your energy and center your trajectory toward love and light. Once you have felt the blessing of unconditional love enter your space with consciousness, you can hold the essence of that feeling up to other interactions. Learn to hold the vibration of love throughout your life because you know its value. Remember our higher purposes of living unconditional love, no matter the outlet. Awaken love by placing attention within your heart and letting it guide you.

We turn next to the polarities of love and how to give love even when we are hurt. We discover we are worthy of love no matter what has occurred, and that it always begins with us. We also ask another to bestow feelings of love so we can feel it and look at love's most pervasive face—loving interactions.

CHAPTER TWO

Get Love by Giving Love

Some were lucky enough to grow up knowing unconditional love as the norm; many were not. The latter may wander and work through their lives, feeling something is missing but not knowing what. If you've picked up this book, perhaps you suspect what that missing piece is. It is unconditional love. This chapter helps you get love by giving it to yourself and others, especially if you feel undeserving or wronged.

THE POLARITIES OF LOVE

We learn by experiencing opposites, or polarities. Many masters have written and taught of the divine dichotomy of self-realization through experiencing opposite extremes. How could we recognize or teach unconditional love if it was all we ever knew? This dichotomy is where we find love, and it is through our tests that our love can be strengthened.

You may feel unworthy of love, or angry at others for their lack of love toward you. You might feel that something must be wrong with the world or yourself that prevents you from feeling or giving love. Maybe you did not receive unconditional love while you were forming your lifestyle or growing your personality and don't know what living a life of unconditional love looks like. Maybe those who cared for you never saw or felt it themselves. Maybe you did get love but could not feel it because of something inside, like an obstacle you need to look at, or learn from. Maybe you wanted to give love to others but could not. You felt hurt or rejected, yet tried and just fell short because you were in your own pain or uncertainty. And maybe any of this talk of giving love brings up a sense of guilt or shame because your upbringing focused on the external instead of the internal, or upon caring for others over yourself. These thoughts are a call to change your perception, to find the answers and healing.

You *are* whole and loved and lovable just as you are—by Spirit and any human who counts. You are worthy of love at its best, and you can learn to find it everywhere. Repeat this to yourself when you feel unloved: *I am whole and loved and lovable just as I am.*

"You *are* whole and loved and lovable just as you are."

Perhaps you are a seeker of living spiritually and wholly, and desire to endow the world with the effervescent love you have bubbling up from your growing soul, knowing it is ready to pour out if only tapped into correctly. Even the strongest who soar on their spiritual path have room to accept the blessings of unconditional love. Love will take you to the next step in your enlightenment journey, and some day it will take you to the far-off places you imagine.

Whatever the scenario, all lives can be changed and made profoundly healthy with active unconditional love.

All of us have felt less than loving feelings toward ourselves or another at some regretful point in our pasts. In the midst of anger or disgust, we need and long for love and peace. Recognize that negative emotions are the opposite of love but can in fact guide you toward love. These situations allow us to look within and search with desire for a better way. It is out of hostility that we find kindness, and through hatred that we finally reach towards love. Only because we have known connection can loss seem so great, and only with separation can we fully appreciate knowing connection or returning to love.

Whatever you have learned, not learned, experienced, had done to you, or done unto another, you *can* have unconditional love in your life, and you can start by learning, as I am, to get it by giving it to yourself. Even if grave feelings of yourself dwell deep down, love is there. Even in high confidence and sure steps, we can turn to this great love for wholeness and splendor. We are not hypocrites because we may stumble on our path or act immaturely, for all roads contain rocky terrain. We are not our pasts or our perceived mistakes. We are not our less-evolved choices or our younger selves. All that is part of who we are becoming each moment.

"We are not our pasts or our perceived mistakes."

May we accept our pasts and mistakes lovingly because it is those experiences that allow us to grow, to realize we want more and differently. We gain light by observing our unholy actions and choosing consciously to love and expand. Learn to apply your soul to the practicalities of life and accept that your process ebbs and flows with wisdom and integration, with care and realization, and without conditions. Once you unlock the magic of this gift, it will surround you always.

LOVE YOURSELF

Learn to love yourself first, so you are full enough to give, and then experience unconditional love wholly as your life touches others. Give light and acceptance to every situation, person, being, creature, mineral, element, and moment. Nothing is as important or valuable as this perception and generosity. Offer it everywhere you go, no matter someone's appearance or personality. See beyond the surface into their spirits. If you are ever lucky enough to review your life, you will be glad you did this, and in the moments you need love, it will be there for you because you imbued the world with it. This will make a difference.

As we discover our new capacities and delight in the journey, let us each remain conscious that learning in the context presented here is simply realizing what our souls already know. We need not learn anything to be our perfect selves; it is simply realizing, going through our process, seeing with expanded awareness, and knowing. It is simply a development of awakening and remembering the knowledge our spirits hold for us until we ask and are able to receive. We are here to experience. All learning and experience is transposable as core understanding. Absorb thoughts and ideas as lessons without a sense of punishment or lack, and utilize all lessons as mere experiences we came to live out.

By reading and even meditating upon profound words of love, we can learn more than we thought possible about unconditional love. Study the wisdom of Saint Mother Theresa, or Saint Francis's popular prayer: "Lord, make me an instrument of thy peace." We can gain great insights from the observations and knowledge of those who have learned and paved the way before us.

LOVE WHEN YOU LEAST FEEL LIKE IT

In contemplating for whom you shall hold this vibration of unconditional love, the first and simplest answer is everyone, everywhere, all the time. A more difficult answer is those who need it the most. You will recognize them as those who are often unable to give it or, more accurately, those who appear to cause you the most pain and suffering. Every moment you are capable of remembering power greater than yourself and reasons for our very existence—this is when to love.

Those destitute individuals who act upon hatred are showing their lack of love and their need for it. Their hatred is a call for love, the best they can muster. This is where unconditional love becomes a quest of the spirit. As Wayne W. Dyer noted, "When your heart becomes pure, your enemy becomes your friend, or even more significantly, your teacher. When you send love in response to hate you accomplish one of the most difficult things for anyone."

Perhaps the most important time to give unconditional love is when you least feel like giving it, or when it is not present. When you see or feel anger, hatred, or sadness, pull out your best effort to love. No one is making you save the world, but your unconditional love is a gift to the Universe when you do what you can to help fellow travelers.

Begin by searching yourself until you reach the point of understanding what you have to give, and what you still have to learn. We can still be accepting of others even when we do not feel put together or confident. The beauty of unconditional love is that it does not take anything from us in order to bestow it. It is like a smile. When we extend this simple contribution, it betters both the giver and receiver. It benefits the immediate environment and the universal whole. This is powerful.

When we interrupt our usual process of hearing and seeing our world through pain, or with contempt, and replace it with one instant of recalling unconditional love, we can be proud of ourselves. When relationships seem laborious we can search our lives while accepting others for where they are. When moments grind on our patience or seem to lack a sense of divine timing, we can employ a bandage of unconditional love.

Though we may not be able to hold the vibration of love for long, our progress is in including love in our array of feelings during difficult situations. We can do this for ourselves in our private heart recesses. When we take any situation or person and encourage within ourselves the best of what could be occurring, our vision will begin to manifest into our reality. No one but you may notice the change, or they may be profoundly changed, but when unconditional love settles into your bones as an emotion to strive for, an energy to hold, any quantity assures growth, complete health, and beauty in your soul.

"Every human we encounter is a soul trying to reach the light."

We can see the best in someone who has just offended us and still walk away to safety. We can understand our own patterns well enough to wonder why we were offended in the first place. We can remember it is all about us and our seeing. Every human we encounter is a soul trying to reach the light. Granted, it may seem that some have outstretched arms and others folded, but it is of the utmost magnitude that we help the light reach brighter and further instead of living in darkness by choosing pride, judgment, or dominance.

When we act with kindness, we fill our energy with greatness. We have nothing to hide or run from, nothing to fear or grieve; we are simple loving beings who acknowledge our beautiful power and use it with tremendous trust and ability. Accept, no matter what. This is unconditional love.

MEDITATION: GIVE LOVE WHEN YOU LEAST FEEL LIKE IT

- Close your eyes, breathe, and relax.
- Think of someone you are mad at, or even someone you might have hated.
- See their guardian angel smiling down on them, loving them, believing the best.
- From this perspective, find one positive thing about them.
- Focus on this perspective shift, and smile at their many positive traits.
- Feel love in your heart from your own angels and try to send it outward.

LOVE FOR OUR GROWTH

When we feel someone has hurt us, it may not comfort us to hear that he or she is here to help and teach us. *No*, we think. *It just plain hurts.* At these moments of profound pain, you have a sacred opportunity to make a life-altering choice—to work on your unconditional love. You can experience a broken heart, a damaged soul, a devastated spirit. You can fall into blame, anger, vengeance, depression, indifference, or immobile isolation.

Alternatively, this can be your moment for a transformation, a leap in growth and self-realization. The phrase "What doesn't kill you makes you stronger," while not soothing in a time of stress, reminds us to work on ourselves through times of trial. You can think of it more personally in this way:

what you do not let destroy you has arrived to propel you into growth, learning, and enlightenment. All for love.

Use the opportunities to discover what lies within your depths, to understand why you are in such a circumstance, and what it is in your nature that vibrates with this situation. What are you currently in need of to heal and flourish? What are you being asked to learn by this loss, transgression, or suffering? If you choose to learn from this evil, you will grow past the ugly awfulness of your pain, experience healing, and transmute it towards the will of the Divine.

Let others own blame and negative projections, for you have bigger and higher work to accomplish. The beauty of this is that by loving anytime you can, you actually help make the world more wonderful. The best and only way to world peace and human enlightenment is through bettering yourself first and letting your better self touch everyone else in your vicinity. And remember, once you can feel unconditional love and integrate it into your personality—your daily being—you may continue without anyone's negative energy attached to you. In your new measure of peace, you may thank these people mentally and give them silent permission to be released from you. Let everyone move on. Hold nothing for them but light, love, and appreciation. This will become easier with each opportunity. You will feel less initial pain and confusion, and recognize the angelic messages sooner. You can get right to your work of self-evolution, and add to the greater good and universal whole, which is why we are all here anyway.

Within feelings of unconditional love, have no judgments, even upon yourself. We are all one. From your soul group of friends who create your tribe, to family—and even strangers and passersby—love everyone, the best you can at that moment. To our enemies, violators, predators, and injurers, unconditional love is mandatory for *our* growth. It may be easier to bestow love upon God, nature, and the Universe, but even the perceived evils, thieves, and ignorants deserve it. This is what we realize as we see love blossom in our own hearts. We are not here to assess or criticize, we are here to love. It is our human gift, need, right, and responsibility.

SHARING LOVE

As we experienced in the meditation in the previous chapter, we can feel love any time we desire by taking a few seconds of intention to maintain this feeling as a vibration. When we hold this vibration, it heals our environment, and when we share it with another it can heal our world.

The following meditation is an invitation to share love with another. I ask that you choose someone you trust and with whom you have felt loved. As your chosen person accepts this contract, the intention for unconditional love is present and already set. If you would like to keep your love work to yourself for now, feel it well up inside you and focus on warming your heart and body with unconditional love. Just recognizing and feeling love creates growth in unseen dividends.

MEDITATION: DO YOU HAVE UNCONDITIONAL LOVE FOR ME?

- After finding another who you trust and with whom you have felt loved, ask, "Do you have unconditional love for me?" If he or she says yes, then ask, "Would you send me some so I can feel it?"
- Both of you close your eyes so you can focus on the love.
- Giver of love: Whatever love looks or feels like to you is your perfect truth. Feel love in your heart. Be

aware of how it feels. After it wells up in you, send it to the receiver.

• Receiver of love: Feel the love come toward you from this fellow spiritual traveler. Feel it fill your heart, fourth chakra, hermetic center, and chest. Take a deep breath, blow it out with relief, and relax into that space. Feel this unconditional love fill even the cells in your heart area. Feel it throughout your physical body. Let love fill your space, forming an arm's length bubble around you.

• Both of you sit with this love for at least a minute. Then open your eyes.

You, your heart space, and your aura are now bathed in unconditional love. Thank this someone who graciously agreed to give to you unconditional love, the most healing and beauteous energy yet realized in our powerful Universe. Take turns being the giver and receiver of unconditional love, and feel how pervasive love can be in the giving as well as the receiving.

This love meditation can also be done within a close group, with one person sending love to all others to feel and fill. Each person can take turns sending love, or everyone can send it simultaneously. Then sit with it as everyone feels love fill the space. Imbibing on love within a group is powerful and can make you feel vulnerable. When you are ready, embrace the opportunity in wisely choosing your feeling-love companions.

This experience, whether with yourself or with others, strengthens awareness of your heart space. This is an important feature for today's humans because we no longer live as just physical beings focused on survival or control of our environment. So choose love, especially when you least feel it. Nurture all your environments with your loving presence, and you will get more love into all of your days. Love for your own growth, and share love for the world. Look for the polarities of love all around you and have humor in these realizations.

As we turn next to the many faces of how love is presented within our lives, remember the importance of loving yourself, for that is where love begins. Living through our hearts consciously enlightens us and frees love's omnipresence. When you have felt this feeling of unconditional love, even briefly, you are taken to your next step in love and awakened to the process of understanding life through love, our greatest gift.

CHAPTER THREE

Kinds of Love

Love is blind
Love is kind
Love binds
It can be learned in so many ways
Or not learned
It may be perverse or holy
New or familiar
It is forgiveness
And releasing
Connecting and reaching
It needs to begin within
So it may be seen or given
It can create joy or pain
Share the ecstasy of creating life
Or unveil the lessons of letting go

So many facets of love exist that sometimes the differences feel blurred. How we love our families is likely different than how we love our friends, yet love is the word we use to describe both feelings. Sometimes what we think is love is actually pride or fear. It is important to detect where and with whom we are feeling love that is corrupted compared to the light we feel as we receive unconditional love. This chapter introduces some types of love you may have experienced, and outlines what we are getting or giving up in each interaction. As we differentiate how each love feels and looks, learning which types of love are components of unconditional love or counterfeit love helps us get what we truly want.

FIRST IMPRESSIONS

You can receive more unconditional love by following your first reactions and responding to your gut feelings with unwavering commitment. It can either be a bad feeling, such as *go another direction*, or a wonderful feeling, such as *I want to consciously connect more with this person*. When you feel a connection or aversion to someone upon meeting, it is wise to look deeper. Anytime you feel something out of the ordinary, bestow the gift of examination. Chances are the inclination was not just in your head.

"A little awareness can go a long way to open important doors in your life and purpose."

A first impression does not have to be a romantic feeling or an instant hatred. Think also of the thousands of interactions you have with those who cross your path. However consequential, do not dismiss your instincts: the encounter was meant to happen and could be imperative to your growth. As you become more familiar with energy, both yours and what swirls around you, what is meant for you and what is not will become more obvious. A little awareness can go a long way to open important doors in your life and purpose.

One dramatic example of such a first impression is love at first sight. Ah, a dream, a wish, a fairytale. Although love at first sight conjures up images of romantic, passionate meetings with our knight in shining armor, I believe this category also canopies those close and deep friendships that are immediate and everlasting. It is instant recognition, a feeling that you have known each other forever. We have all experienced this wonderful connection, and here lives true enduring, unconditional love. This profound love at first sight is an instant affinity often linked to past lives. You feel drawn to each other after a chance meeting. You know higher forces brought you together at just the right time.

Of course, as fate on this planet offers platters of well-rounded experience, we may also meet those with whom we have an immediate dislike. You may feel a sudden sense of discomfort, or even recoil from the person. In these situations you have a present opportunity to heal past indiscretions by preceding your karma with loving development. This may even be the underlying reason for this person entering into your experience. We get more unconditional love when we can clearly decipher where it is not. But still hold unconditional love for this person if you can. Recognize something good in them, something divine within their life, and as you walk away, send blessings to yourself for this recognition. Holding a genuine feeling of acceptance for their soul will bless them and will also bless the blesser.

We attract these "hate at first sight" people for different reasons at varying times. I believe anyone with whom we have experienced past pain or betrayal is brought into contact with us so we may learn to shine light, both on ourselves and the person who has hurt us. There is something we must recognize and learn, change or heal. An interaction with another may be all we need to reconcile souls, even souls with long past histories. Our pasts and mistakes can be healed instantaneously if we are open and loving enough to rise to the occasion.

Seemingly coincidental contacts are endless suppliers of personal breakthroughs; we just have to make sure we utilize the depth of potential messages instead of reacting to the personality. When we are able to shine love on a person who rubs us the wrong way, the power of unconditional love is reaffirmed to us. When we feel the love in a stranger's smile, the power of unconditional love is verified. "Chance" encounters, both good and bad, have much to teach us if we are looking.

Sometimes we have more internal phases in our lives. Our minds and bodies need respite from the noise of the world. It is okay if you are not a socialite. When you need to meet others and have an impact outside your normal routines, the Universe will arrange it with ease. Do not push or worry, for each person has different paths and requirements. Trust yourself and the Universe. What is yours will come to you.

Focus more on what you will do and how you will react when your next step comes. Are you ready to see love and extend it without condition? Are you ready to discover the messages offered you, even by strange travelers? Are you ready to recognize and seize what is destined for you? Shine your light and make it bright so any who need to find you will be drawn right to where they are supposed to be. Learn to express love so that any encounter cultivates it while also bringing meaning, disarming potential foes, or connecting with the soul friends you need.

PASSIONATE LOVE

This type of love encompasses both the throes of passion and loving an idea or cause so much it moves you to dedicated action. Passion may temporarily dissipate within the doldrums of routine. Too much of the same may be comfortable, but might not lend itself to the dynamics of passion. However, we can be creative in expressing and discovering new passions within comfort, as well as with age and perspective. As the role of passion in our lives changes, it is a powerful form of getting unconditional love into our lives.

Romantic passion may have started with quiet or daring interludes in the middle of the afternoon, and over time morph into a meeting of eyes as your song plays on the radio while running errands together. It may be touching toes under the covers as the family jumps, reads, or plays on your bed on Sunday morning, a cup of coffee brought to you in bed, or help caring for the home without being asked. These are all signs of passion in real life.

As a passionately sexual relationship matures, that passion may be filtered into worldly pursuits, family matters, or personal accomplishments. Wherever it goes, it ignites us, and it feels great. Take charge to fire up your enthusiasm, and position it wherever it tickles your fancy. Reaching for passion in any form activates getting more love.

Passion for a cause can leave you feeling drained or overwhelmed as the initial excitement gives way to the day-to-day work and the sometimes slow nature of change. When it feels difficult to find and live your passion daily, recall the moments of excitement that helped you find your passion. If you can, record them as well. This will lead you back to passionate energy. Allow any deep calling you feel to fill you. Allow yourself to throw caution to the wind. You can breathe passion into existence by yourself or with another. No matter where or with whom you share this fervor, when you bring unconditional love to passion, it is a potent force.

Be wary of the kinds of passions that might not be for the highest love. Notice if something else might be disguised as a passion. If your passion turns into addiction or harmful behaviors, realize it may only look like passion and could be destructive. Make sure passion is not an excuse for constant distraction from challenging inner work, or relationships that need tending. In all areas, temper passion with compassion.

This aims us more truly at getting the kinds of love we really want.

"Find your passions and follow them at a sprint."

If you have experienced passion even once, you know it is an ecstasy rarely matched. Passion may explode inside our bodies or electrify our heart's desire with ambition. It is a moving force that makes things happen. It creates life, ideas, and Universes. So go for it! *Feel* it coursing through your veins and take the plunge. Be it a physical liaison (within our truth and loyalties) or a longing to serve with faith, find your passions and follow them at a sprint. Passion will keep you alive, make life worth living, and manifest your desires.

SEXUAL LOVE

A sister to passionate love, which can be directed anywhere, sexual love profits the body. From physical intimacy to explicit sex, this form of love can be promiscuous or deeply personal. Divinity advises that sexual interaction is best when filled with unconditional love, and I wholeheartedly agree. Unconditional connection on a sexual level makes you feel expansive and brings hyper awareness of unconditional love, thus attracting more of it to you.

You can and should enjoy everything that comes with unconditionally loving sexual experiences. Sex reduces stress by releasing endorphins and increasing great chemical hormones such as serotonin. It also relieves aches, pains, congestion, and much more. Perhaps most importantly, intimacy allows us to feel close to another human in deeply personal ways that open our heart chakras, which is more conducive to a happy, healthy physical and emotional existence. Sexual love is about oneness, connection, trust, and procreation.

When you find your soul mate and begin to explore sexually, it can be the most fulfilling and ecstatic communion. Truly knowing your partner creates a deep and magical intimacy. The honesty, openness, trust, and commitment developed in your relationship allows the single act of sex to explode your bond toward the stars and Divinity itself. Making healthy choices in this arena opens access to getting more unconditional love. These are the purposes for which sex should be "used." It is meant to be sacred, though it can and should also be extremely fun.

Albeit a powerful card up your sleeve for control and persuasion, sex should never be soiled by lower motives. While some may think sexual love is about power, it only manifests as this pale shadow of love if one does not take the time to develop relationships. Without the trusting element of all-encompassing love, sex can leave you wounded and bereft, not to mention ill. Sex can be a game to some people, but at its highest capacity it is never to be handled lightly. It is a gift of flesh and pleasure come to offset the difficulties your spirit entangles with as a human being. Without unconditional love, sex cannot reach the depths and dynamics for which it exists. With unconditional love, sex can be exciting and fun, ultimately connecting, and enchantingly exquisite.

If the sex you are having is not feeding your soul as well as your body, it is worth moving mountains to uncover what is missing. It is both important and necessary to share your feelings and thoughts with another before engaging in this physical act if you want more out of it. Get more unconditional love by asking for what you need.

Sometimes spontaneous intercourse with someone un-known can be fun and exciting, but the best possible energy exchange occurs when the other person knows what you like and dislike. This mutual understanding usually exists in long-term relationships where there is communication. If it seems embarrassing or vulnerable to discuss preferences, choose a time when you are both in a loving and safe place—it might not come across so well mid-coitus. Come from your place of unconditional love instead of emasculating comments about how he or she does not know how to please you. Knowing how to please each other comes through communication and trial. Allow this to be fun.

With all the proper and beautiful qualities of intercourse set aside with politeness, it is also important for you and your partner to experience orgasms. While you gain many benefits from the entwining of your bodies and auras, and the sensations of skin on skin, the physiological gifts received from orgasms are incomparable to much else on this planet. If you or your partner are not having orgasms regularly, research the topic and seek whatever help you can to figure out what triggers your body's release. This is something only you can do for yourself. Give yourself the unconditional love it takes to find satisfaction, and you will both get more.

If you have had negative or harmful sexual experiences, strive to get them healed, professionally if necessary. If you have been part of sexual infidelities or experimenting gone bad, then seek healing on every level, from therapy to energy work. You may need to start with more holding, cuddling, or kissing in order to feel safe enough to open up and allow another body access to your temple. If this is the case, it is even more important to find a patient, understanding partner and consistent communication.

Perhaps you or your partner need a little extra talking or cajoling to get in the mood. Foreplay is well worth the effort. Adding ambiance with candles or sweet aromas is usually helpful. On those days where either of you feel you might not have it in you, do not discount the snowball effect of kissing. Remember in your youth when it was all about making out? Sometimes just kissing, unfortunately often neglected in long-term relationships, brings your body in line with you or your spouse's physical desires. Recall what intimacy was like when you were first with your partner. When was the last time you explored your partner's body as you did in those first years of innocent discovery, caressing every inch with loving touch?

I am not one of those monk-like humans who are above earthly pleasures. I love sex. Making love with my husband is always glorious. After having children, we have less time and space allowed for such pursuits of splendor, but every time we head that way, we remember we should do it more. In tandem with our energy work, we have come to some rewarding climaxes and connections, to say the very least. Sometimes we even seem to jump space as our enmeshment lifts us spiritually. It is exciting to compare notes on what chakras are opening or being activated, and to share what exhilarating new dynamic is created within our ignited energy. Our truth is that making love is a priority paying unseen dividends in our thirty-one and counting years together. It always helps us get back to unconditional love.

Enjoy the sensations that come with your human form, for sometimes it seems as though there are not enough benefits outside our spiritual bodies. Physical pleasure can be enlightening in itself if done right. No matter how intimacy enfolds you, allow each soul and body to create its own desires and boundaries without judgment. Keep the best of integrity and unconditional love within your sexual encounters to harvest its amazing and countless rewards. You deserve it.

SOUL MATE LOVE

'Tis the loveliest of loving forces here on earth. To have love with a soul mate means you can always be yourself, guts and all. Soul mates understand and raise one another at every turn. One look can convey this infinite connection, and intimate knowing pervades the relationship. Imagine how close two souls can be traveling together through lifetimes of forever, and be grateful. Gratitude always helps us get more unconditional love. Extra light is put off when soul mates are together, and they are the example of what everyone can attain actually living a life of unconditional love.

There are as many viewpoints on what a soul mate is as there are people searching for their own. Some believe in them and know them to be true, some disagree completely, and some believe we have more than one. While I feel for the cynics who may not have connected yet in this lifetime, I also agree with the potential for numerous soul mates of varying degrees. I believe we have soul mates that appear as friends, rivals, parents, or children, but mine is the one to whom I am married and give my heart.

I was lucky enough in this lifetime to reunite with my soul mate, Paul, at a very young age. I am sure we planned this after previous lifetimes of waiting in loneliness or impatience. We needed our togetherness early this time around for our ultimate happiness and purpose. It may not have always been this way, and we may have spent other lifetimes platonically, but I am grateful beyond measure for our union and timing this existence. The unconditional love he gave me came at just the right time, as I had been contemplating suicide. Please know that if you have had similar thoughts, there is always hope, and many can help you find it. From the spiritual perspective with passed on souls, I've witnessed that suicide does not make anything go away or get better. Call someone for help! The Universe loves you. Unconditional love may be right around the corner, and getting it in the very next moment may save your life.

He showed up in my life when I least expected it, which is often the case with marvelous manifestations. Although I always had an innate belief in soul mates and true love, I was not looking for my life mate—I was only sixteen. Nor was he specifically searching, but our unwritten agreement in Spirit led the way. I did not hear bells or music of the spheres upon introduction—he was several years older than me—and I was not expecting any sort of magnetism. But we let it take shape, and for that we always remain full of unconditional love.

Within weeks we had intimate and significant conversations that let a certain light shine between us. It was meant to be. Upon this growing connection, I saw and felt colors that connected our souls. It was very soon after meeting that as we strengthened our friendship, we *knew* we would be together forever. Many months before even our first kiss, we found comfort in innocent handholding and saying "I love you." Our intimacy was deeply spiritual.

Soul mate connections can exist no matter the outward label of the relationship. My soul mate is my spouse, but another's soul mate may be a very dear friend. They are connected in an unseen, unshared union, a special type of blending energies. There may have been lives where Paul and I missed each other completely, and there were most certainly times when we adopted other types of relationships for optimum personal learning. This is a profoundly special lifetime where we get to be bonded as husband and wife—a sort of deep reward, if you will.

If we ever physically lose our true love in flesh, I believe we can reach another deep connection so we do not have to feel alone, though I trust soul mates are continually bonded in Spirit. A lifetime contains numerous unifications for our growth, such as a first or second marriage, stepparents, and other substantial contacts. Others are close sister or brother souls with whom we may have experienced significant events in past eras. You may have deep-seated feelings of recognition and love for many—congratulations for getting love into your life. I have one particular and extraordinary link, unexplainable and unprecedented, which I share with only one other spirit currently in human form. Whether you think there is a greater plan and commitment between souls, or you are with whomever you choose here and now, for this present time, your definition and your own truths are all that matter.

Even in the present, there are beautiful and unique qualities that define who you love and who you choose to share your life with. It has not always been roses in our marriage— some lessons come aggressively. I know that we have fought and cried, as well as celebrated, worried, and communed. We are in each other's lives to teach and guide, to support, understand, and assist. Paul has been monumental in helping me understand and better myself, just as I have done for him. We understand our purpose together as mirrors to reflect that which needs to be brought out and healed.

We try consciously to appreciate each other while we are together instead of only in hindsight. We know deeply that what we see or dislike in the other is always about ourselves. We continually strive for unconditional love between us, and we get it. We have made and amended agreements for lifetimes, and always we illuminate our own as well as each other's pictures and programs (or habits), good or bad, so they may be looked at, integrated, moved, and released for growth.

We are grateful for the strength and awareness that binds us, and in the end our relationship will have changed the world.

I am eternally grateful to have cultivated this relationship, both in spirit and in flesh. Some of it has been excruciating, I can now admit with amusement. But most of it is deliciously divine. It has arrived and continues to build into exactly what we need and want. We are blessed that this mystical union has brought us two beloved children, also soul mates of long-time kindred spirits. I treasure our time and sustenance. It is a matter of extensive continual growth over millenniums, and unconditional love at its finest. May we all experience soul mate love in its most beautiful and fulfilling potential, and may we always feel connected to something greater than ourselves.

SPIRITUAL LOVE

Spiritual love is the love we feel from Divinity, whatever faith we believe in. This is pure love resonating from where it emanates. This is the essence and origination of love. Feel what they, divine beings, really feel for you. It is a beautiful, easy, quick, and everlasting way to get unconditional love.

Divinity walks beside us with unconditional love. Unseen forces for good support, guide, sustain, and love us always. Spirit is a steady luminous presence in our daily waking, working, musing, and rest. This power of heaven is available to us in all moments—we only need to reach and ask for it. When we connect with our own spirituality and a higher force of love, we are enveloped in our highest ideals, we are our potential, and we progress as our souls become filled with the light of God and the angels.

Spirit has made itself easy to reach and utilize, but belief in a higher power is an essential first step. If we think we are alone we will feel that way no matter the love offered us by Source. What we see and believe is always our choice. If we look for it, we will see evidence everywhere that confirms this compassionate and generous good is bestowed upon us lovingly from above. We do not need to have specific degrees or resumes to feel spiritual love; we only need the desire and openness. And when we know it is there, we want to be better for the highest good of all. Better than we were yesterday and better than our little self ever thought we could be and, most importantly, better in a way that creates unconditional love for where we are today. Spiritual love supports this.

Once we send forth our wish to serve a greater purpose, like love, we will be amazed at the opening of the Universe. What we aspire to will be linked with grand synchronicities all around us as we begin to trust that angels are always near, and the Universe is loving. We will begin to know ourselves, and to feel the immense love vibrating in the earth and from above. We no longer need to search for our spirituality as we realize it lies dormant within us, innately. We already are everything we seek, we just need to uncover it, simply allow it to be free.

Spirit is everywhere. It joins us in the breathing of the wind, the flowing of waters, and gives essential life and light to all equally. We do not need to *be* any particular way to live as our spiritual selves with God's love. Unconditional love is the perfect gateway to experience our higher self. The thing about Divinity and receiving more unconditional love is that Spirit is the perfect, always-present example of unconditional love. And when you feel the feelings of unconditional love, no matter the source, you actually draw more of the same to you.

When we are quiet and tranquil, Divinity has a much easier time reaching us. When we keep this loving connection, we attune to the world around us and the vibration of our planet. We can then hear with pure ears and learn to act upon those feelings of peace and presence. We can link and receive through prayer and meditation, as well as from our most valuable internal source, our intuition.

When we are in harmony with our souls, we are guided through every moment and action. This kind of connection is tremendously helpful, as if a great master was alongside us as a continuous escort, always loving us and helping us feel love. Such a connection really is that astonishing and attainable. Our influence will have a measure of magic, and no matter how simple or complex our vocations, we will influence the world energy with a lovely radiance. When we walk hand in hand with Divinity, whichever face we attach to its essence, our lives hold greater meaning, purpose, and beauty.

To be truly *seen* is an immeasurable and genuine gift. Unlike humans who might love what we do selectively instead of just loving who we are, Spirit always sees us and loves us for our whole selves. Spirit is always available, always loving, and is an ever-present cheerleader of our success. Whether we are married or not, in the company of a party of close friends or not, we can always contact a divine companion or guide for assistance. We can get quiet and be guided toward our innermost aspirations any time we choose. Spirit does not care if we have eaten an entire chocolate cake, cut in line at the supermarket in a rush, or said less than loving words to someone out of fear or frustration. It accepts us as we are, unconditionally, and it rejoices in our efforts to learn and feel more peaceful.

It is through Spirit's unconditional love that we grow into loving beings ourselves. The universal consciousness knows we strive to be more generous and light-hearted, and it always sees the best in us. It follows us through lifetimes and past difficult lessons still to be acquired. Trust in a benevolent and unseen force, and believe in the feelings you receive when you intend a higher union. Experience reverence by noticing the beauty that surrounds you in this moment, and surely you will witness spiritual love sharing your space.

MEDITATION: PRAYER FOR UNCONDITIONAL LOVE

"Oh Supreme Being, please connect my heart to your heart of unconditional love, and fill me with your unconditional love. Thank you."

- See pink light coming softly to you, filling your heart.
- Feel it fill you, your space, and your life.
- Breathe in unconditional love, and breathe out unconditional love.

CONDITIONAL LOVE

An oxymoron in itself, conditions are the antithesis to love. This is a "spoiled" type of love. Conditional love is a choice that stems from desires of control and ego satisfaction, although the choice may be unconscious. If one has not yet recognized their lower patterns, like selfishness or indifference, and healed them consciously with introspection, they cannot give what they do not yet possess. Conditional love destroys relationships, self-worth, and families.

In families, where the parents did not have examples of unconditional love in their life, conditional love is where you are loved or "good" if you do what Mommy and Daddy tell you. If you are an obedient little girl or boy you receive approval, but if you veer from the desires of this authority figure, you are not loved, you do not get what you need, and you begin a cycle of learning that certain actions warrant love and others do not. You will not grow up believing in your innate goodness, or right to be here as you are. You may begin to feel deep down that you are not lovable or adequate, and never will be. You will make choices that please others instead of yourself, thus getting into dangerous situations and losing your sense of self.

Parent-to-child conditional love results in children either choosing to follow their parent's wishes to their own detriment and missed dreams, or not being acceptable or loved by their parent. Even if some growing children do break free to live their own lives, their sense of guilt at having disappointed or even angered a parent or authority figure can be a huge weight, which may take miracles to heal. The most attainable miracle is to learn unconditional love for your dear self first, who definitely deserves it. This can be a daunting task if you have been brought up with only examples of spoiled love, but it *is* possible.

The best thing about conditional love is that you are learning what you do not want. This makes it easier to get what you do want. Can you communicate how you would like to be treated? Sometimes just asking for unconditional love brings the connection and understanding of what you are looking for. When you express your need for it, they know better what you want, how that looks for you, and therefore, how to give it to you.

Conditional love in friendships can be equally devastating as our foundation is ripped from beneath us. These were the friends you gave to and sacrificed for, only to become aware that your efforts were never appreciated, never enough, and rarely returned. You helped these people and cared for them intensely, loving them despite their conditions. Nevertheless, in an abrupt and unexpected turn, they may have lashed out at you the very instant you could not give anymore. Conditional friends can be suddenly accusatory, unforgiving, and even abusive as they conveniently forget all you bestowed. Most of us have experienced at least one relationship that mirrors these conditions. Hopefully we have all learned from and healed these types of losses.

Wherever you experience the manipulation of conditional love, you must stand up in truth for unconditional love. Recognizing counterfeit love helps us get what we need. Making healthy choices invites real love into our lives. Seek the gift of real and whole acceptance. Open, honest, truly loving communication can mend the bond and enlighten, or at least bring fairness and kindness.

Sometimes there is a damaging goodbye and loss, in which case you may look back one day with grateful hindsight. You can always work on yourself and do your best to move into forgiveness and unconditional love, no matter another's actions. After years of separation, all may be reunited with everlasting loyalty, understanding, and of course, unconditional love. Their companionship may yet again bring joy. If this is not the case, and it frequently is not, then you have at least removed yourself from harm's way. Good job. When you are in an unhealthy relationship get more unconditional love by releasing, or changing it. For more on how to examine the health of a relationship see Chapter Eight, and keep focusing on what you do want.

The blessing within conditional love is that you have gained great knowledge about what you will or will not tolerate in your life. You have raised your self-esteem and hopefully some degree of forgiveness and release. You are surrounded by gifts of insight into unconditional love. You know better and will give and receive better, thus showing others by your example how to live a life of unconditional love.

UNCONDITIONAL LOVE

The blessings of love. The way God meant for us to love and be loved. This love is omnipotent and omnipresent, awaiting our connection to it and use of it. This is our greatest resource and recourse. This is the reason behind our existence, and the purpose for which we think and grow. Live your life through unconditional love, and you will want for nothing else.

It is our natural state to love unconditionally. It is simple and easy. But general society does not want you to think it is easy. If you love unconditionally, how will the money moguls sell you products to "make" yourself acceptable or appealing? How will they get you to buy more so you can keep up with everyone else? If you know that we are all wonderful just as we are, and we always have been, how will the world control you through fear and consumption?

It will not. It cannot. You will find freedom and begin to live your life for the reasons you were meant to. Happiness will be found in lovely gratitude of the sun shining in your window or a pleasant talk with a fantastic friend. You will not need for anything because you will have inner peace, and you will be spreading it.

Our own fear is another obstacle to loving unconditionally. Fear is the ego's control over us, protecting what *it* wants. The irony is that when we release our fears and learn to love unconditionally, anything we ever needed protecting from falls away.

Do not buy into the fear of judging other people or looking out for yourself to ensure you have enough. You will. It is our birthright, and the highest hopes of the Divine that we all have everything we need. Give unconditional love, and your fears have no power. Unconditional love is the greatest power in our Universe. It transcends struggle into abundance, happiness, health, love, and light. The secret to all these blessings is simply to bestow them.

If you have any doubts about the power of unconditional love, turn to the Law of Attraction. Begin to grow something simply because you get what you put out. We do need to be genuine if we want unconditional love to be present for us. Without trying to trick the all-knowing energies around us, simply initiate giving any amount of love that you can find within. I promise that with integrity, even if it is not much to start with, the love you do give will flourish and be returned exponentially.

It is much like Dr. Seuss's Grinch, whose heart was three sizes too small. When he heard the music of all those in Whoville singing on Christmas morning, even without presents, he was overwhelmed with wanting to give. Soon he returned everything he had stolen, and he was welcomed and warmed with the restoration of the Whos' unconditional love.

Whatever energy you are harmonizing with will expand. After you see your uplifted feelings spread like magic, you begin evolving to a place where you are giving love freely, not because of the irony of wanting more, but because you want the world to have it. You discover that unconditional love pours out from as well as into an open heart. Living through unconditional love becomes an opening of everything your soul ever knew.

When you experience negativity or are hurt, it is usually because someone did not conform to your conditions. By giving unconditional acceptance, and loving them where they are, you allow both you and the one you conditionally loved to heal, and paradoxically, grow. The worst thing you can do is take offense or give it in response to unkindness. All hatred is a call for love, so answer that call with uncondition. See the plea and repair another's vision of fear instead of causing an additional problem by acting out of defense.

You will stay stuck in the negativity if you believe the other person is somehow awful. Look at their soul. When an element is missing in a situation, it is much more productive to give it rather than just keep expecting to get it. If they cannot see their own way to love, then help them see it by showing it in your actions. It will do so much more to teach them and uplift the situation while at the same time raising your own vibration.

Negativity cannot affect you when you are loving. It does not matter what anyone else is doing, not doing, or even doing "to" you. Everyone walks their own path, and they all lead to unconditional love. How another chooses to get there and in what time is their lesson. The best thing you can do is love. So be brave. It takes more courage to look in the face of conditioning and choose to give rather than to take the commonplace action of judgment or blame. It is easy to find fault with another or yourself. It is universal to be blocked by challenges or comparisons. Break free of limitation and stagnation by learning to love unconditionally.

There is coming a point of a critical mass of love as more and more people wake up to the universal realities underneath all the illusions we were taught. The scales are tipping in favor of joy over struggle and love over fear. Many of us are learning that our light shines from within and that it is very easy to spread. We are learning how to create what we need and to manifest love for our brothers and sisters. We are arising to the beauty of unconditional love, and it is making our dreams come true. Be a part of the healing, of the love, and of the perfect future we are all supposed to have. We will have it because we will build it.

So reach out with open, loving arms. Let others know you are striving to see their beauty, even if sometimes you momentarily forget. Keep seeing where the lessons for unconditional love present themselves in your life, and master those lessons. You will change your world with this one element. Witnesses of your radiating light will feel better for simply being in your presence, and their light will spread. It is a beautiful, glorious world inside our gift of unconditional love. This is the direction toward which we were destined to develop.

The core of your being knows that seeing the world through the eyes of unconditional love is both attainable and transcending. Even if no one else is aware of the change at first, you will know you are on the right path. Feel the magnitude of this behavior well up inside you, springing forth into every aspect of life. It will change who you are, and it will heal your life. Your life will be blessed with peace and understanding as you fulfill one of your most important purposes: to help our world mend by loving and healing yourself.

MEDITATION: EXPANDING
UNCONDITIONAL LOVE

- Close your eyes and breathe calmly.
- Ask God, or whoever you believe in, to connect with your heart and fill it with love.
- Feel it grow full. It may even be warm or tingly.
- Feel it fill every cell in your body, absorbing into your essence.
- Continue to feel it enter, and then make it bigger.
- See if you can expand it to the chair you are sitting on, or even the room.
- Keep this feeling with you and come back to it often.
- Send love following as many thoughts as you can today, and forever.

CHAPTER FOUR

The Two Most Common Sources of Love

Those who know us best have the greatest opportunity to give us unconditional love. The first place you felt and showed unconditional love was likely within your immediate, or root, family. As you grew up, you took what you learned about love from your family and applied it to your friends and other relationships. This chapter references the types of love from Chapter Three in real-life scenarios of family and friends and will give you the tools and understanding to receive unconditional love in your closest relationships, no matter what kind of love you were given as a child.

FAMILIAL LOVE

For millions of people, "family first" is a deeply ingrained mantra and way of life. However, for millions of others, families put the "dys" in dysfunctional. Those you grew up with—Mommy, Daddy, brothers, sisters—taught you, right or wrong, all you think about how families work. They bring blessings, but by design can also bring out the worst in us.

When you grow up and create your own family, your spouse is there because he or she was chosen by you. Your children, if you have them, are shaped by you. Therefore, a larger part of the family you create is yours by choice, whereas the families you are born into, well, you are often stuck with. Obviously, there are more spiritual arguments—that we chose where and when to be born—which accurately teach us what our soul-self wanted. We enter into myriad agreements for the path of each life, and all players carry their personality contracts, becoming part of the larger picture of growth, karma, and choices.

Your family has lived with you through illnesses, traumas, joys, puberty, and life changes of all kinds. They know everything about you, or at least did once. Ideally, immediate family members are the most accepting source of love for you. But few of us have the ideal. Use the following meditation to ponder what family love looked like to you as you grew up.

MEDITATION: FAMILY LOVE

- Get quiet.
- Think of when you were young, and what family love looked like to you.
- Do you see distinct scenes playing out in your mind's eye?
- What feelings are strongest when you think about your family?
- Do the feelings vary widely depending on certain memories, or do they stay consistent?
- What three words would you attribute to these images or feelings?
- Send love to these pictures, feelings, and yourself.
- Give thanks to each family member for doing their best, no matter their lessons.

All families are dysfunctional in one way or another, and the root cause of this dysfunction is a lack of unconditional love. Many parents and siblings create obstacles to love if they are not understanding and communicating with love. A well-intentioned parent or grandparent who has his or her own views and hopes for a young one may end up interfering and judging, all the while misunderstanding the unique beauty of the child. A parent may withdraw love when a child, especially one learning to stand on his or her own, disagrees or behaves differently than what the parent expects or wants. An abandoned or abused child may feel any type of love is out of reach for him or her.

Any time love is withdrawn, it is not unconditional, and it can cause damage that kids carry with them forever. This type of trespass stays with you, interrupting the good flow of life until it is understood and healed, often at a deep level. Luckily, unconditional love can heal these wounds. You can get unconditional love from a dysfunctional family by staying close to a family member who accepts you as you are, remembering good memories and experiences, and fostering open communication. Appreciating family helps you recognize and cultivate unconditional love.

Family is created as the place to learn and always have unconditional love, but if this has been withdrawn for whatever reason, at whatever age, then that soul will need much assistance to become whole again, and make sense out of it all. Usually there is at least one family member, or revolving ones, who are there for you, and this is a good place to start your search for unconditional love within your family. If you have a small or unusually closed off family, cultivate your life and path to find this necessary unconditional love in many friends and trustworthy others.

Another way to find unconditional love in a less-than-perfect family is by remembering the family traditions and happy memories that bring you warmth. You recall the same stockings or decorations hung each year during the holidays, the spots where you always know the Easter eggs hide, or the taste of the gingerbread cookies or pumpkin pies that only your family makes in certain ways. How nice to have others who knew your clubhouse passwords, who can laugh about all the bad things you did that went unnoticed. Who else shared the punishments and groundings when you did get caught? Remember the neighborhood games and the feeling of summer break? When you are grateful for past loving memories, you get more love.

All these traditions, and so many more, are the memories that are shared with a lucky, close few: your family. These are the gifts and very treasures exacted for the price of the steep playing field that comes along with the responsibility of families. Although layered circumstances within a family unit may cause trials, try to enjoy what it offers because family, like it or not, is here to teach us more lessons than we can learn anywhere else.

Every family has glorious traditions and close laughs, as well as hidden secrets and dark memories. Family get-togethers can be a source of security as you share inside jokes and genuinely care for each other's souls, or a source of pain and loneliness if you feel misunderstood or unable to be unconditionally loved. Communicating with your family will bring you a greater sense of yourself, the agreements you uphold, and the life you came here to live and learn from.

So no matter where you stand with your family, get past the traumatic lessons and contempt by focusing on those who love you no matter what, remembering the joyful times, and being your true self in your communications. As we know all too well, families can create the most solid and healthy foundation for you to thrive in, but can also teach you worthlessness, continued unhealthy patterns, and conditional love. Work towards unconditional love.

This means let those in your family do their best, be themselves, and learn their lessons, all the while offering real unconditional love. The main purpose of the family, or nucleus unit, is not to force one's will upon others within the group, but to love them by allowing them to grow out in the ways they deem fit for themselves. We can intend that wise and safe decisions are made or learned gracefully, but interference for the good of all is quite different from insistent will.

One day you may have the luxury of creating your own family, your second corps. Know that what has come before you strengthens you. We then have our illustrious chance at evolving "the sins of the parents" so they not be visited upon our children's children. We get to recreate an everyday household the way we would have liked. We take with us the traditions we delight in from our childhoods, and if we can, we leave behind what did not work for us. You have more choice in how your unit runs, how many hugs are given each day, and how important laughter is in filling the dwelling. You can believe in your children, and see in them the greatest light and potential. You can communicate with your spouse peacefully with many kisses and smiles.

When siblings grow up and create their own lives, the adult children must learn to update how they see each other. One may be blossoming and adding their light to the world, but the other only sees the ruined sweater from childhood. Get unconditional love by respecting growth and loving each other for who you have become. As families of all kinds grow and change, with siblings becoming adults, adding spouses and new generations, grandparents and others passing on, the rug slips out from beneath us once again as all our known and conquered approaches that once worked are now outlived.

We may not appreciate our parents or grandparents for all they have done for us until we are older and become parents or grandparents ourselves—or we may not appreciate their sacrifices until it is too late. Make time to spend with aging relatives, for they are a strong source of knowledge and love. Even with strong threads of unconditional love, making sense out of how drastically families can change throughout our lifetime alone can be mind-boggling, as we must constantly adapt to new roles. Examine backwards and forwards the unconditional love that flows through your family dynamic and look for instances in which to impart even more.

Families are so close that ties really do bind and create your blueprint for how to be in the world, but they are also close enough to hurt you where it counts the most. Give thanks for and to those whom come together in your family with unconditional love to help the drug addict, the kooky misunderstood outcast, those looking for love in all the wrong places, or those furthering the negative patterns with which they were brought up. There is value in all of us, and in how we connect with those around us; it is supposed to be this way.

Every family has a unique environment, and it is a mix of love and sharing, trespasses and wounds. All of these are considered normal parts of family dynamics and can be managed and transmuted with unconditional love. If unconditional love does not exist in your family, or feels more conditional than some would care to admit, then thank yourself and your search because you will learn to find unconditional love where you need it most—within yourself and the circles you keep.

FRIENDSHIP

For those searching through their fundamental years and running into confusion as to why their household sometimes seemed painful, you may find refreshing solace in Richard Bach's words: "The bond that links your true family is not one of blood, but of respect and joy in each other's lives. Rarely do members of one's family grow up under the same roof." Or, put more humorously by Dr. Wayne W. Dyer, "Your friends are God's way of apologizing for your relatives!"

Friends are our reward for being human and are the passage through which we discover ourselves, our purposes, our deficits, and our potential. While any creature on the planet can find a mate in order to procreate, friendships are a divine gift exclusively for humankind. Without them we would be relegated to our own perceptions and limits, and we would surely not get very far. As messengers and teachers of unconditional love, friends dispense our abilities to be and do greater things than we could accomplish alone.

The face of friendship can appear in many ways, and we will explore three such types of friendship in the rest of this chapter: acquaintances, growth friendships, and trustworthy others. You can obtain value from each type as each in its pure form endeavors to demonstrate unconditional love. As we display our own varied levels of intimacy, our connections to others are a looking glass for the self. An encounter may be fleeting, last a short while, or span most of our lifetime, or many lifetimes, but each brings boundless gifts and gateways for which we should be both grateful and studious.

Utilize all opportunities of friendship as they are unique to our pursuits. They can have an everlasting effect upon our circumstances and life as a whole, and these effects can be created in an instant or grow slowly with age. You get more love by nourishing friendships and by being and sharing with all kinds of people who uplift you. What will be shown to you through the eyes and energy of your friends is priceless and should be treasured with great gratitude.

Acquaintances

We can be taught many things in a short period of time through acquaintances, and this is the first type of friendship. These are passing engagements that leave a lasting impact— ephemeral epiphanies and connections that are not meant to grow beyond their initial noteworthy impressions.

Think of an instance in which you crossed paths with someone through circumstance. You cross a busy street with another pedestrian, and a loose link is made between both of you while seeking the same end result. Your paths are lightly crossed. You do not really expect anything from this meeting. But such situations are a good place for synchronicities to enter your flow, and you may realize some small message or confirmation from one of the passersby. You may share a smile at a necessary moment. He or she may inform or impact you in countless ways. Usually they will not be aware that they benefited you. The exchange may or may not move you profoundly but it will remain an imprint in your field nonetheless.

This type of bond is quick and colorful, full of surface energy and subtle hints of connection. At this level, your outermost aura will be affected. A small seed may be planted as the result of a chance encounter, or they may be the recipient of the recent energy you are taking in or creating.

I have experienced two of these acquaintance encounters recently, and both prove illuminating. One was at a Keane concert, a band I love and find absolutely magical. I don't usually get out for events like it, but I love live music and could not pass up the most ethereal voice I know (since John

Denver's death). My husband and I stood in the rain to get seats, and had a good time shooting lively conversation with those thrown into our circumstances.

Laurie was the woman sitting next to us when we finally made it inside. She opened the conversation, and soon we were talking like old friends, laughing and sharing parts of ourselves. I gained the courage to ask her name later in the night, and we even hugged as we parted in the late, rainy, lovely evening.

Although part of me secretly wished she could be my new best friend, and she did look strikingly similar to a recent friend I had lost, this short encounter was fun partly because it came with a sort of freedom from the lack of expectations. Also, as a fairly serious and prepared introvert, it was really good for me to come out of my hermitage and be swept away with a taste of spontaneity.

Most importantly, I celebrated overcoming past difficult relationships by being open with light and without an attachment, which is a big lesson for me. I could enjoy the moment and the connection without wondering where it would go or how I could keep it. Getting out around other humans can be a glorious experience. Thanks, Laurie, wherever you are!

The second acquaintance encounter occurred at a party our neighbors had. Our family stopped by for a short while, met some of their friends, and enjoyed some easy laughs, stories by the fire, and brief connections. One man told me how the hummingbird was his totem. I, as a devotee of all creatures great and small, thought that was a pretty fascinating spirit guide. After that night, I began to see hummingbirds everywhere—even on a stained-glass decoration I received from a friend. I looked the hummingbird up in my dear beloved reference guide, *Animal Speak,* by Ted Andrews. Its lore spoke of tasting the nectar in life and remembering to enjoy the journey.

From one unique conversation at a party, I gleaned valuable information that served as a timely reminder in my life. I hear a hummingbird as I write this, enjoying the nectar of the flowers I put outside my window. I shall endeavor to find joy, believe in the impossible, and be rich with light and sweetness.

Another acquaintance encounter made a difference in my life during high school. Most mornings as I walked the short distance to the high school for early marching band rehearsal, a friend named Joe would also be walking to school. We had good conversations and connections in those ten minutes, several times a week.

I was, of course, a very angelic child and not rebellious at all (at least compared to my brother), but I got in trouble for sneaking out—a product of my ridiculously early curfew. My parents grounded me from everything for a few months, including school for a week. This consequence made no sense to me. I had tests and important musical performances that week, and my plan was to sneak out my window and get to school so I could talk to the counselors and convince them to talk to my parents and let me at least attend school.

I found out years later that my parents had a bet about whether or not I would sneak out. My dad lost. Early Monday morning, out my window I went. I ran straight into Joe. What a shelter Divinity had brought me, as I was terrified of the swift and sometimes serious punishment we endured at home. He ran all the way to school with me and made me feel safe, and I was able to get the school counselors to convince my parents that grounding from school was not proper retribution for anything.

What a strange place I got meaningful unconditional love

from. I am not sure Joe ever knew how much his companionship meant to me that misty morning. Thanks, Joe G. I hope someday I can rise to your aid, friend, or to another in need, in the circle of kindness.

So many people pass through short moments of our lives, unknowingly having an effect. We rarely realize the impact we all have on one another, and it is the unknown ripples that are such a beautiful reason to bestow unconditional love. Even in the first level of knowing someone, we have countless treasures and awakenings laid at our feet. Pay attention and extend kind gentleness. You may be rewarded at just the time you need someone to hold your hand and run with you. T. H. Thompson and John Watson offer a good reminder: "Be kind. Everyone you meet is fighting a hard battle."

Growth Friendships

The second type of friendship is one of intensity. Where an acquaintance may be a candle catching your eye or a blanket of warmth, the level of proximity of growth friendships ignites into an inferno, a roaring bonfire for all to behold. Flames of this magnitude have the strength to both create and destroy, and these relationships are explosive. They are powerful and life-altering. Some of these souls are familiar old friends come to reunite with you, but more often this is the space in which new ties or karmic pay-backs are formed, perhaps for lifetimes to come.

These relationships are created for the sole purpose of true, penetrating growth. If you are not focused upon your own development and obsess instead on the mistakes of the other, then you will get burned. If you do delve deep inside to discover the gale forces of destruction and creation, you may be wise enough to arise from the magnificence of your lessons just as the phoenix rises from its own ashes.

These affairs of the heart can become very intimate but are usually not lifelong—that holy space is held for a fire that does not burn itself out as these often do. Growth friendships are forceful and passionate, but because of this, arrive with less consistent staying power. Even so, identifying the bounty of unconditional love flying through these formative years can lift us.

When this association outlives its purpose, you will observe, right within the grips of your life, if there is unconditional love or not. The pact made between you ends when you have learned what you each needed. It seems callous, but it is also beautiful as your souls rely on certain aspects of the other.

The end of the friendship may be abrupt and painful, or a tight bond may fade into the background in which you only connect with each other at milestone times. Either way, these are the people who usually force us to learn and grow and cause enormous change within us as we get closer. Reaching for light and understanding in all relationships helps us get more love. And so does recognizing when it is not present.

If you do part ways, you will always remember each other and be able to feel your combined energy if ever you choose to. I often send them light and love. But the face of this bond transcends greater bounds than most anyone ever expects, imagines, or understands. You might only realize their importance in hindsight. If you learn anything, your benefits will be worth the appearing loss and emptiness when the relationship ends. As you evolve, you become a little more cautious, far more giving and accepting, and you will end up finding your real life-long friends, born out of these dynamic lessons.

I had a best friend in my twenties. We were two peas in a pod, although our age differences were such that she was a flower girl in my wedding. Years later, she moved to my town, and I found her to be beyond her years in thought. The ten years between us seeming to disappear, we became quite connected. Telling in itself, neither of us had thrived in friendships with women as we had instead been unusually successful at cultivating male friendships. She was the closest thing I had to a best girlfriend in my early adult years.

Neither of us had a great deal going on, except for me raising a family, which she lovingly helped with, so we were usually together. We were closer than most young women had the capacity to be. For most of a decade we talked every day, sometimes as many as six times, just to compare notes on our relationships, how long we exercised, what we were contemplating for dinner, or how we were feeling about the day. We were even on the phone together screaming when the towers came down in New York that fateful day. We had similar and deep experiences and feelings, which we spent endless hours sharing.

Our relationship ended in a way that to this day I do not understand. One misunderstanding of poor timing, and we never met face-to-face again. With a new baby coming into my family, and one slight on her changing path, we spoke on the phone only a few times in the following months. After having my second daughter, my husband and I stopped by to connect and amend, but she had her boyfriend shut the door in our faces. It is nearly impossible to repair a relationship without open interactions. We were both upset about something, but it boiled down to pathetic miscommunication.

I miss her sometimes still, but not as I ached in those first years, especially after I heard she had moved. It was such a disconcerting loss. I was bewildered at the sudden nature of our departure. I learned eventually to feel only love in her absence, even as I grieved our loss.

Our friendship taught me about how forgiving grudges

needs to balance pride. She was always there for me, and I realize we were depressive and co-dependent, and struggled with our own deep issues. We became healthier inadvertently through her walking away. She probably taught me more about evolving relationships than anyone to date. Although I have connections now that are amazing and real, none have ever been as constant as her companionship—an incomparable gift aided by our young age.

Another perfect example of this second type of relationship occurred a few years ago within the pipe band realm. Although the laymen, who sees a bagpipe band on an occasional St. Patrick's Day, would never suspect it, this world of pipe bands is a colossal, intense alternate reality. That world appears to be the field in which many past life clan battles are replayed, and frighteningly relived, with all the great animosity and betrayal likened to falling kingdoms completely intact. Disguised anger, hostility and revenge, and even loyalty so tangible it is as if you innocently stepped into an ancient war—all played a role in my pipe band experience.

It was not always a space of such chaos and enmity. Many of us who fled the new unsettling energies still have yet to figure out what occurred to change that bonded world of "love for music" so radically. As I said, this matters here as its own epic in my life only to the extent of trying to explain in what ways I have met, until recently, most people in my life, within all levels of intimacy. Understanding that world would considerably help anyone understand me and my demons.

I grew up in that world after being introduced to it by my mother when I was nine. A powerfully concentrated arena of extreme intensity, my bagpipe band life defined what friendships were to me as I was growing up, except for early dance and school friends. It was my great playground for learning, a friendly communal haven. They were my tribe, and my whole world.

I became a very successful leader of many drum corps. After weekly rehearsals most of us would go out for a drink for relief from hard work and serious expectations. These were some fantastically joyous, illuminating, and beautiful times.

A new member joined us for the post-rehearsal get together, and I was delighted as I had felt a compelling connection during the rehearsal with him. As we left the restaurant, a group of us stood in the parking lot still conversing, laughing, and enjoying our buzz. We stood by his VW hippie bus, reading all the amusing bumper stickers celebrating the earth, trees, magic, and some of my other favorite categories. As we said goodbye, I remember running up to him and throwing my arms around him. I told him how glad I was that he was back, and I was grateful that he had returned home to us. It might have sounded weird to many individuals, but he knew and felt exactly what I meant.

As the next two years progressed, I cannot begin to explain the turbulence and shift within the hierarchy of the band. Although my winning drum corps was strong, close, and growing, I lost a lot of piping friends through grave misunderstandings and assumptions. This included my stepfather as well as my own mother, a long-standing piper and teacher.

The band totally reformed, and this friend took over as the pipe major. I grew very close to this "old friend" of mine, and we developed a devoted and loving working relationship. Since we were both leaders, we talked several times most days in order to prepare rehearsal schedules, competitions, or performances, as well as to compare life and personality insights. We grew into the best of friends and leaned on each other with confidence and trust.

Our deep relationship ended two years later when my husband, daughters, and I reformed our entire lives, leaving the whole of the pipe band world due to changes he made. In essence, he made it okay for us to walk away, and his actions made it clear that it was time. In trying to release our old pipe band lifestyle, we have only been in contact a few times with him and those left in that realm. He was a divine catalyst of my life transformation by allowing us to recognize this alternate and liberating path. His impact on the course of my life was even more important than I could have imagined. We owe him a great debt for opening our eyes to our potential, even if at first it appeared through negative circumstances. We fulfilled our soul's agreement, and I am eternally grateful for his insightful interjection.

My husband and I engaged closely with the lives of a couple also met through music. We loved spending time with them and got into all sorts of trouble. The end of our long relationship erupted in profanity and obscenity after many issues surfaced, one being that we were unable to be part of their wedding party. We explained my recovery difficulties after the birth of our second daughter, and our financial difficulties at that time meant we could not prepare the parties and honors we felt their wedding deserved.

The inability to communicate, despite our long history, left a devastating hole in place of bonds I thought would stand the test of time. Their refusal to stay in contact with us (at least on his part, I would find out years later) startled me away from being able to heal anything between us. And yet, the break was probably for the best because, in hindsight, I can see we were all a mess without realizing it. We needed to grow up.

Today I have a fair-sized, enlightened, and supportive tribe of true friends. As fate would have it, after ten years and their divorce, that wonderful girlfriend returned to our lives, and today we share great unconditional love. What a gift of maturity, connection, unconditional love, and never giving up.

The main point I want to convey is that after healing from the hurt and loss of these ended friendships, I gained a very large perspective of learning. I looked at my stuff, dealt with the darkness, and was eventually taught unconditional love. I grieved them and went on. I learned to be a better friend. I learned the importance of honesty and communication in getting unconditional love into my life.

Holding light for them really did bring waves of everything I needed back to me. The severity of these lessons and friends affected the jagged and unevolved parts of me, deep into all the colors of my personality. They penetrated like an arrow into my center and carried with them all the shifting, swirling shock of a sonic wave. But because I gleaned so much about unconditional love from all of them, I healed, and the power of those friendships is undeniable and valuable.

Trustworthy Others

The third and most superb echelon of friendship is the most beautiful of all. It calls you home to safety, like the warm glow of a lantern seen through the window of a lovely cottage within a dark wood. When you are welcomed inside, it is the content crackling fire and hearth. It warms the entire room with a reverent radiance. The comfort of this space sustains your well-being, and here you always get unconditional love.

Here you come together with your real and resilient trustworthy others. You talk all night, cackling with glee, exposing your deep insides, and breathing fully, easily, and genuinely. You awake the next morning as if from an exquisite dream but realize you are still wrapped in the heavy quilts of friendship, cared for and wholly protected. The birds sing outside in the forest, and the embers still glow. You smell potent pine needles and fertile earth as you share a warm fulfilling drink, reminiscing about your late-night communions, connections so piercing that you could not find words to explain; a sense memory recalled in feelings, but so hidden it belongs only to those special others and you.

Your self is transparent, and you see through their eyes far into vulnerability, but rest still and sure in security. You hold each other's souls and dance with their spirits. You have made this eternal bond, a connection for a lucky and chosen few. This is unconditional love, this is true friendship, ceaseless and encompassing. You whisper divine tales of magic and esoteric living among others, unrecognized for the goddesses and stargazers you have become by growing together. Your union with these people is sacred, known in unspoken understanding.

"Friends see immense capacity in you no matter what you are going through."

These friends see immense capacity in you no matter what you are going through. They accept your bad days and weeks, and help pick you off the ground if you cannot see your way forward. They know you are spiritual even in discontent, so you never need to prove your light or worth. They see your light through any temporary darkness, no matter how solid it looks from the inside, and they remind you of your greatness when you have forgotten. Your home does not need to be clean, nor your clothes ironed—they just enjoy being with you, and truly love you under all conditions.

The only evident disadvantage of these brilliantly entwined relationships is that the people are of such a higher consciousness that by definition they are very independent.

They are by design busy with worldly deeds, healing the planet, and discovering themselves. These magicians are occupied with raising the children that will save our world and passing the bill to save our environment.

These are the friends who you see fairly infrequently but upon reunion feel not a moment of time has passed. You cannot always call on one another for simple, consistent, or convenient conversations. I have yet to find a higher light being who has much time to get together for no big reason, though maybe we should endeavor to change this.

How does one find their trustworthy others? We can learn to make new friends at any place where we share common ground with others. Most relationships are the result of our place of school, work, or inhabitance. Find allied communities where you are gathering with like-minded others. Be your true, loving self and others will be attracted to you. Learn to approach others who seem interesting and go out on a limb to ask about getting together. You may be surprised at how great friendships can begin from something little, so late in our lives. Everyone can use another friend, and graciousness can do much to foster this. We can expect wonderful connections as we actually reach out, take a chance, and hope for the best.

Many folks can cultivate families or close friendships, but not often both. It takes conscious effort to keep relationships alive as we follow our paths and create our mature lives. In the words of Ralph Waldo Emerson, one of my favorites, "Go often to the house of thy friend, for weeds choke the unused path."

Most importantly, be a trusted friend to yourself. Learn to love yourself and foster forgiveness. Those simple attributes could save abandoned or forsaken friendships. Are you expecting someone to meet your criteria in order to shower them with your love? Have you focused on the negative instead of holding your friends in high esteem? Do you give unconditional love and believe in everyone's intrinsic goodness and capacity?

We cannot place a value on those who allow us to truly be ourselves. Extend that same understanding and love to your friends. Be generous with your absolution because grudges are heavy indeed. Remember that judgment and bitterness come from inside and are brought out by divine messengers, known as friends, so that we may become healthier and more complete by seeing and transforming those flaws. Be outwardly thankful, and be generous with kind regard to those with whom you share unconditional relationships. That bond, and any that come after its related knowledge, is a treasure appraised with limitless honor and prestige.

As H. Jackson Brown Jr. astutely reminds us, "Remember that everyone you meet is afraid of something, loves something, and has lost something." So, be a friend, and extend compassion. When we learn to be better friends, we have better friendships. We cannot get very far without others. Friendships are our doorway to unconditional love—both the mastering and receiving of it. Be grateful for these opportunities. Share what you can, allow and accept generously, and give your best.

MEDITATION: FRIENDSHIP

- Take a minute to recall a kind gesture made by a friend.
- Let gratitude well up inside you with this memory.
- Breathe and expand that feeling into your space.
- Appreciate the richness friendship brings to your life.

- Remember a kind gesture you gave to a friend.
- Decide one kind action you could take today to spread that feeling to another.
- Do it and smile.

CHAPTER FIVE

Love Yourself First

Too pleasing,
too teasing,
or too humble?
A bumble.

Being too arrogant
or being too giving,
both are detrimental
to balanced living.

Have pride in your dreams
but not so much it seems
that you would hurt another
or leave your strength with a lover.

Go ahead and play.
Know you are okay.
Believe in yourself today
and within loving balance stay.

Don't let others down
and on your own efforts don't frown,
for you can turn it around
when self-love you have found.

Be you too great,
or be you too meek,
both have big stakes
and both are weak.

So love all of you
and then love them,
but trust inside
is the most important gem.

Self-love before anything else! You cannot save the world until you save yourself. And so it goes that you cannot heal the world until you heal yourself, with unconditional love. By growing the possibilities to love yourself completely, you engender trust to the greater capacity of love within our world.

Initiating this process of self-love might seem daunting if you have stumbled onto the disagreement over whether we are all flawed to our cores or are simply perfect as we are. Are we here to awaken through our growth or to recognize the divine in ourselves? Beginning any edification process takes us down so many avenues, and through so many doors that it can be internally mystifying. Am I perfect in love, or am I eternally flawed?

Unconditional love found within our depths, then released onto everything we see and do—this is the answer. It creates true acceptance and light for everyone and everything. You are given light so you can see what needs love. We are all the same universal light, here to recognize ourselves in each other. Unconditional love accepts everyone as their current selves, and it fosters individual growth. Divinity heals our flaws through its benevolence and expands understanding as it experiences itself through us. Our mission and irony is to realize flaws are an illusion, even as we grow. Become divine through the encompassing path of unconditional love.

We may see "flaws" in our earthly adventurous way, deep into our centers, whether we admit it to ourselves or not. We would not otherwise be on this planet to learn and transform our hidden spots. All this and more emerges from the most important of all lessons: unconditional love. But it is in learning and discovering how to unconditionally love *ourselves first* that unlocks this expansive gateway. Self-love, and only self-love, will allow us to unconditionally love others, and thus our world.

> "Until you truly learn to love and accept yourself, you will never realize how many subtle sabotages you are creating in your life."

Until you truly learn to love and accept yourself, you will never realize how many subtle sabotages you are creating in your life. Missed light and blessings may abound because your deep self did not feel valuable enough to reach out and grab them in deservedness and appreciation. This limits our havingness. Sanaya Roman states this unsettling revelation in *Spiritual Growth*: "More of you have lost your effectiveness in carrying out your higher purpose through self-doubt and too much humility than for any other reason." This chapter seeks to show the steps to achieve self-love and how to see opportunities in the obstacles that seem to prevent us from loving ourselves.

STEPS TO ACHIEVE SELF-LOVE

We begin with simple steps that will help you love yourself, starting with being aware of your level of self-love, and then moving to feeling worthy and deserving of self-love, loving yourself despite perceived flaws, and finally being easy with yourself. I love this quote from *The Key: And the Name of the Key is Willingness* by The Center for the Practice of Zen Buddhist Meditation: "When you love yourself in your unhappiness, you are no longer unhappy, you are loving." What a beautiful thought to begin our journey to achieving self-love!

Personal level of self-love

A good place to begin in recognizing your level of self-love is to be aware, for how do you go about refining and nurturing self-love if you are not even conscious that it is missing or suffering? Take some quiet time, and delve into your feelings of self-love.

Are you looking for love from another person to make you feel whole? No one can fill "the other half of you." No man or woman, parent or child, amount of money, or even great friend or job can start your whole, healthy, self-loving process. If you think you can find what you are looking for in anyone else, or any other place—when you receive more recognition or lose more weight—you are very wrong. Stop running, stop wasting your precious time, and love yourself first. This is healthy, not selfish.

Do you put yourself down or call yourself names? Either

verbally or mentally, if you catch yourself being derogatory toward your person, actions, or even mistakes, then you are not loving yourself. Most of us would never treat another in this fashion, so notice if you speak to yourself in ways you would not to a friend or a child. You wound yourself deeply with any self-condemnation, so remember, learning from our mistakes is sufficient awareness with unconditional love. Do you take great care of yourself because you know you are worth it, or do you take care of others, and take a back seat? Might you feel undeserving of really having your dreams come true? Might you be afraid of your light? Look into other ways you might notice when you are not unconditionally loving yourself.

MEDITATION: SELF LOVE

- Relax into a peaceful state.
- Be alert to your internal messages.
- Breathe and find three positive messages about you.
- Fill your heart with light from the angels; they always see the best in you.
- Try diligently to witness your own beauty every day.

Worth saving

Learning the secrets and powers of unconditional love is certainly one thing, but it will not be possible if you have not first had the revelation that you are worth saving. Doubts about our worth come from a personal lack of faith in our own abilities, and from the judgments and opinions of others. Only solidity in our foundation of unconditional love can overcome these doubts. We must rise to our own value, our potential for learning and being, and initiate our inner observer.

I remember the precise monumental moment I came to the awareness that *I am worth saving!* Though my search for worth was not conscious, when I became conscious of the truth of my worth, I felt a shift from victim to victor. I began to see how this responsibility and epiphany changed how I reacted and acted within the world. The moment this revelation entered my personal space it created a permanent imprint of enlightenment and hope.

I am not proud to admit that as a young girl I entertained many fantasies about being rescued by knights in shining armor. I created imaginings of being weak and in danger so I could be saved. I remember getting the most attention from my family when I was ill, and I unconsciously played on that knowledge. One day during a disagreement with my mother, I had the thought that she would forgive me and reach out to me if I was sick—I had a sudden wide-eyed wakefulness at just how sick that thought was.

From there I began to realize that I could be loved and attended to even when I was healthy and strong. My family did not always mirror this to me, but I was determined to have that idea transcended in my life. Thank goodness! It took years to recognize that not only was I in that destructive pattern, but I needed to change how harmful it had been in my psyche. And recognizing one dangerous pattern led to discovering and altering many others.

> "I can increase my own strength, and I can increase my own love."

Learning to love and value my own courage and abilities, I slowly began to prove to myself that I could survive and succeed. I can increase my own strength, and I can increase my own love. My sense of fulfillment and confidence became greater. If someone else could save me, then surely I must be able to save myself.

I toughened up to the petty societal views placed on my conditional importance. I learned to value my adequacies, and I soon began to expand that energy to all the love and goodness I desired for the world. I made a positive difference by training to love myself and relishing in my strength and wholeness. I no longer had to be the damsel—I could be the warrior. I could fulfill my need for attention and love myself, even if this potency repelled others. It finally became more admirable for me to respect myself than to lust after the approval and appeal of anyone who did not also relish in my power. I could be strong and loveable. I could be powerful and loved. And so can you. You are worth saving.

MEDITATION: YOU ARE WORTH SAVING

- Go within.
- Start with a small seed of any feeling of love you can imagine, remember, or hold onto.
- Remember one good thing you did or one pleasant situation that included you.
- Grow this love for your wonderful, talented, and capable self.
- Weave these images into your daily thoughts, feelings, and deeds.

Being Deserving

To take one more detailed step towards loving ourselves, and knowing we are worth saving, we may need to look into our true thoughts on deserving. All the things you want will only begin coming your way when you *feel* deserving. If you have been expending lots of effort and energy with less return on your dreams than you would prefer, you absolutely need to search how you feel about yourself. Your goals may not be manifesting just yet due to a subtle lack in your feeling deserving. And you cannot save yourself until you know you deserve it.

You may not yet realize you have issues with being worthy of everything great, or you may be painfully aware that you have a spot of self-loathing somewhere hidden. Whether it is not fitting into old jeans, horrible misunderstandings in a relationship, or continued inability to speak up for what you know, let us remember to return to abundant forgiveness for ourselves at these times. Some people conceal self-blame and disappointment better than others, and some are not really conscious of it, but even those who appear confident and successful may have a deep-seated esteem issue that keeps from them all they deliciously desire. Any kind of addiction is a red flag that somewhere, you feel you don't deserve better.

Perhaps you think you have done something bad, and no longer deserve happiness or health. This could not be further from Spirit's truth. The awareness that you have done something "wrong," or at least limiting, is exactly where learning begins. Divinity cheers as you can both see it and eventually love yourself enough to change it. If you do not love yourself, it will be much harder to receive love from anywhere else. If you do not believe you deserve the best, you will probably not have it. Up your level of havingness by loving you.

See the good in yourself. When you do something that is new or difficult, take a moment to make sure you acknowledge your bravery. This counts on your own scale, and only your scale matters. When you walk the higher road or choose the better choice, even once, be proud of your progress. Smile in the mirror at yourself as this gift to yourself heals you. This will help instill your faith that you are good, can do well, and deserve everything you can imagine. When you make a mistake, do your best to make it right, and realize all the experience brought.

You are deserving. All you need do is get out of your own way. Believe in yourself. You are part of God. Sit with yourself, release anything that disallows your peace or beauty through breath, energy work, or any proven catharsis, and just feel deserving. Not much more than this need be done to initiate the encompassing of love and worth.

MEDITATION: GOOD FEELING

- Close your eyes, breathe, relax, and smile.
- Find one good feeling or happy thought about you.
- Hold it as long as you can.
- Breathe into the color and feeling of this thought.
- Let another thought join it, and another.
- Enjoy this until you feel good about yourself.

Loving Your Flaws

Recognizing the lessons we came here to complete is another step to loving ourselves, and our missing or dark parts are the guiding path. Being overweight or bearing scars, having outbursts or appearing withdrawn—these aren't flaws. These are merely outward manifestations of needed experiences yet unrecognized. Our flaws for this lifetime are simply misplaced parts to fill up through learning and sharing. Each person's insecurities, limitations, and issues bring to light where growth can occur—they are why we are here. So don't feel guilty or bad for perceived flaws. They are simply the lessons we are on earth to learn, and by owning them, we learn unconditional love.

"Our flaws for this lifetime are simply misplaced parts to fill up through learning and sharing."

It is no small feat for some of us to love ourselves as we are while we are a work in progress. And to accept our beauty as we are still unfinished is a dichotomy of divine magnitude. We can all love ourselves fully while reaching higher potential as humans. We are here to remember self-compassion and brotherhood. We all need to heal, and to be healed.

Forgive yourself for anything you may be holding against yourself. Perceived or real, you did your best, and received from the circumstance what you needed at the time. Now you might need loving forgiveness for your supposed shortcomings. Take a breath, and be sure to allow for some space in which to instill the beginning of this valuable shift. You need not share your inner work and struggles with anyone else. It is deeply personal to locate your smallness in order to heal it, and your frightened ego needs a safe place in which to be vulnerable. Trust yourself first, and then be discerning about who you may reveal any of this to, until your self-love and confidence has really strengthened.

Ease with Yourself

It is easier to love yourself when you relax. Your feelings can be elevated as you consistently witness your hard work and small steps. Take notice, encourage yourself, and enjoy this feeling. When you have opted to respond to hatred with love, in any situation, to any degree (which may sometimes only be silence), you are getting it, and making a positive difference.

When you choose a few moments of solitude to refocus and relax yourself, you are being love. Appreciate when you make gains in your level of development, even minute expansion in your allowing of self-love. It is far too common to be hard on ourselves for small trespasses not equal to our own obsessions with perfection. So be on the lookout for single steps in the right direction. Have gratitude for these. No one ever got very far by beating themselves up.

After leaving my busy life of the pipe band world, I afforded myself boundless opportunities to develop self-ease. As I turned away from this world I competed in, led, and shined in for twenty-five years, many condemned me, thought me selfish, trouble-making, and many other horrible and, to me, untrue perceptions. It took me months after my escape to set these false and skewed opinions aside. Obviously leaving behind a complete and successful lifestyle, which defined my sustaining relationships, required much releasing, centering, faith, and quietly brilliant revelations. Enjoying this sojourn took practice, as peculiar as that now sounds to the rejoicing of my soul.

When I walked away to find myself, heal my battle scars, and seek to discover my deeper purpose and meaning, it was an unbelievably colossal new course. I wanted more than anything the solace of being given unconditional love. I had been serving others so obsessively that my internal sensitivities had languished. I did not find unconditional love until Spirit assured me it was safe to search inwardly (where I could find anything I truly needed).

At first I kept feeling like I was not doing enough. This

feeling was probably escalated by the fact that others felt abandoned by me. It appeared selfish to walk away from this life altogether. Taking time to do internal work was discouraged. It took much longer for me to not only allow myself the time, space, and attention, but to believe and convince myself that this too was valuable work—and that I deserved it.

The feelings of laziness persisted. I was tied up in frustration over this need to be moving, knowing where and what was before me, and to be achieving, even if my many accomplishments in the pipe band had not gotten me where I wanted. I was no longer teaching and leading. I was not affecting the lives of fifty people three times every week or performing for great audiences. Bestowing my gifts internally was foreign to my personality and the life I had so devotedly created and managed. As it turns out, that time of self-discovery was not only mandatory, it became, finally, full of beautiful revelations.

Only through this deep work with allowance for my humble self-importance did I find myself and touch my own blossoming potential life. I gained my inner spirit as a more constant outer persona. I found my true center, desires, and purposes. I learned how to treasure me, create balance, and release. It took quite a lot to get myself in my own picture, but in discovering that I can and should rejoice in myself and my powers, I have greater ease, desire, and ability to enjoy others.

You must be in a calm state of allowing in order to receive, and you must be breathing and flexible to facilitate ease in your life. Take the well-known sturdiness and strength of trees allowing for great flexibility and flow within the wind in order to not be broken. If you are difficult with yourself, you will appear difficult. It may be routine to be caught up in expectations of life being the way you prefer, and then having outbursts of anxiety to rage when life goes another way. But this is not a fun way to live, nor conducive to the light, your growth, or especially your desires for unconditional love. So take a minute to breathe, look around with soft eyes, and see how many wonderful things you can appreciate.

Life is usually more simple and smooth than we allow it to be, and we are usually greater than we believe. Take all feelings inward and treat yourself with the same sense of relaxation and acceptance. Let it be your mantra to be easy and positive with everyone, especially yourself. Look for the pleasant, and you will find it. It is way more peaceful and inspiring to just relax with yourself and your world than it is to be all tied up in knots—for whatever reason: simple or complex, petty, subtle, or even monumental.

OPPORTUNITIES TO DEVELOP SELF-LOVE

The irony about cultivating self-love is that there will be abundant opportunities in life for you to do so. These opportunities may feel like obstacles. Through soul agreements, you may draw into your experience all those individuals who create spiritual weights of unloving against which you must depend on your own discovery of love. There will be many people and experiences that invalidate everything you do and are, allowing you to truly develop self-love.

These awakenings arrive from teachers in the clothes of commoners, sometimes even the clothes of aggressors. These opportunities allow you to be there for yourself and to learn to depend on your own love and personal validation for fulfillment. So take heart if your environment sometimes feels like love's opposite, for it is in that space that you will discover your ability to cultivate love. We discuss a few of the obstacle opportunities below, and how you can learn and love your way through them.

Others' opinions

Once you begin to believe in yourself and your power to help the world through unconditional love, you then have to learn to rise above the judgements of others. A nice storybook ending would be if everyone were totally life affirming to you when you showed love to your independent self, but the truth is that there are people on this planet that will disown, leave, blame, or judge you—no matter what you do. The simplicity of "be true to yourself and others will love and accept you for who you are" is often shown to be false, for when we stand up for our own truths, we may elicit fear and surprise in others. This has to do with them and not you.

You may have had relationship after relationship where the other person put you down, disregarded your greatness, or did not see who you truly were. If everyone was accepting and validating of who you are, you would have less opportunities available in which you needed to create love for yourself. The best thing to give in dealing with these types of people or situations is unconditional love and, for your own protection and sanity, space. But the best thing you can give yourself, for your needed good, is your own approval, unconditional self-love, faith in goodness, and compassionate understanding. It is up to you to recognize your Divinity when others cannot. Remember your nature, which comes directly from Divinity. You are a loving child of God.

We must persist in loving ourselves when others cannot. Our growth of unconditional love and beauty shining from within our own hearts may someday become the beacons of light to which those others will awaken and respond in kind. Even so, we cannot wait for others. Our loving awareness allows and calls for us to both find and lead the way.

Society's lessons

Our society has fervently taught us that one must lose for another to win. That we cannot disagree and at the same time understand is a profound misfortune, but through inner illumination and assistance from our friendly Universe, we begin to uncover the essence of unconditional love. We can all win; in fact, we must.

Society may withdraw its approval if you do not conform to what is deemed "normal." Unconditional love beginning with the self is about seeing everything in line and in harmony for greater harvesting. We can all be uniquely different and lovely at the very same time. My good does not take from yours but actually allows it to blossom in even greater ways and quantities. Goodness opens the door for goodness, and love of any kind widens the path for all love.

Addictions

Any sort of addiction is one definite way to know you have ill-favored feelings lurking inside you. These feelings make it very hard to love yourself. Be it food, alcohol, drugs, lifestyle, or another person, having any addiction involved in your life will create a ping pong effect of guilt or even self-loathing. Even while you are learning, growing, and having some successes, until your addiction is healed through self-love (and sometimes professional help), there will be a quiet, dark voice reminding you that you are not seeing or living your true worth. This could keep you from achieving your potential. Be aware that if you are not taking care of yourself, you need to work through your ideas about yourself, and you need to spend time breathing through the belief that yes, you do deserve love. Everyone does. Seek healing and unconditional love for self.

Feeling unlovable

Fear of not being loved or lovable, whether amplified by others or not, is a self-created debacle that might stem from an innate sense of realizing just how magnificent we can be, yet feeling far from that magnificence today. Less aware people seem luckier because they don't know that they could be doing or being better. The weight of Divinity that some of us have been virtuous enough to touch a few times is not a weight all care to know, let alone invest in. For Divinity seekers, the guilt to always evolve sticks to our guts. We are well aware of every minute we are not being our highest selves. We know immediately when we are having difficulty unconditionally loving something. We know each choice that does not follow our best aim, even when we try to with all our might. And this knowledge makes us feel unworthy of greater love.

Give yourself a break. As long as you are trying to elicit unconditional love, you are indeed adding to the light of its wonderful vibration. Don't expect perfection, which is the next obstacle.

Perils of perfection

I can go for weeks being very loving and light. I walk on air and am in the flow of life. Nevertheless, when I stumble, I still sometimes spiral down simply because of my self-talk or high expectations. Some of our expectations may border on perfectionism.

Our greatness can be quickly overshadowed by the overwhelming knowledge that always being perfect is actually impossible on the earth plane we inhabit. And what would "perfect" look like anyway? Indeed, it would be different in the minds of all. Do not be so demanding of your evolution that you can seldom forgive yourself for not being perfect.

Redefine perfect. You have another opportunity each moment. Love is a process. Unconditional love is a gift of transcendence equal to magic. Realize that the conundrum of berating yourself and making yourself feel less worthy, valuable, or good will block your ability to be healed, which does not then allow for the forgiving and unconditional loving of others.

Dysfunctional patterns

We all know in relationships, especially close relationships like with family members, how easy it is to pick out and comment on a hundred things someone else does "wrong." This usually means they're doing something not to our liking. But how many days have you caught yourself being reckless with kindness, compliments, and encouragement toward those same people? These are people we claim to love, or have committed to, and yet dysfunctional patterns in our treatment of them are abundant.

"The one primary relationship that dictates the flow of all others is how we treat ourselves."

If we are sometimes unconsciously strict or rigid to those close to us, those same unconscious cycles are created inwardly first. The one primary relationship that dictates the flow of all others is how we treat ourselves. As we break the dysfunctional patterns in how we see and love ourselves, our eyes will be opened to how we treat those most important to us.

Although realizing the depth of our mistreatment of dear ones can feel like the ultimate in guilt, use it as a light of pride for your new steps into the uncharted instead of one more reason to feel let down by yourself. Awakening is so wonderful that we only need to let go of having previously been asleep. We may have needed the rest, but today is our time to move— no judgments.

MEDITATION: OVERCOMING SELF-INDUCED OBSTACLES

- Take a real moment to get in touch with yourself, because you deserve it.
- Close your eyes, breathe, and relax.
- Pick one self-induced obstacle that prevents you from loving yourself.
- Create in your imagination a bubble in front of you and put that obstacle in it.
- See the obstacle loosening from wherever in your body or space it might be as it fills the bubble.
- Once the bubble is full, take it to the sun and explode it. This is releasing.
- Now look deep into your heart, where we hold our core picture of ourselves.
- See this picture of your potential this lifetime. Make it beautiful and add light.
- Know you placed this picture there in love. Expand it, and let yourself become it.

HAPPINESS THROUGH SELF-LOVE

By simply recognizing and working to overcome obstacles, you are opening the door for lighter energies. You do not need to *do* anything to make these come; you only need to let them arrive by clearing the path. Slow down, relax, and breathe. Stop beating up your wonderful and developing self, and Spirit will help with the rest. Believe in your intrinsic goodness. Heal and fill yourself with love so you can do the part you were meant to in coming here to help save us all. Feel it swell inside you again and again. You will be a shining example for all others on our path, and you will be happy. By forgiving yourself, and loving yourself in all your humanness, you help everyone from earth to Spirit. You then live out one of your higher purposes, and teach by example, one of the very best assets each of us came to learn.

Repeat to yourself often, or in quiet moments—*I am a beloved child of God.*

Take solace in Divinity's help, however you believe it arrives. It is a big job to recognize and work on total transcendence of how you learn to treat yourself, but I assure you of its unlimited value as the most important building block to your ability to receive anything else, including basic happiness. God, the angels, and the entire Universe are always here to help us.

They give all the tools and support needed to be directed towards joy and the peace of the world. Everything you need in order to save yourself is right at your fingertips, and available. Don't be like the man waiting on his rooftop in the flood, calling for God's help to be rescued, yet he denied the rescue offered by the boats and helicopters. If guidance goes unrecognized or unutilized because it appears differently than expected, then how can we be helped? What is done or not done with this assistance is ultimately our choice, and ours alone. Choose to love yourself unconditionally.

GUIDANCE TO HELP YOU LEARN TO
LOVE YOURSELF

- Remember you are unique and important.

- Remember that God and the world love you and need your contributions.

- Take time to list 100 attributes about yourself (who you love). This can and should include physical, emotional, mental, and spiritual accomplishments, kindnesses, and sentiments. If you do not feel you are worth that much time yet, find five things for which to be grateful about your life, choices, or self every night before you fall asleep.

- Smile when looking at yourself in the mirror no matter what you think you "ought" to see there.

- Pamper yourself, within your means, in small ways as often as you can. This can include buying yourself flowers or a new book, or treating yourself to healthy splurges and fun exceptions.

- Acknowledge your dreams and goals and take time to sort out the small steps needed to get started. Call for information on that class you have been interested in. Take risks, and step outside your comfort zones. Read about Kaizen techniques (Robert Maurer). One small step will make you feel proud and get you to where you want to go.

- If you have a friend or family member who belittles or does not appreciate you, allow yourself to say no to the next get-together. Don't feel like you have to explain why you aren't coming. Instead, do something for yourself that you may have been putting off, or that makes you feel good.

- If you are home for most of the day working, parenting, or for any other reason, take time to care for your physical self. Brush your hair and teeth, put on lipstick or earrings, and wear something soft that makes you feel good. If you spend most of your day away from home, treat yourself to your favorite restaurant (within your means), walk to your favorite nearby spot, or take time to sit with nature so you can breathe and dream in the fresh air. Twelve minutes will make a difference!

- Give love to others. Call a friend in need or reach out with a card or text with condolence, encouragement, or congratulations. If you cannot or do not want to connect in person, then breathe and connect with them mentally. Send a thought of light or love.

- Ask or pray for God and the angels to help you. Trust that you deserve it and look for evidence of their assistance everywhere.

- Pat yourself on the back when you have done well or tried hard. Immediately and completely forgive yourself, and keep trying towards love if you are not sure you were up to your very best.

- Spend time with individuals who share your desires and support your dreams. Appreciate and seek out those who do love you unconditionally. Let them know that it touches your heart and enhances your life.

- Find life and love-affirming quotes, memorize them, and fill your head with them for use the next time you are experiencing difficulty. One repeated positive mantra can have a soothing, hypnotic effect on ruffled feathers or a trying day.

- Exercise, eat healthy, and drink water. This makes you feel good for taking care of your body, and it makes your body feel good and work efficiently, which makes everything else easier and more uplifted.

- Meditate and bring in divine love and light—it exists in abundance!

- Have a corner in your home or room where you can display your most special accomplishments. Whether it is a diploma, award, medal of victory, monies made doing what you loved for the very first time, list of attributes, or an old assignment for which you received a golden star—look at them often and remember your worth and value.

- Give yourself your own golden and blue stars when others do not recognize your mounting feats, as small or large as they may be.

- Lovingly but firmly stand up for yourself.

- If all else fails, take a bath, make a favorite childhood comfort food, hug an animal (or your teddy bear or a tree), and cover up in bed knowing that this too shall pass, and tomorrow is another day. Focus on the good things you want, and trust they will come.

- Add to this list.

CHAPTER SIX

Joy over Struggle

Thank you, Archangels.
I have learned from you and been led by you.
You have let me know I am good
And on the right path.
You are looking out for me,
For which I am grateful.
I have been touched by your wings.
I have purpose,
Breathtaking power,
And a clear heart awaiting communion.

I have cried in enveloping confusion,
And ached with disbelief.
I have lost and languished,
Been misunderstood,
And shaken,
And have felt alone holding up the earth.

Now I have unwrapped your treasures.
I have opened the gift of unconditional love.
I have cloaked myself in trust and acceptance,
And I know I am safe in your keeping.

I have sent light and filled myself with it.
And I have learned beyond my imagination.

Now I try and I express
A profound healing and hopeful energy.
I am cleansed, and I resonate with love.
Where once so much pain swirled about me,
I have found peace.
Through trusting in your Divine timing
And flowing with the Universe,
I have experienced a true and expanding present.
Blessings in each moment are magical before my eyes,
And nature whispers and cheers with its ethereal music.

Abundance and connection abound because I allow
with tenderness.
I rejoice in faith and believe in intrinsic beauty.
I have rectified my past wrongs,
I have released what is no longer mine,
And because of your gentle guidance
I live through joy.

In 2000 we moved into a quiet and pristine town of less than two hundred near St. Mary's glacier in Colorado. At nearly eleven thousand feet in altitude, the old mining town had existed from 1880 to 1889. We found the long commutes, isolation, and forbidding winter (consistent fifty-mile-an-hour winds from October through March and many feet of snow each week) well worth it. In fact, one of the reasons we moved there was to enjoy more snow—it snowed on June 15th, the night we moved in. I was ecstatic.

We had a backyard forest of pine and aspen trees. No one

could see us, the sky was clean and clear, the trees were our friends. We were deeply connected to the earth and streams, to the Faeries, elves, and light beings. They were protected among our forests by our love and commitment to nature. We enjoyed the heck out of the yard during spring, summer, autumn, and parts of winter. You have rarely ever seen such untouched beauty as thrived in our precious high mountain valley.

Eight years after finding this heaven, the son of a wealthy and prominent family bought more than four hundred acres of land near us with the purpose of turning it into a lucrative snowboarding park covering our whole mountain, right up to our view. They wanted to kill thousands of trees, empty and drain our lakes to make more snow, and invite hundreds of people to traverse the ten-mile, narrow, windy, steep, and very dangerous road. The erection of immense lights for night skiing would take the beauty from our unreal starry skies, and blaring music would eradicate the extreme silence. All for recreation and money.

The police, EMS, Roads and Bridges Department, Division of Wildlife, and the majority of residents opposed the development because the land was zoned residential. Few I knew supported the rezoning, but some preferred to bring in additional revenue to the area. It was determined that zoning would be voted on by our town's three commissioners. In defense of the land, and our way of life, I spoke at meetings and contacted wildlife preservationists, radio and television stations, and local and state government for help.

The commissioners voted two to one to pass rezoning. One understood the dangers of our roads and saw the value in our quality of life. The other two practically had dollar signs for eyes. One thought a twenty-run, four-lift snow park honored our community's past, as there had been a single-run personal ski acre with a standing lift there in the fifties. As it happens, the lakes a dear ancestor of mine helped create were the very ones to be drained for the new loud snow machines. It seemed only certain parts of history were worth restoring.

A picture of me from that fateful day was on the cover of our county newspaper. I sobbed with head in hands as they read the verdict. As all our efforts and hopes for retaining anything lovely crashed to an end, our community hugged each other, and watched everything we had worked for slip out of our control. I fell into despair as I saw our way of life destroyed. I wondered how we could afford to move, and I had grave concerns in our ability to locate a place with trees, peace, and quiet. I went through anger, hate, injustice, devastation, and every terrible feeling one can imagine.

I had nothing against progress but was outraged by the lack of appreciation for sparing one small town their slower, more meaningful, and endangered way of life. I wondered when our world consciousness would include preservation of scarce and pristine natural beauty in the definition of progress. I stayed in bed for as many days as I could get away with. I cried constantly, and my chest literally ached. I was so absorbed in my anguish that I could not, nor did I want to, recall or utilize any healing techniques. As it turned out, I needed to go through these feelings of loss and ruin for many reasons, which would only be revealed with full participation, surrender, and hindsight.

Slowly, I remembered my lessons, my book, and my path. I was grateful my children were healthy, that we even had a home, and for numerous overlooked gifts. I began to come to a place of understanding that our local town was based on tourism, and that although disappointed, some people were excited about the snow park. I could understand them, even if they did not understand me. After all, with unbelievable amounts of snow, it was a brilliant place for outdoor winter entertainment.

I began to see that maybe this was the Universe's way of helping us move to a sunnier and bigger home with less dynamic winters. I began to trust that something good would come of this wreckage—that it was happening for a reason. I may not have fully recognized it yet, and I may have been rather shortsighted in how the bigger picture would unfold, but I began to release my resentment and taste for revenge. I knew there were lessons in the struggle, if I looked deeper. All these things I had just learned from pain I vowed to begin learning from joy.

> "All these things I had just learned from pain I vowed to begin learning from joy."

I contracted with myself to trust the Universe more and to find my way by being open to possibilities. Just like leaving the pipe band world, the only world we knew at the time, would later open us to healing, maybe this snow park would end up being the best thing that ever happened to us. Our town could run out of water within ten years, and we could be stuck there unable to survive, or by moving, we could be saved from the increasing dangers of our road with so much added traffic. A move could place us in a more environmentally friendly community or bring us great new friends.

I wanted to live in this sacred and remote place we were so lucky to find, but something better could be in the works. This insight was more believable after reassuring conversations with my inspired friend Linda, who could see the bigger picture. I really did not know the answers or the future, but

I was willing to be open. I was willing to see good and joy around me and let my perceptions of this "problem" be healed with unconditional love for everyone involved.

It was an arduous process, but the angels lined up synchronicities that opened my mind and healed it. The instant I believed I could live through it, the very moment I opened to the unknown, I noticed the Universe flowing toward me with everything I needed. I received repetitive signs that we would be taken care of, and that something great was coming.

In the time being, while I tried every day to stay connected, remain faithful and present, and find the good, my trials continued. Stories of the coming attraction were on the news, but I was less and less thrown off balance or filled with fury when this occurred. I was increasingly grateful for all the joys in my life. I became much more aware of the small things I had taken for granted. I talked to the trees, warning and blessing them, and I prayed we would be spared the pain of hearing thousands of them fall to their deaths.

Several times a week when reminders of the impending development popped up, I waffled between sadness and hope. I was being reminded to be vigilant in searching for my joy and in believing this was all bringing something good. I would be proud at my grasping of this concept when I looked back with certainty in a few years from a better place. I was letting it go and was even happy with my growth and trust. I felt inspired and lit, even if it took time and a lot of introspection and entreaties to get there. I knew through that pain that I was closer to learning lessons with, through, and from glorious joy!

CONSCIOUS JOY

One must be very conscious in order to learn from joy. While pain jolts you out of apathy or unconscious living and gets you moving, searching, and solving, you must possess greater wisdom to look at a happy day or contented life and be able to learn. Learning from joy is a wonderful way to live and grow, but our society has drifted far from that perspective. If you have the correct tools, it is noticeably helpful to start or maintain this place of peace, for where you already are, you simply need to persist. If you have fallen prey to discord or sunk into depression, it is much more difficult to see your way out.

The good news is that if you have experienced such exaltations and felt in sync with the world around you even once, those feelings are part of you and can be reached and resurrected upon request. So remember them and write them down in any sort of book of joys or gratitude journal, along with the feelings these wonderful encounters and events elicit. Feelings are stronger than thoughts and are an easier sense memory to be recalled and repeated at will.

Although I have enjoyed countless moments of pure joy in my life, I am not yet evolved enough to learn without pain. I have many, if sometimes brief, insights and inspirational glimpses of happiness and goodness. But there are always moments of pain. I wrote this chapter as a profound inner sojourn to recognize and deeply root out the reasons for the penetrating pervasive pain I feel some moments.

When I struggle for answers, or it appears my life has come crashing down as it did when the snow park was approved, I must turn to trust in the Divine; that this is part of a bigger, better plan for me. When I feel decimated and fear for my life and the lives of my loved ones, I must turn to my tried-and-true tools for help, brought to me by my favorite books, most productive meditations, master teachers, and a reality check in the present.

TOOLS TO LEARNING FROM JOY

If you research the topic of learning within joy, whether from your favorite books, personal experiences, or intriguing conversations with friends, you will probably find some form of the ideas I present in the following paragraphs. Along with engaging in such a conversation with my husband during my snow park desperation, I received an almost immediate synchronicity in which I came across a sentence in a book I was reading that exactly matched his belief about how one can consistently learn from joy. I am always humored and honored by such synchronicities sent from above, and they have become a recurring and common blessing to me as I advance in my path to light and love. They are confirmations that I am on the right path.

The most basic reason for living unconditional love, as well as joy, is the Law of Attraction. We get what we expect and what we put out. We usually get some aspect of what we believe—if we believe learning has to be hard, we will not be disappointed. Or, if we are just going through the motions of life unconcerned with learning, we will be nudged by a Universe that demands it. If we ignore the nudge, we will be shaken, then kicked, and so on, to a place we do not want to go to but to which we have all gone at least a few times. Let us do ourselves and those watching a favor by learning from joy instead of pain, for it is much easier and kinder. As Gandalf said, "All you have to decide is what to do with the time that is given to you." So, do you spend it in struggle, manifesting negativity over and over, or in harmony with your Source, manifesting what you truly want? These ideas may help you to recognize and learn within joy.

Seeing the Good—Gratitude, Visualizations, and Affirmations

If you are struggling and wondering why you might be experiencing the world through pain, it might be because you are seeing things in the negative. This detection and self-questioning is a delightful sign of hope and progress. While some realistic understandings of imperfections might be necessary to being human, a chronic belief in bad is not healthy. You might think bad things happening is the sum total of all your karma because it feels that big. You might beat yourself up (suffer over your suffering) because you are mad that you are not evolved enough to always see the silver lining, but change your focus to any love and joy you can.

Do you feel like bad things naturally happen to you, or that you are being punished? It is hard to get out of that mindset and to blithely believe that good happens if you have made a mistake, but the real truth is that the Universe is innately good and helpful. Could the answer be as simple as that? Is it a matter that you just do not trust the Universe enough to see all the good?

"Whether you believe in a friendly or hostile Universe will dictate much about your life."

This goes back to the Law of Attraction, but more basically points to your belief in the world. As the brilliant Albert Einstein observed, whether you believe in a friendly or hostile Universe will dictate much about your life (and what comes to you).

So, when a "bad" thing happens, it is much more likely to be a lesson than a karmic repercussion (unless you've knowingly and repeatedly hurt others). You are not being punished; the Universe loves all of us unconditionally.

Whether you can understand the lesson in the trial of the moment is of less consequence than your faith. Trust and look beneath the surface—everything brings results that will create a further learning opportunity. Fulfill your obligation in that opportunity to gain knowledge and focus on the good. You will get what you focus on, whether you want it or not.

Although this type of Pollyanna attitude may seem trite or even fake at first, it is a slow and significant switch in your most fundamental thinking. By searching for the good and joy in everything, you actually bring about more of it.

MEDITATION: GRATITUDE

- Find your space.
- Search for the feeling of gratitude, and a positive thought you can believe.
- Think of five things for which you are grateful— anything at all. Include a gratitude about yourself.
- Note these mentally or in a journal.
- In down moments, come up with five new things you are grateful for.
- Do this every day and feel your life change.

By training your mind to see the good and be grateful for it, you will begin to search for the good on a regular basis. If the day has not been all we desired, give thanks for family, their health, and even that the day is over. This is okay. On other "better" days, take ten minutes to write down as many appreciations as you can come up with. When I cannot manage to write them down, I make my gratitude choices mentally as thank yous to the Universe while I lie in bed before falling asleep. I usually end up continuing to ten or fifteen before I drift off.

Visualization is another tool of positivity. It has been scientifically proven that your brain cannot distinguish between something actually happening and your mind running through the actions in your imagination. This is a fantastic gift. Begin to see what you want, in the present moment, inside your mind's eye, and you will be harmonizing with the vibrations of your desires. Your energy will attract even more if you *feel* what you are seeing. See and feel it as if you already possess or are this desire. If you picture things working out well, even things you previously had been dreading, you will lay the groundwork for that energy to penetrate the situation. You bring it toward you.

Visualize your dreams coming true. Visualize your day. See everything going swimmingly—happy, guided, easy, connected—and thus you create the energy for it. Take a moment each morning to lay out your desires for the day, to Spirit. An entreaty for what you really want does affect energy. It is called intention. Feel it, and be creative. You get what you place energy upon.

Visualization becomes easier and more vivid with practice, and it really does produce results. Hold onto positive thoughts of your creation as long as possible, and another bright thought will join it. Soon you will have created enough energy to get it moving into reality. Place pictures of having what you desire in your head space, bathe them in light, and add the feelings of excitement, passion, and gratitude that will result. This powerful combination, which only takes a minute or two, shifts your process of creating.

Affirmations produce this same sort of internal belief and stimulation. Repeat words of conviction and desire as if you already exhibit the quality or objective. If you catch yourself saying things are difficult, you are using your effective tool of speech to be negative. Instead of complaining and spreading more negativity, write, read, and then speak positive sentences dealing with your specific issues. Sound is a powerful element, so make sure its use is constructive. Your self-talk, whether mental or verbal, determines your experience, so use positive fortification in as many ways as you can to shift your outlook and belief systems. My little book of ideals and optimistic goals immediately lifts me and shakes me from my doldrums.

Trying these simple techniques will change your life. And when you fear you are unable to learn through joy in some ominous moment, your mind will already be primed to begin focusing on the good. You get what you see. You can shift your thoughts with your own strength of simply wanting to feel better. Growing really can be easy, and it should be; there is no reason we need to struggle in order to get love. When you think good things, remember good memories and feelings, or believe the best will happen, you actually multiply those marvelous aspects. More good will come to you. You will live a life of rose-colored glasses because those are your choices, and it will be real.

Be in the Present Moment

One of the best tangible sources to living with joy is simply being in the present moment. If you are gifted enough to recognize the offerings of this existing point in time, then you are blessed and very wise. The present moment has much to offer if you stay with it and look around in expectant curiosity.

Without worry or anxiety, memories or reminiscing, there are so many things within reach to enjoy. It may take a few slow breaths and relaxing seconds of solitude inside your thoughts, but you can turn on this flow of good feelings and gratitude for as long as you choose. *The air outside is so fresh. The sun feels great on my skin. The breeze gently refreshes my eyes. My body feels comforted and calm. I am healthy today. I can smile and appreciate how good things are right now.*

When you allow yourself to be here, now, where else would you ever want to be? It matters not what your circumstances are; in every place, you can find a piece of serenity for yourself. There is always something wonderful about your space, even if it is only within. The present moment connects with appreciation to enhance our joy. If you are not lusting after anything further than your senses, you may learn constancy and peace in these places.

"When you allow yourself to be here, now, where else would you ever want to be?"

In our conversations with trustworthy others, we can search out what helps them to learn joyfully. One such opinion in my circle about the joy of the present moment was this: "The key to learning through joy could definitely be meditative focus on living in the now—really learning to live that way." Such profound insights from others are what we find when we have deep dialogues like this.

Being in the present may feel particularly difficult during times of turbulence, but when we stay present with our adversity, we move through it easier. It is important to learn from adversity, but to also learn through it. Do not bind yourself to these lower emotions, and do not ridicule yourself for the experience. While you are there, learn what is being presented, so you will not have to repeat the lesson. Remember, the only way through is through.

Every time you truly gain insight from an incident, you move close to a measure of joy. Eckhart Tolle said, "When you have reached a certain degree of presence, you no longer need negativity to tell you what is needed in your life situation—but as long as negativity is there, use it. Whenever you notice that some form of negativity has arisen within you, look on it not as failure, but as a helpful signal that reminds you to be more present."

When you use your life and experiences for study, you thrive within whatever is happening. Whether a trauma you must get through with persevering strength or the bright elation of a dream realized, you accept the place, and search for meaning. When you focus your energy on being with the present moment, no matter its bounds or stories, you receive benefits meant for your soul. By flowing with the moment, you are resonating peace, and this will allow for recognition of joy. Perfect presence permits profound and proximate pleasure.

Trust the Flow

Trust that you are being divinely led and supported. I believe this is a key factor in learning: when we are struggling we can let go of the struggle part, look for the learning, and then remember joy. When turning to joy, the struggle falls away. Learning does not need to be hard. When we are learning, we are no longer struggling. Then we release the effort or pain, and live joy with ease, still learning. Instead of making challenges in life so ugly, trust divine flow so you can simply learn and let go. If you are led by fear, or feel anguish when worrying about challenging occurrences, then your lessons will arrive painfully rather than joyfully. Relax.

"Trust that you are being divinely led and supported."

When something happens, and you find yourself observing

and defining the experience, you must remember that it is not yet over. Even if something appears bad, it is only one step in your life flow. Your events are not over until the end of your life, and some would argue not even then because of potential lifetimes lived with your same spirit. Time as we see it does not exist any place else. When you feel something is done, it can still change in the blink of an eye. Gain a far-reaching perspective to get unconditional love.

When we connect with Spirit through prayer or meditation, we have a better chance of hearing the guidance meant for us. Through studying our own spiritual communion, ancient texts, and other holy happenings, we can gain trust through our increasing faith that we will not be led astray. Our Universe and guiding spiritual energy are all-powerful. It keeps planets revolving around the sun and sustains life in a never-ending chain, and it has you in mind among its larger scheme. Trust that it knows. Be more intimate with the guiding forces around you. Be more aware of where it is sending you and why. It gives limitless signs and synchronicities. If you learn to hear your intuition and follow it, you will watch life unfold as a beautiful and joyful script.

As we develop our trust in a good and gracious Universe, we gain clarity that allows us to learn with joy. We do not need to judge anything, and this is a powerful stance. When we accept what happens to us and look for its message, then nothing is ever really "bad." It just *is*. And it is meant for our higher good and greater joy.

When something transpires that triggers anxiety or stress in you, experiment with a new perspective. We do not have the all-seeing power that our Source does. It is paramount to our peace and joy to trust in this higher power. This seeming problem could end up being the very best thing that ever happened to you.

Think of a moment that threw you off balance. What were your assumptions about the event? What were your reactions to what happened? Now imagine what you may have missed in your initial assessment of the situation. Did you learn new information about the situation later? If you hadn't had those assumptions, how would your reactions have been different? If you felt negatively, then you may not have been open to seeking the message behind the event. Did you trust this was *your* vision, a message timed perfectly for you by the cosmos in order to show a bigger picture? Something your soul was looking for? You can stay centered no matter what is happening in your life by flowing with the Universe rather than against it.

MEDITATION: FLOW

- Find your relaxed state.
- Become conscious of your breath.
- Through breathing, relax your intention on flowing with the Universe.
- Feel your breath keeping you moving, simply flowing along.
- See experiences passing by your mind's eye.
- Just watch and let them go.
- Allow the light of the Universe to come in through your breath.
- Follow where it wants to take you, effortlessly.
- Breathe with the Universe, however it is flowing.
- Let this meditation center you as whatever is for your highest good comes to you.

Pain impacts us when we create resistance by refusing to release what no longer serves us. Let go of what does not work and be open to the newness of learning through joy. What a prize in itself! The Universe never chooses pain, just experiences. How you receive or resist them is always your choice.

When I really connect with the world around me, I feel subtle inner urges. The instant I act upon these and follow through with their direction, I am led to the next step. Sometimes I keep this going throughout the entire day, and the wondrous happenings within these moments are monumen-tal. I get huge insights and answers to some of my deep searches, and I am led right to where I need to be. Trust in universal joy, and find it by listening to what is being whispered. You are loved and looked after. With trust and allowance of flow, there is never a reason to feel pain, only openness to what may be next and why.

Engage in Right Action

The final tool we'll discuss is the course of right action, which is another way of saying "Do what you know you should." If you are on track with your path, learning what you need to know, acting from integrity, and generally doing your best, then Spirit will applaud your efforts with joy. It is often when we are out of sync and not listening to subtle clues that we are affected by pain.

In the world of energy, there is always a nudge before a slap. If you are living in harmony and evolving, your higher order will call for joy. Taking cues from our light Source and being directed along our highest path lets us learn with joy as a reward. All the right pieces fall into place as we consider the best for all concerned. It does not mean lessons will not be placed along your path, but if you are truly listening and following your best good, there is simply no need for pain to enter. Sanaya Roman in *Spiritual Growth* reminds us, "To grow with joy it is important to follow inner messages and make small easy changes." Consciously learning from joy will disengage and counteract the jolting experience of learning more extremely through pain.

If you are taking part in circumstances you know are not healthy, then you are probably aware of it. When you put toxins into your body and life, or indulge in emotional intoxication, some level of you knows you are not in as good of shape as you could be. These unhealthy circumstances range from screaming, fighting, spending time with lower energy people, choosing unhealthy lifestyles, and eating bad foods, to having a serious drug addiction or living in abuse or illusions.

You can learn to speak your mind with tenderness and concern for other souls. You can act with gentleness to those around you, yourself, and your body. Drama and laziness can be reshaped with excitement in living more consciously. In our society it might be very difficult to eat as healthy as you would like. With fast food available everywhere it is a daunting task to say the least. You can still make better efforts in caring for your body.

There is no need to feel bad or guilty when you know you could be doing better. Just be aware that you are choosing a path that may teach you through pain and harsh awakenings. When you engage in conflicts or lower vibrations, you open the door for various toxic energies, substances, and even people. This could knock you off balance. Until you follow your highest calling, you know there are always going to be negative consequences to your negative choices. When you do act in accordance with proper action, your consequence is joy.

We all reach for comfort in times of low vibrations, and many of us have only allowed ourselves to learn from pain.

When you are no longer willing to experience life that way, your soul will have had enough, and you will be able to change. You may even be forced to. There is no bad way to learn. Your path is yours, and no one can say it is wrong or bad. Know that if you are feeling pain and meeting lots of obstacles in your path, it can change toward joy the moment you make different choices, even in thought.

You can fool yourself into believing you will continue getting away with bad choices or behavior, and you might sustain that mindset for quite a while. But sooner or later what we put out will catch up to us. You cannot hurt others, alter your energies through lower chemicals, or purposely manipulate with maliciousness, and then live a life of joy. Perhaps you are attracting some extreme lesson into your experience, and that may fulfill your soul's requirement. Choose better with love, and acknowledge the power, immediacy, and consistency of karma.

We only harvest the fruits we plant and nurture. Anything you give time and energy to, you are tending and cultivating. There will be some reaction to your action, but it is fully within your control. Give what you want to receive. Do your best and expect the best. If you are refusing to learn and grow, then do not be surprised when your pain repeats itself. Right action—not perfect, but the best we can see and give—allows for the best possible chances of harmony and joy.

THE ENDING TO MY SNOW PARK STORY

I strove to apply each of the tools discussed here to learn from the pain I felt when the snow park was announced. I searched in desperation for the good: my home was peaceful, full of love, and there were many wonderful things in our lives. I tried to keep perspective and remain in the present moment searching for gratitude. My pain came from my mind, from thoughts of things not there, and I breathed a little better hearing my girls giggling in the next room and smelling the comforting dinner being prepared by my caring husband. I was grateful, and I did my best to trust. I knew this obliteration was mine; it was in *my* mind, and it was there I needed to heal it.

I also realized through the help of a fellow clairvoyant friend, Sean, that the pain I agonized in was perpetuated by other triggers and not necessarily just what was occurring before my eyes. This situation was lighting up similar events from my history. My hurt in the moment was magnified by painful memories that had not been completely integrated or released. This information allowed me a little space, and this helped immensely. Though the pain felt earth-shattering, it was a large opportunity to process similar information. Out of pain and into experience, let us look at it and be able to grow.

Sure enough, the Universe came through. In our tenth year by St. Mary's glacier, the same year the snow park was to open, we lost the main power conduit to our home, and our carport collapsed under the weight of snow. We had been nudged to move by numerous other obstacles and tragedies, and these two hardships proved the last shove. I did not know how I could find a peaceful sacred space of quiet because I was so attached to my land, but we moved down to nine thousand feet and started renting a much bigger home while we let the rest come to us.

Among normal humans and altitude again, we soon came to find life even better, and within a few years bought the home we now inhabit. It is high enough to be clean and quiet, and the town is lighter and more spiritual. We found a more magical forest, and the miracles in our life feel even greater. As soon as we made our way to our new life, the plans for the evil snow park fell through and it never opened. How's that for a humorous yet rewarding Universe!

In our journeys to learn from joy, do not be fearful if you have a bad day or react to someone's inconsiderateness with hostility. Just recognize that you can choose differently in the future, and this will precede your karma. You are trying, and you love more; desire is the key ingredient to right action. We are not perfect by nature, but we are commanded to learn no matter what. Acknowledge when you are able to learn from joy or to love unconditionally, and also when you could have just a little more.

Positive thoughts and actions are much stronger than any negativity around us. Keep at it—that is all that can be asked. Give yourself a break, but realize you are creating your life. Some things happen as lessons we may not have even known we needed, but there is no punishment, just learning. So find ways to study joy. How does it teach you? When does it come into your life? Where do you feel it in your body? The more love and acceptance you extend without condition, and the more you follow your ideal path, the better your opportunities for joy.

THINGS I'VE LEARNED THROUGH JOY

- My intuition works! When I get quiet, listen to, and follow it, I am always rewarded.

- I know I walk hand in hand with Divinity. Connection and confirmation are pleasures available to all and are always brought with joy.

- Giving unconditional love instantly brings joy.

- Taking care of myself—giving myself downtime, space, TLC—is important.

- Small indulgences or healthy treats continue my feelings of abundance and worth.

- Remembrance of magical moments leads me back to peace.
- Doing nice things for others and then appreciating and focusing on their joys brings joy.
- I can change my life and create what I want because the Universe is friendly and abundant.
- Boundless joy is everywhere, and I can choose to have it, even if others cannot.
- Joy feels good in my body, and hugs always help.
- Animals never question pursuits of pleasure and peace.
- Nature offers joy every moment we look.
- Releasing unwanted energies is my choice, and holding preferred emotions is my right.
- Add to this list.

CHAPTER SEVEN

Forgiveness and Love

Today I remembered who you are.
Even though you forgot some time ago
When you found fault judging me,
I forgot too
When I defended.
Today
I remembered,
No one needs to justify their holiness,
Only to evoke it.
I remember,
Our souls are entwined,
We are the same.
And, for this moment,
I see you for who you are, utterly.
We are both love,
And nothing else is real.

As you progress in the direction of unconditional love, you begin to see that to truly get it, you must forgive. For real healing, forgiveness is perhaps the very biggest gift that unconditional love carries. You can only enjoy the full teaching of unconditional love if you have thoughts and feelings of unconditional love. You cannot preach it while you harbor resentment toward someone whom—you feel—has hurt you, even if you have grounds for justification. Forgiveness is a process that takes time, awareness, willingness, and implementation.

You will come to a point where you might be able to send love to the offender, and at times even feel love when you think about him or her. Then suddenly a past reminder will surface, and some pushed button is violently activated. Until you have mastered the lesson this person or situation is to teach, you will re-experience pain and various negative feelings that act as signals requiring your higher realizations.

Forgiveness is like history and healing—as one layer is dealt with, we continue working through the next layer, and the next, until eventually the issue is uncovered in its entirety, fully seen, processed, and understood. As you get more deeply into unconditional love, these hurts or angers will become less frequent and less intense. This means you are succeeding.

The path of unconditional love, like enlightenment, does not mean you will never encounter ignorant, selfish people who may hurt, judge, or project onto you. The meaning in your interaction with these people lies in the way in which you handle yourself. It is about living with peace and light, *learning* to love, especially when it is challenging. Discover the essence of your experience with non-judgment, holding the best view of everyone as often as you can teach yourself to.

This chapter invites us to delve into the ever-important arena of all kinds of forgiveness. We look at blocks to forgiving, as well as the all-important act of forgiving ourselves. We consider what empathy has to do with this lesson, and how important can be our angelic viewpoint in living forgiveness.

As we learn steps to forgive even the little stuff of our daily lives, we grow pure forgiveness by unconditionally loving.

BLOCKS TO FORGIVENESS

While you are working on your feelings of pain, trying to come to terms with what you believe happened, you are hoping the other person is working as hard, looking at your perspective as well. Often they are not, and this leads to the first potential block in forgiveness: you cannot rely on others taking steps for your own growth toward forgiveness. It is always about you and your evolving experiences, and truly never about the other person. Our focus is on feeling good —feeling unconditional love, no matter what.

"You cannot rely on others taking steps for your own growth toward forgiveness."

The second block involves the timing of forgiveness. Even with the best of intentions, forgiveness can take more time than we want. Sometimes it can be instantaneous, almost miraculous, as if you received sudden revelation. Sometimes it arrives as a gift to your long seeking. When you have integrated some of your lessons, forgiveness can be quick utilization of knowledge gained. But for serious trespasses, true and lasting forgiveness can be a long, thorny path you must tread repeatedly. Continue working to be wiser, to see clearer, and to bring light into yourself with unconditional love.

Although time does not necessarily heal deep wounds by itself, time to get away and think more clearly about whatever the situation is will help. Time allows you the space to witness the situation from various angles. Use time to gain perspective.

Putting yourself in the shoes of the perceived transgressor will help open your eyes, and perhaps eventually, your heart.

Third, an attitude of superiority. Strive to forgive without arrogance—which looks like someone forgiving because they are the "bigger person," more enlightened, or only pitying the other person—which is not true forgiveness. Superior attitudes will not feel healing to your body; the real feelings of forgiveness ease tension.

And last, watch your speech and thoughts about someone you want to forgive. Thinking and speaking negatively about them builds more negativity. Affirm positive words you can believe, like *I am healing every day. My life is just fine. I learn and let go. I release, love, and move on.* Notice all these are about our own work, and never the other. That is all we can control.

ANGELIC VIEWPOINT

The angelic viewpoint is a valuable tool in the lesson of forgiveness. Not only does it put you in the shoes of the perceived perpetrator, but utilizing the view of God and the angels is deeply transforming to those perceptions that separate. The Universe sees the best in everyone, and loves them for who they are, unconditionally—including you. You may think someone's attack was not justified or kind, and it may have hurt you quite a lot, but the point is to focus on what lesson a certain experience is presenting to *you.* Remember, God sees only love.

One of my Divine teachers, Margaret, read me a passage in Neale Donald Walsch's children's book *The Little Soul and the Sun*, and I was moved to tears. The story shines a bright light on forgiveness. If you are in a place of needing to forgive, I urge you to absorb the perspective brought to life by beloved little souls in heaven awaiting their new bodies and lives.

The story goes that one little soul wants to experience something new called *forgiveness*, and this becomes his greatest joy. As he wonders how he will do that, another soul, with whom he has shared many lives and different experiences, steps forward to offer his help. He tells the little soul that he will lower his vibration so he can give his friend the opportunity to learn forgiveness. He will create a situation in order that the little soul can fulfill his wish of experiencing what forgiveness is like, and he does this simply because he loves him.

The little soul cannot believe that a spirit so bright and dancing would be willing to become heavy enough to do this not-so-nice thing just to help him fulfill his desired experience. The little soul dances all around singing, "I get to be forgiving, I get to be forgiving!" His friend reminds, just before they go to Earth with their agreement, that when he does this terrible thing as a favor for the experience the little soul wishes that the little soul in return *must remember who his friend really is.*

You see, his friend must lose himself in order to play his part to offend the little soul, and if the little soul does not remember their pact, and his wish, then they will both be lost for a very long time. (This is one way darkness encroaches upon our lives.) If the little soul does not recognize his angel friend, they will both need another to come along and remind them who they are and what they were doing, so they may awaken from the heaviness to their light and love. God reminds them with a smile before their departure, "Always remember, I have sent you nothing but angels."

And *that*, out of all the wisdom I have found on forgiveness, is the most beautiful and profound by far. It touches my soul to think that a person I was so hurt by could have loved me enough to keep their promise to me so I could know this new thing called forgiveness. It is quite a shift in perspective.

We are all just doing our parts. We are all fulfilling our heavenly pledge to learn the things we chose. If you place yourself in that picture for just an instant, you can for one twinkling flash feel a rush of understanding accompanied with unconditional love. How kind of another to forget themselves momentarily and be hurtful so that we might gain experience and wisdom.

And if we do fail to forgive, fail to recognize our soul friends, then we will remain lost until we remember each other, or until someone reminds us who we all really are. What a sublime, thoughtful view. It makes you wonder how many great spiritual relationships we have cast aside out of mistaken importance placed on personalities and surface issues. We need to look much deeper at what comes into our lives. You must touch others with unconditional love if they are to remember themselves.

MEDITATION: FORGIVENESS OF SOUL FRIENDS (HINT: WE ARE ALL SOUL FRIENDS)

- Close your eyes, breathe, and feel peaceful.
- Think of something terrible you feel someone did to you.
- Look over everything you think this person did that hurt.
- Lovingly look over everything you did in the situation as well.
- Recognize the other as your angel friend; he or she is fulfilling a promise to help you remember and learn.

- What have you learned from this experience? How have you grown from these circumstances?
- Now do your part and see the other's holiness.
- Feel love in whatever way you can reach, and grow it, maybe even to the offender.
- This is forgiveness. Feel it.

Situations in which someone injures you will repeat in various ways, through various messengers, until the experience is transcended into your soul's requirement for growth. This person or people are simply the vessels by which God or the Universe is showing you yourself and honoring your pact. Thank their soul for sharing with you in this important experiment toward your selected experience. As long as you stay in judgment that something is "wrong" with the other person, your heart is closed to forgiveness and love. Let go of vengeance, rectification, anger, hatred, and opinion, for these emotions only add to the pain of the world.

"Awake from the grand illusions that anyone is less or more than another."

Everyone is doing the best they know. Everyone is in their own process and discovering their own realizations. Their realizations will usually not be the same as yours. By harboring anything negative towards them, you are also creating error, because everyone involved is a beloved child of God, just completing their assigned roles at their personal pace. If someone forgets his or her holiness and connection to the Divine Source by being attacking or defensive, it does not mean you must also forget Spirit by playing along in that game. Awake from the grand illusions that anyone is less or more than another.

In any situation that requires forgiveness, both parties are being taught the same lesson: to return to unconditional love. Focus on healing. Love is the only fundamental energy in our Universe, and God's greatest gift to us is our ability to accept and express unconditional love.

PURE ACCEPTANCE

Forgiveness opens the doors to real peace and a better world and is the essence of unconditional love. My grasping it is one of my main paths in this lifetime. I have had a lot of situations come into my life to allow me to grapple with the importance of forgiveness. Sometimes it took destroyed relationships and teary tantrums before I understood I was being unloving by holding negative opinions of those I felt had hurt me. I was taking the easier road of judgment instead of striving for non-judgement or unconditional acceptance.

Have you ever met someone who lives in pure acceptance? Because of our conditioning, it is difficult to even be aware of acceptance as an option when we are offended or hurt. Someone who lives in non-judgment makes no business assessing anyone. They just love, and it is a priceless and wondrous atmosphere to behold. My first teacher of meditation tools, Tanya F., bestowed this gift. It changed the way I saw the world and the way in which I believed the world could be.

It is a huge shift in consciousness to be able to experience rejection or harm separately from the person committing the act. By doing so, we can accept the person and love them, and not let their hurtful action define who they are. They were the messengers, and I added to the problem by failing to recognize their beauty and perfection, even in their unfriendliness (the way the situation presented itself to me).

I have had unbearable treatment from some with whom I shared my greatest and most vulnerable self. I have spent years in despair and introspection failing to understand reasons behind suffering. But after much time, work, and resources, I am stronger and more whole for all of it. I forgave because I finally understood the situation, why it arrived, and what I was to realize from it all, instead of judging it. But this takes a continuous shift in focus for sure. As long as we dwell on the perceived problem, or the person we think acted unfairly or unkindly, we are off track. The real meaning behind any experience is unconditional love. Remember that we are all connected and inherently beautiful. Accept everyone.

EMPATHY AND FORGIVENESS

I have always been acutely sensitive, especially as a child. When another person ached, I could feel it. I have a high degree of empathy and used to get so overwhelmed by people's pain and chaos that I could not even go into a grocery store without picking up many foreign energies.

Once when I was younger my parents had to both drive separately to some destination. All three of my siblings chose to ride with one parent, and I began crying, feeling that this had hurt the other. You can guess who I rode with. As a parent myself, I now realize that "lonely" parent probably wanted to have a few moments of well-deserved space and quiet. Because of this sensitivity to others, it has been easier for me to understand another's perspective and apologize or forgive. If I feel responsible for anyone's pain, I am crushed.

So, while I could believe that people hurt me, or were thoughtless, I could never accept hurting or thoughtlessness from myself. I came to expect this misunderstanding and throbbing from the world, which I now know helped con-tinuously to create those experiences. Thank goodness I have been able to measurably shift my focus from that place to a friendly universal perspective, though not before great gains from turbulent comprehensions. I know from many lost relationships that I never intended to hurt anyone, and this helped me realize that no one who hurt me probably meant to either. It is rare to encounter an individual who actually wants to cause harm. We all handle things the best we know, and early on, most of us do not know very well. We would love to have always had an evolved perception of learning through joy so we would not have been wounded or wounded another accidentally.

Nevertheless, in my twenties especially, it was these very wounds and breakups that helped me achieve that more evolved perspective. Now I know a little better, but it is still a process of witnessing, realizing, and shifting back to unconditional love. I am grateful that it comes much more quickly now, and I understand the deeper fundamental nature flowing through my experiences. And because of these reasons, I also appreciate beyond words the feelings of being forgiven. Each of us has done countless stupid things on our way to knowing better, and it is a special gift to be forgiven so we may keep moving forward, realize higher truths, and learn clearer love and joys.

FORGIVING YOURSELF

It has always been easier for me to forgive others than to forgive myself, and I suspect I'm not alone in this. In order to forgive yourself, you need to love yourself. If you are hard on yourself instead of loving, it will be enormously more difficult to forgive and love another. If you judge yourself, you will judge another. When you allow others to be as they are, you extend that allowance to yourself. This is priceless for your peace and happiness. From personal experience, I know

"When you allow others to be as they are, you extend that allowance to yourself."

the impact of self-talk and how we treat ourselves. It took me years to realize the causes of my inability to make better life choices.

In my quest to lose weight, I would lose most of what I wanted, then gain some, lose some, plateau—just like the majority of humans. The missing link, at least for me, was when I finally realized I could not lose weight or find serenity while I was calling myself fat. Even if mostly in jest, I was being very unkind to my body by calling it names. This is something I never would have said to anyone else, so why did I beat myself up in such a way?

This was a big lesson in self-love and forgiveness. I am not perfect, but I could at least learn to be kind and understanding to myself despite it. It is amazing the things we do and say to hurt ourselves when we would never imagine hurting another in the same way. How we feel about and talk to ourselves expands outwardly to others. By loving, honoring, and appreciating my body, I create the energy that allows others to do the same. We can be forgiven for what we feel inside are our worst failures, but only by shining light from within. Then others can be warmed by its glow.

Forgiveness starts from within. Whatever you hold toward yourself, whether it be judgments, criticisms, or love, it will radiate outward to others. Forgive yourself for your perceptions and be reminded of divine unity. We are all one. What you experience resonates in all humankind, and you can only give away what you have overflowing from inside, so cultivate the very best you can where you are.

If you feel you have caused a trespass, do everything to heal it and transmute it toward love. Then forgive yourself.

We are all human beings and by design are here to learn and grow. The only way to do that is through trial and sometimes mistakes. Give the light of communication and ask Divinity to be forgiven and to help you forgive. If you can sit down and make it right, do so. If you cannot reach the other, then work on yourself so you learn this lesson and do not repeat it. If someone else chooses to live amid illusions, it may bother you, but it is their choice for their life. Let them have their stuff and use it as a lesson to search your own illusions. Then there is nothing to forgive, only stuff to learn.

What bothers you in another is a key to unlock something within yourself. Surrender your pains to our embracing Divinity and reach out to be as loving as you can, even to yourself. Everyone makes mistakes, but learning from them can be missed. You will be righting the error by asking for a forgiving perception of your life and everyone's; this way the error will not be carried into the next situation.

Forgive yourself, and treasure your willingness to do so. You will go a long way to understanding that others are just as deserving of forgiveness and love. It will only hurt you to be unforgiving. It will only serve to separate you from your Source, and from your true purpose. It will not bring anyone realizations to be resented. If anything, your example of forgiving what seems unforgivable will jump-start many others along the road. This is an immeasurable gift to our world.

Love yourself for every effort you make, and even if it takes years and spiraling ups and downs, you will heal. Any who inflict harm are desperately in need of love. They must have found you because their spirit knew you were capable of seeing the best in them, of forgiving them. They saw in you seeds of unconditional love.

You have the ability within to heal completely, so begin with your competent and beautiful self. It will make the world a better and lighter place to allow peace within, that you may spread it outwardly. God and the angels love you unconditionally, and you could never do anything for which they will not bestow forgiveness. So feel it and swell it.

MEDITATION: SPACE TO FORGIVE

- Close your eyes and sit with any feelings of unforgiveness.
- Release these feelings down into the ground through your feet.
- Allow all negativity to flow into the earth, to be grounded out and recycled. Doing so literally creates space within your energetic field.
- Now fill that space you just created with love from your heart, or love from anywhere.
- Add light to that space like a beam from God.
- Breathe, and release, and fill again and again.
- Feel gratitude in your heart for this healing.

HANDLING INCONSIDERATENESS

How we handle everyday irritations can be more important to our happiness than anything else. After all, it is through our actions each day that we create our lives. You may practice spirituality and give generously to charities, but what is your immediate reaction when something does not go according to plan? You might preach peace and love, but do you then kill an insect sheltering in your home, scream at your spouse or children, or feel your stomach twist into knots over an unhappy surprise phone call?

Many of us have worked on the big things in our lives, but the small recurring experiences may be a bigger and more mysterious block to feeling the way we would like, as smaller problems go frequently unnoticed. It is darkly humorous that we sit and meditate upon "working on ourselves" and then we are totally undone by something infinitesimal. These are important clues to what is holding us back from receiving unconditional love.

When we lived in the town of two hundred at eleven thousand feet, the only access to the place was a two-lane, ten-mile-long road. Over those ten miles, the elevation rises three thousand feet. It turns and twists, with four switchback hairpin turns, meaning drivers can't see to anticipate oncoming traffic. It has virtually no guardrails and has more than a hundred-foot drop-offs any number of times until you reach our valley nestled in the continental divide.

During daylight and summer, it takes twelve minutes downhill to reach the highway. During winter, the steep grade, thick snow pack, ice, and sideways blowing snow make the route very dangerous, and the same route can take forty-five minutes. Few cars use the road, though certain times of year invite loads of tourists. At several points, the road is wide enough to allow for a wide shoulder, where a slower car can move over and considerately allow a faster car to pass.

We drove slowly on the way up because we do not like to push our cars. But we always, *always* pulled over when someone behind us wanted to go faster. I kept a vigilant look out my rearview mirror to see anyone gaining on me. (I knew how much a schedule could go awry if getting behind the wrong car.) I planned where I could pull over to let others pass. Who am I not to let someone be in a hurry if he or she wants to be?

Despite my own personal care in making sure to get out

of the way of faster cars, I seemed to get behind every slow person possible when I was running behind schedule. Some folks noticed and acted appropriately (especially with flashing lights and honking from me), but some seemed completely oblivious. Worse, some took my clear frustration as the chance to teach me a lesson by going even slower. I just do not get this attitude. If someone wants to go faster, and you can safely move to a shoulder to let them pass, why would you not participate in these unwritten considerations? Who likes to have someone riding on his or her back end?

A thirty-minute difference in making it to the highway meant thirty minutes of steaming about thoughtless people. Now, I do not rant and rave or drive like a crazy maniac as these paragraphs might suggest, but I did have to examine why it bothered me when others did not extend the same civilities as I did them. I began to experiment with different strategies to avoid boiling my blood every time I drove to the highway. I tried breathing techniques, looking out the window to connect with the trees and river, and extracting compassion for the driver ahead. Nothing worked for long.

I don't have that drive anymore, but small inconsiderate events keep happening—which leads me only to myself. I know fundamentally that I continue to create these situations so I can change my experience and acquire deeper patience, but that realization does not always help me, or occur to me in the moment. I do see the universal humor of trying to spread unconditional love around the world while also losing faith in intrinsic human goodness because of a speed limit, elevator door, or line at the store. Therefore, it remains important for me to grasp and transform this aspect of my mindset.

We can be put off by strangers and companions alike. My husband leaves our kitchen cupboards open all the time, and it drives me crazy. Just this morning he went outside and left the glass door unlatched to slam and bang in the ferocious wind. This was made into a bigger deal by the fact it was before six in the morning, and the door was near my young daughter's bedroom window. She had been sick, which meant both she and I needed rest.

After grumbling to myself at his unbelievable thoughtlessness, I could feel the stress in my body. That was not how I wanted to start my day, nor did he want the defense and anger that was sure to ensue upon his return. So I started to be grateful that he was snow blowing so the car could get out, and he was probably meditating also . . . what an ironic concept!

No matter how put together we think we are or want to be, spontaneous situations are revealing because they are the realness of life unfolding. These reactions illuminate our true spontaneous dispositions. Day to day we are defined by our knee-jerk reactions, poor though they may be. We can all be graceful when we are prepared, have rested well, or have things following our clever plans. True temperament shines in the small details or real-life happenings, right there in front of us. Whether or not my husband was inconsiderate, it was obviously my lesson. He was a Divine messenger for my attainment of peace and growth. I am sure I forgot to thank him, to say the least.

It is ingrained in us to recognize negative circumstances and hold that focus rather than see the little miracles. When we begin believing that we can create our world, we gain a great power over our lives. We can choose to consider others with kindness, knowing it takes nothing away while blossoming in the nurturing environment. Consider those less fortunate who show gratitude for simple luxuries and small occasions—they are creating a world of abundance for themselves. I myself have learned to center more on the good than bad, which is a feat for me, and it is a beautiful place to start healing, as well as lower our blood pressure.

Truth be told, there were exponentially more times we flew unencumbered down our road (safely) rather than the stressful alternative. Focusing on the times when things go right helps remind us that good things happen too. We can remember to be grateful for the millions of blessings in our lives and not to fret over the little stuff.

After appreciation, I turn to compassion. Maybe a person I labeled as unconscientious has just lost someone or is traveling through a current void in his or her life. I recall times I was so upset about something that I did not recognize others around me. And if someone cut me off, maybe they were on their way to the hospital.

This connection through familiarity reminds us of our entwined destinies and purposes. This pattern of thought not only calms me, but also gets my mind concentrating on empathy instead of the previous unwanted feelings, which may not have been fair or loving. We need to take great responsibility in our collective consciousness; the energy we create with our feelings, thoughts, words, and actions resonates throughout infinity.

With compassion surfacing, I remember to confer with Spirit. Trust and divine timing are two invaluable perspectives I have employed when I feel impatient or angry. When I connect to Spirit and have faith in a friendly Universe, I know that everything is happening just as it is meant to. Who am I to question holiness? I know that my living in harmony with nature and the world will always put me in the right place at the right time.

Here enters a huge element of trust. If I am late to the airport, maybe I was meant to miss that flight. If I was not on the schedule I planned, then maybe there was someone who needed help along the way who could only cross my path at that time. We could be late enough to miss a fight or an angry co-worker. We must trust the infinite possibilities of our world.

When we ask to serve humankind or beg to be led by Spirit, many doors open for us in unexpected places. We need to trust and be glad that we are being answered. If everything always went according to our own schedules, we would be limiting our choices and experiences to what we already know. We are aware of very little in the grand scheme of things. Our Universe has abundant divine plans and recognizes how to do everything for the best of all concerned.

"We only come to recognize our own limitations through interaction with others."

To all of these solutions and tips, I would add a final one: evoke unconditional love. If ever we are abrupt in our reactions, we are not in a loving space. If our feelings are unbalanced or our thoughts judgmental, then we have thrown ourselves into a closed and unlit energy. Call to mind the love you would want bestowed on you, feel it, fill with it, and give it. We never know what another is going through, but all of us need more love. Practice patience for those all around you. This is not only sanity saving, but benefits the other person, and most importantly, you will be saving yourself. As Saint Augustine said, "The reward of patience is patience!"

And although my husband often leaves the door unlatched to bang in the wind, and it can be maddening, it is a giant life lesson. When unhappy emotions are brought to the surface, we can thank the person or situation for leading us to something we needed to become aware of. This person is only a messenger, and the sooner you observe yourself and grow, the sooner your peace returns.

It may not be comforting to hear our life is our experience, and we are responsible for how we react, see, and live, especially if you feel certain that blame sits on someone else's shoulders. But once realized and implemented as truth, this path will liberate you. Take your blame off what you perceive wrong with the other, and while remembering you are the irate one, forgive yourself. They appear quite serene while driving ten miles an hour in front of you—you are the one in restlessness. Cover all bases with compassionate understanding and be proud of yourself by offering love with no conditions of how one must act in order to receive it. We are all deserving. We are all here to experience, and we are all worthy of forgiveness.

CHAPTER EIGHT

Evaluating Relationships with Love

I sent you love today.
I cried out, finally missing you,
and I spoke loving words, long lost.
I wished that you could understand me,
as I finally have understood you.
For I realize what I saw
was not what you saw.
And I wish you truly knew
what you believed to be me wasn't.

I am so different
than the person you assumed and blamed.
And yet, as I feel attacked and wronged,
knowing you feel justified in your vengeance,
I still understand, forgive, and release your illusions
with love.

So tragic what was destroyed,
I know it needn't have been so.
But I finally arrive on the other side of pain and
confusion.
I find meaning and acceptance,

appreciation even,
for our time together.
You walked away with anger,
and I bought into it.
But today,
from a place of peace
and sought-after kindness,
I finally cried tears for you.
With loving thanks and farewell for now.

As we continue on our path of getting unconditional love, we may think that such love will heal all problems within our relationships. As we've discussed, relationships exist to show us the dark parts of ourselves that need to be brought up into the light so they may be healed. We only come to recognize our own limitations through interaction with others. So, full of love, we strive to put ourselves in the shoes of the other person, and learn from the lessons that come up. But it may be that the other person is not in a place where they can accept healing or love. Sometimes it is not up to us or even them.

You can unconditionally love everyone you meet, but if they are not also in that place, you certainly cannot change them. You can give them wave after wave of unconditional love. You can have deep compassion that their own pain or fear added to their intolerant actions. You can even forgive them over and over and over. But if something wrong persists, it might be time to end the relationship. This chapter discusses how unconditional love can be applied in relationships and when it may be time to sever the bond.

TO END OR NOT TO END

We each must love ourselves enough to let go when the timing is necessary. With the exception of death, most relationships end for one of two reasons: you hurt someone, or someone hurt you. The one cut-and-dry scenario is abuse: you need to end a relationship if it is abusive. If you are being abused in any way, you need to seek immediate assistance to move to a healthier circumstance. We must first keep ourselves safe.

If abuse is not in the picture, then how a relationship is perceived really comes down to one or both parties being displeased. Most of us do not desire to hurt anyone and try diligently to avoid it. When we wound another, it is our work to heal it, to earn forgiveness, to communicate as best we can and bring mutual understanding.

Asking for forgiveness and making up to someone you have hurt is utterly easy compared to the alternative. When we have caused a trespass, we know hopefully that we are responsible. We can find humility, and therefore make it right, or at least try. But how do we reconcile when we have been deeply scarred by someone else? They may not realize they have caused mutilation to your heart, or they may not care. When something is this pervasive, how can we find unconditional love?

First, we begin with ourselves: heal and balance, love and nurture. Something in them caused harm, or perceived harm, and that is theirs to rectify. Deal with your own insides, and conclude another's influence on your truth. Then we can start cultivating unconditional love for them. This may take time and searching. Since we are not yet enlightened, it can be difficult to respond to hatred with love. But it is exactly this response we need to learn. Distance will help, and lots of release. You can understand them and have compassion while still feeling blindsided by their terribleness. As we discovered in Chapter Seven on forgiveness, it may take years to heal if this was a serious incident, but you will return to harmony and love if you work at it. Let it go and leave all of it behind, except for the lessons learned.

The ways in which a loved one may harm us are in-numerable, but they all have to do with their own issues, not yours. When someone dear to you makes you doubt your goodness, loveliness, or potential, they are getting into their own issues and projecting. If someone you trusted believes misinformation about you or your actions, they may never have the ability to enjoy the real and beautiful you. If someone planned or continued to hurt or betray you, he or she is not a person you need. Be sure your information is correct and preferably firsthand, for many a good friendship or family has been destroyed because of false words or misinterpretation.

I have had the majority of severed relationships in my life occur because of someone believing a mistruth said by another. Instead of lovingly speaking and hearing the truth straight from me, they chose to believe another's lie, and therefore did not choose with accuracy or heal with unconditional love. It is very sad when a tie is broken because of fallacy, but if one truly believes evil falsehoods about you, you may be far better off with others who honor your good heart and steadfast truth. It seems as though these situations should end after grammar school, but if you have a group of unhealthy adults together, the dynamics can bring out schoolyard cliques and attitudes.

Barring any large betrayals or mistruths, we can look into ourselves to know how to heal within a loving, albeit deep or potentially difficult, relationship. It can be a confusing moral dichotomy. Have you done all you can? When do you know the difference between needing to do more and try harder to forgive, or needing to get out of the situation, and being okay with that decision? When is your ego lacking in compassion or your pride taking over, and when are you hurting yourself by holding on in futility? Does this person need your gifts to grow? Are you or people you care for going to get seriously hurt if it either ends or continues?

Sometimes we can limit time spent together to very small doses while increasing our strength and detachment so we do not suffer in their presence. Other times their neglect and denial are so painful and permanent that we are hurt and wounded by having a single conversation with them. Can we change how we take in the information or interaction with the person in a way that allows our truth while holding unconditional love for his or her humanity? Can we simply approach our connection with him or her in a different way? Can I remain neutral to his or her conflict or indifference, and appreciate something about the connection, or does interacting at all cause major distress? Does it take time away from my life and how I want to feel because it is just too damaging or limiting? Do I need something different? Keep asking yourself questions, and be honest in answering them.

If you feel continuously low vibrations upon every interaction with a group or person, then they are not adding to your light. If it is always a struggle, or you feel you must defend your given rights on every occasion, then you need to get out, at least temporarily, so you can correctly assess and save yourself. If you are not sure whether the relationship is unhealthy, spend time with different friends or meet new people and compare the feelings you are left with afterward. If you are unsure about a primary relationship, then take a few days away at a hotel or with friends or other family members and evaluate how it feels to do so. Does being somewhere else bring you peace, allow you to relax, think of yourself, or get excited about your dreams?

Likely your vibrations in relationships are not consistently low. When in doubt about whether to continue a relationship or not, the best place to look for answers is of course through Divinity. If signs keep appearing and they resonate internally with a sense of knowing or relief, then you are being guided. Look for divine repetition. Look for synchronicities. Sit outside and breathe. Take a moment to feel your heart. Ask silent questions, and listen through peaceful breathing. I promise you will have knowing. If you are aware, and receive repetitive messages to leave a job, place, relationship, or group—whatever it is, listen and trust that you are being helped.

When the Divine Universe is sending out messages of guidance, it is a calling. There does not need to be judgment or pain, just innocent, inspired movement in a different direction. In hindsight, you will see the beneficial and magical lining up of events and circumstances that brought you to where you are. With unconditional love, you will feel good about your choices no matter what the other person chooses. You loved them the best you could, and when it was not getting through, you loved yourself enough to move to where you could be valued and could make a better difference.

We can also turn to energy work to release our programs, which are beliefs we unconsciously live. They may have been created mistakenly, but we are now stuck in them. It could be as simple as clearing our own space so the relationship can reset with clean energy. We will learn techniques of specific releasing methods in Part Two. Whether it is associations with friends or kindred family affairs, there will be much to consider before you will know what is best for you and the other on a soul level. You may determine that the other person needs your light and example of growth while you have a private understanding that you cannot and should not trust them with your deepest sacred feelings. Connecting on this spiritual level may be enough to save everyone involved from loss.

If you are contemplating terminating any type of union or are on the receiving end of being disowned or left, you need to deeply consider both the history and the future. Family dynamics often involve a great deal of karma. There may be lifetimes of lessons and learning if you are having troubled family relations. You may have been stuck in this pattern for so long that it is paramount to your soul that you sever ties. But don't just run. There may also be beautiful gifts of healing if you communicate, love, and work through the issues together. You will keep reliving this model of pain and lesson through lifetimes, as both child and parent, until you learn unconditional love, or even self-love.

MEDITATION: EVALUATING RELATIONSHIPS

- Close your eyes and breathe into a calm space.
- Take stock of any relationship you have ended or are considering ending.
- Beyond the personality and situation, what deep feelings lie here?
- Breathe deeply, and release this negativity with each breath out.
- Be honest with yourself, and ask some internal questions. Have you tried open and real communication? Has everyone gotten to explain and share their feelings? Have you done all you can to make things right? Can you feel unconditional love for them? Take as much time as you need to fully answer these and whatever else comes up.

- If you can walk away with love, put this person in a bubble, and let them go.

- Remember good times with this person, and focus on that loving connection.

- If you are still angry or hurt, do more work, ask more questions, and be available to work through the issues together if the other is willing.

ENDING IT

Once we have searched our hearts and higher selves for answers, sometimes the truth is relationships need to change or end. This can be an immense lesson, but it does not have to be painful. If you focus on the messages and joys brought by the relationship and take care of your needs, it can be less distressing and even liberating.

Sometimes friends are lost, a family member becomes an outcast, or a relationship is terminated. This can occur because of growth in one party and not in the other, differing directions or interests, a simple misunderstanding, or a gross betrayal. Sometimes we just grow in different directions, all the things we had in common changing as we change. You might feel drained around a certain set of circumstances you no longer wish to be a part of. You might just feel an increasing distance in your bond.

At the same time, you might find new people who share your newer visions and dreams. Your vibration to your other acquaintances may simply be shifting toward a dissimilar resonance. As people get busy with the details of their own lives, their older connections may quietly fade, to be reclaimed along another road. Often it is very tender as well as confusing.

A handful of individuals have passed through my life in

such ways. Some seemed staples to my existence. Some were easier to learn from and let go of than others. Some I still miss and send love to, even as I remind myself to release. It hurts. With some, I have not completed karmic cycles, and we will end up rehashing similar situations in future lifetimes because the end was not dealt with healthfully. I would, however, like to precede this karmic pattern with growth.

It may appear to others that in ending a relationship, you are running away from someone or something, or being immature, but follow the information you receive from your internal or spiritual Source. You need to remain loyal to yourself and your truth first. If you need to, feel free to remind others that you are just moving toward something else. You are the only one who can know what or who is best for you. Set boundaries you are comfortable with and stick to them.

Love them and move away kindly. When feeling weak or seduced into replaying an unhealthy role in an outmoded relationship, gently remember why you chose to walk away. Work to heal or transform that role in you. Continue in a good direction. Remember, sometimes no matter how much you look at it, work on it, grow, or change—if the other party has not followed your progression, you are doing the best thing possible for everyone's spirits involved by separating. Even after you have healed, you do not want to go running back into their lives.

Sometimes you can reach out from a distance to see if the energy has shifted. But there is a good chance that restarting will just lead back to the original difficulties which caused you to leave initially. Sometimes we stay in touch that we might continue our learning of unconditional love while giving the space that others need. This occurs mostly in family situations, because we usually choose our families for more reasons than meet the eye. It may only be after lifetimes of growing that we recognize our patterns and weaknesses, and can therefore alter our associations.

No matter the reason for the end of a relationship, whether mutual or heart-wrenching, remember the good and the lessons learned, and allow yourself to fill with the healing power of unconditional love as you take care of yourself and transition to new spaces or relationships.

TAKE CARE OF YOURSELF

Deciding to leave or change a relationship all comes down to this: do you have the ability to stay connected to this person and still remain safe and healthy and growing, or not? A vital part of any relationship is your level of okayness. This must be about you and what decisions allow for your peace and security. If you can share your truth calmly and without expectations, then great. If you cannot, then this decision is simply your own plan for personal success, and it is in your best interest, and perfectly reasonable, to keep it to yourself.

Communication works wonders, but you especially need to be aware that sharing any real feelings may not elicit the response you desire. Your heartfelt communication may not make anyone suddenly "get it." You may state your perceptions of the difficulties and your arrangement for what sort of connection will be acceptable to you, but any expectations of the other person understanding your perspective may further hurt you. This is another possible reason on your list of reasons as to why this relationship is in question in the first place.

I always felt I had to speak all of my truth to enjoy my relationships, and to be myself. But I have learned that I can still glean education and love from these contacts, and they from me, while not wearing my heart on my sleeve. My preference is to have fewer intimate connections that are very open, revealing, close, real, and true. But there are advantages to keeping in contact with those whom I would not choose to share with deeply. I have learned to have relationships with different levels of bonding and benefit while still holding true to myself.

Try to speak truly if you want, but know that others may not be able to hear you. Many people enjoy the control they feel from power struggles. Choose not to be a part of others' pitiful manipulations. Love yourself enough to trust your feelings. A friend most likely is not hurting you on purpose, but some will. You are special and must ensure your own health and happiness. We are all usually doing our best, so hold light for others even in turmoil, and from your heart; give unconditional love even if you have to walk away.

When a bond has been broken, either to you or by your choice, our work has just begun. We now have the freedom to ask some important questions. How do you feel afterwards? What are the lessons you are learning now because of the disconnection? What can you heal in yourself or give to yourself? Could this broken bond change with time or personal introspection? Do you feel relief? Are you now safer or stronger? Are you still missing something? Are you in need of looking at your own anger or patterns? Has your truth about your feelings changed?

Whether a blessing or curse, after I have separated from someone or something, I tend to only remember the goodness and fond feelings. This reaction helps me hold unconditional love for the other person, but I also love and forgive so easily that I blindly forget the deeper truth. I may long for those past heartfelt connections, forgetting that I had already learned what the relationship wanted to teach me. Once you have learned, there is no reason to repeat frustrating interactions, misunderstanding defenses, or any of the negative reactions that caused you to tag that relationship "unconditionally love but move away now" in the first place.

MEDITATION: LETTING GO

- Relax, close your eyes, and take a few nice breaths.
- If you have communicated, searched, and worked, and know it is best to release this person, congratulate yourself for learning, trying, and knowing.
- Ask what agreements this relationship might have had on a spiritual level.
- Feel gratitude for all it taught and brought you.
- Let Spirit know you would like to amend or end this agreement.
- Imagine you are signing a new contract. Let it read as you like, and then sign your name.
- Roll up this document, place it in a bubble, and send it to Spirit.
- Follow this action with thoughts of love.
- Release any remaining energy, repeatedly if necessary, and bring in unconditional love.

GROWTH THROUGH THE END

Being unable to fulfill a relationship in preferred ways can be sorrowful. How grand it would be to have stuck with each other one moment longer, listening and sustaining a circle of laughter, drinking tea, with smiles and flowers. All the potential sweetness you could envision—pure listening, pure connection, responsibility and rectification, real truth from open hearts—would be ideal. However, everyone learns, lives, and grows differently.

Differences need not be detrimental, but the route of strife, separation, blame, projection, negativity, and hatred is the path some choose and need for their own growth. Here is where we can interject unconditional love—love for the relationship we had, the good times, the lessons, and acceptance that a change needs to come for everyone's higher path. Let that and our light of hope at least be some consolation as to the appearing loss. Let joy overflow that we finally choose easier, happier ways to learn. It is only in our growth and evolving consciousness that pain ever had a purpose. We can experience change through hopeful joy.

> "It is only in our growth and evolving consciousness that pain ever had a purpose."

Relationships are simply here to mirror behavior and teach lessons, and you must admit they certainly do that! Who knows, it may come to pass that learning from them and releasing them with unconditional love will, in the end, reunite you. Many paths lead to the same place, and it may be temporary that you both move in different directions. You both need to teach and learn different lessons that cannot be offered through your current status. Distance allows insight. Remember to choose a friendly universal view, for the Universe will always unite or release what is best and right for the energies and paths of all concerned.

We each have occasions when we are either more attached or detached. This is okay, as different times in our lives can require either more space or stronger support. Remember that closeness waxes and wanes as does any other cycle in life. We might preface the stark *ending* of a relationship by replacing it with the word "change." With karmic cycles, self-growth, and awareness, we can simply see the bond altered. It continues in a different form, for a different time.

Keep in mind that we do not know what comes next. We need not judge anything as a true end, just a modification. Labels can seem more daunting than the real flow and flexibility of life. Sometimes we just need a break from deep enmeshment with another so we can see ourselves and work on our own stuff. And if you felt you needed to end a relationship to work on your own stuff, you may yet find a reunion. We keep many people and thoughts in our energy field, and often focusing on our truths may be enough to change a dynamic for the better.

Choosing or needing to end any relationship should never happen lightly. However, you also need to allow yourself to remain healthy, and follow your own dreams. I send hope, love, and forgiveness to the other person so that somewhere down the road, light can heal us both. Like the old adage reminds us, "Love them and let them go." They may or may not return. I do my very best to release my attachment and let the Universe take care of our potential meeting. Whether it is tomorrow, twenty years, three lifetimes, or just a peaceful understanding of goodbye, it gets easier to do my part to unconditionally love and trust Divinity's timing and plans.

LESSONS I LEARNED FROM RELEASING WITH UNCONDITIONAL LOVE

- It feels great! Freedom and relief after turbulence is wonderful.
- You will keep your integrity and self-respect.
- When God closes a door she/he *always* opens a window. New and better people *will* come into your life.

- By honoring my time, energy, and self, I give others the example to do the same. We teach people how to treat us by how we treat ourselves.

- Communication is the most important tool if any relationship is to work.

- It is more important to focus on myself and my lessons than on anyone else. Focusing on myself allows me to hold and radiate more light.

- I have great love for everyone, even if I have to hold it silently; it makes me feel peaceful and whole to know this about myself.

- Releasing makes room for better energy.

- Ridding your life of those who cause pain allows for personal healing to begin and demands self-responsibility in your work.

- When others who are not honoring you leave, it is a blessing.

- As you release and heal from any discord, you have more time to focus on happy and important things that are actually meaningful to your life or the world. You may not realize how much time you spent stuck in pain or hurt until you are freed from it.

- If someone does not deserve you, find someone who does. They are nearer than you realize.

- Unconditional love does not mean unconditional presence or permitting.

- Unconditional love could heal the entire world if we let it.

- Add to this list.

PART TWO

Growing What Comes to You through Love

IT WILL COME TO YOU

What you love,
What you loathe,
What you want,
And what you do not want.
All this will come to you, and more.
What you think about,
What you seek,
What you resist,
And more than you yet realize.
What you put out will come back to you,
And what you ask for.
What you run away from,
And more than most can imagine.
What you focus on is paramount,
Where and with whom you spend your time matters,
And your intentions are of consequence.
We create our lives
And what we see and experience.
So select conscious light,
And choose to live with love.

The words of this poem can seem daunting, but, as you will discover in Part Two, they are empowering. You *can* affect what comes to you. How you spend your precious energy, your action, and all the seemingly unimportant moments between will influence what shows up in your life. You can turn it to your liking. You can create each day to be beautiful. You can grow your life simply, and condition yourself to have more with no conditions.

As the first part focused on the tenets of unconditional love and how to get it in our lives, this second part attends to cultivating what we have planted. We concentrate our personal energy on observing how our outlook is helping or hindering us, so we may then heal and evolve those perceptions according to our goals. Everything in our lives resonates with what we think and therefore create. What we choose to receive vibrates with our individual thoughts and actions accumulated over time. Learn responsibility, pure faith, and unconditional love in your choices, even in thought, so you get what you want every time.

Answers, love, success, and everything you desire can come—you can make complete the world in which you live. Become whole. Seek out and name your dragons. Believe in a positive force to overcome them. Victory will be yours. It already has been in some measure—remember that! It will grow as you let it. As you assist yourself with faith in good and in everything you give energy to, more and more benevolence will enter your space.

Trust, and trust shall be yours. Show patience, and peace comes into each moment. Believe, and others will follow in belief. Be the spark for yourself, your acquaintances, and your world. Such great energy grows exponentially, and when ignited with hope and eagerness, real magic begins. That there are endless keys to getting what you want, where you want to go, who you want to be and feel like, is reassuring. That they are within your reach and available to improve your life, even beginning today, is even greater.

So lift the burden of fear or hopelessness by opening your mind. Changed thoughts will guide and enlighten you toward what you seek. They will help bring you what you want and keep from you what you do not want. In the coming pages, we will explore the power of perception, growth through manifesting, and the importance of uncondition. We will look at our passions and inspirations, how our observations can benefit us, and the role attachment might play in our success, happiness, and security. Here bestowed are higher connections and priceless meditation tools to enhance your world. And we turn to nature, always, to help heal us. Think about the steps and states of mind presented to you, and as you act with them in your conscious view, what you choose to release and change will dissolve, and what you want and need will come to you.

CHAPTER NINE

Manifesting, Growing, and Waiting

Here we learn how to grow unconditional love through manifesting. When we accept the truth that we create the world we inhabit, it becomes important to know what kind of world we want. Our desires will manifest in our reality. Our feelings can be a gauge to determine if we are getting closer to or further from the world we want. If we feel stagnant or experience a void between creations, this too is growth. As we take stock of our shifts and what we desire, we find patience, the void, and our creations are all one.

YOU ARE A CREATOR

All life is creation. As created and creative beings, we are always creating; it is the nature of our earth and humanity. Whether or not we realize or purposely create, we are still continuously manifesting. We are co-creators with a higher power—you may call it the Universe, God, Source Energy, or Divinity. All life is in constant movement, and it is in your best interest, and that of the world, that you use this power of creation wisely. Consciously or unconsciously, you create what you think about and desire—which means you can create what you want if you are intentional.

Although we came here connected to our Source, knowing our goals and how to achieve them, we lose our way from time to time because of our upbringing, society's media, and other forms of illusionary thinking. Luckily, many enlightened souls lead us, beautifully lighting our path so we may stumble less on our way to manifesting a better world.

One light along my path of enlightenment is *Ask and It Is Given*, a book by Esther and Jerry Hicks from the teachings of Abraham. In this exquisite source of knowledge, the authors explain how we often think we are creating what we want but are actually so focused on the lack of having it that we are instead creating more of what we do not want, simply because *that* is where our energy is focused. They give practical tools to relearn how to know what you want, and to make sure *that* is the creation of your manifestations. Any desire you have that is good, feels good, or betters your life or the world is a positive intentional desire worth pursuing.

Think about what you truly desire. If you could have it all, what would that look like? Would you remain in your current profession because it makes your heart sing? Would you keep most of the relationships you have because they are supportive and uplifting? Do you have dreams you have not yet achieved? Is there a different life you would be living if you *really* believed you could create it? You can! So begin to ponder what you would like to manifest if you had confidence in your abilities or the Universe. Remember Source will create whatever you intend, but do so with high integrity and positivity, because you cannot trick it, and it will not harm.

OBSERVE YOUR FEELINGS

By becoming aware of what you are thinking, and especially how you are feeling, you will know if you are either going toward your desires and manifesting what you want, or going away from your desires and thus manifesting more of what you do not want. This knowledge is priceless. If you feel good, peaceful, or positive, you are probably heading in the direction of your desires. If you feel frustrated, depressed, or worse, you are probably heading toward what you do not want. Stay in close observation of how you are feeling and learn to notice when you need to redirect your life to where you want to go.

VISUALIZATION: GETTING CLEAR

- Find a calm space and turn inward.
- Visualize your perfect day.
- What does it look like? What are you doing?
- These are clues to your innermost desires. Follow them. Note any new wishes.
- When you picture them happening, how does your body feel?
- Continue with what feels good, and visualize your wildest dreams come true.
- To get in touch with the desires you want to manifest, pay attention to your feelings.
- Ask yourself questions, and as you visualize, you begin to create.

Once you take stock of your life and how it measures up to your unlimited desires, you are clear about the kinds of things you want to show up in your life, and you are focusing on them (and not on their absence), it is simply a matter of allowing all this good to come to you.

It may sound silly. Of course you will allow the good to come! But upon closer observation, there are many forms of resistance to this allowing. If you are angry with someone, or are judging or blaming, your energy is not in a place of allowing, even though you may insist you want happiness, peace, or this other great thing. As you cultivate unconditional love, you live more frequently in a space of openness where all your dreams will come true.

If you hate something, you are not ridding your life of it—you are binding yourself to it. If you are upset with a personal relationship, it will continue to haunt you even if you think you want it to disappear. You cannot just put things out of your mind. You can forgive a person and let them be released from your life, but you cannot let them go from your mind and spirit unless it is truly with good-heartedness.

These feelings of fear or angst are bothering you for reasons of your soul's growth. Understand these energies and resolve to not bring them with you into your next manifestation. If you know enough to look at your feelings, this situation has brought you the gift of insight and learning already. You must replace lower vibrations with conscious change. Just like a bad habit, you cannot simply end it; you must replace all those moments and thoughts with something new and better. Life ends things in order to bring new things. The Universe knows what is best, and you learn, through allowing, what you are meant to do—such as loving unconditionally.

LIKE ATTRACTS LIKE

The Law of Attraction, brilliantly presented in numerous books and movies such as *The Secret*, states that "like attracts like." This is the essence of manifesting your world the way you choose. You become and attract what you think and feel about. Your thoughts and words are powerful. What you intend is a command to the energy of the Universe. This simple, profound knowledge is now in your hands, within your grasp.

Become in tune with the vibrational harmony of your

desires, and they are on their way to you. You do not have to possess all the answers or know how what you want will arrive; you only have to engage all the corresponding thoughts and feelings. Hold these vibrations in your meditations and visualizations as long as you can, and additional energies will attach to them in kind. As you feel them and concentrate with joy, they will gain in strength, and you will be in the creation process of your choices and desires. Your world is what you make it, and realizing this makes all things possible. We take an evolutionary leap when we begin to believe that we create our experiences.

MEDITATION: MANIFESTING

- To manifest, be clear about what you want.
- Sit in stillness and see your desire in your mind's eye.
- Feel the feelings you will have when you receive this blessing.
- Feel it as if you already have it.
- Add light to this picture.
- Believe you deserve this, and know it is for the good of all.
- Play with this picture, and see all the ways it will help you or the world.
- Focus on gratitude, as this energetically helps begin manifesting. Feel gratitude for all you already have and have created.
- When your picture of your desire feels and looks good, let your request grow in positive feelings and light.

- Then trust it, and let it go to Spirit. Take actions in alignment with this desire.

When you have focused on and felt your desire, you send it to the Universe, and it will hear you. When we feel genuine gratitude, this energy resonates with the splendor of the Universe and connects us to the life we want. Be in these states often, and remain open for many blessings and surprises to come to you.

ESSENCE OVER FORM

When doing any sort of creation-oriented energy work such as meditation, affirmation, visualization, or even just general thought manifesting, it is key to tune into the essence of your desire instead of any specific form. While it is important to be all-encompassing in your requests, you can do this more purely than you might realize. If you are demanding the details you think you want, you may receive things you did not consider. When you focus on or ask for the *essence* of that which you seek, you actually allow it into your life sooner, and with greater ease precisely because of its simplicity.

By stating that you want a partner who earns more money, you must be aware that this does not necessarily mean that your current companion, who you love, will get a desired raise. The Universe could very well cause a series of events to remove this current person from your life so you may receive a new partner that fits your previous request of only more money. You could also win the lottery and live happily ever after.

If you think you are helping yourself by being very exact in your request of marrying a man that is tall, dark, and handsome, you might wind up with a tall, dark, and handsome man who abuses you, or steals. After all, the Universe found what you asked for.

Instead of Robert or Rachel so-and-so who you think will give you the feelings you desire, the underlying wish is more likely for that of unconditional love. Request the essence—for instance, "the perfect mate for me" or "my perfect job." When you release specifics, you free the sources in the Universe to give to you the foundation of that which you are seeking. Being caught up in details slows down the natural process. Remember that "perfect for you" means many things, including that your mate or new job will find you for your own good.

Along with stating a clear desire to have simply that which will work well for you so you do not have to get involved with the details, you can get more precise and faster results by focusing on the feeling condition that you want this specific "thing" to bring you. Instead of asking for jobs based on desired money, or even to win the lottery so you have more money, focus instead on vibrating with prosperity. Bring the energy of prosperity to you and into your life. Feel the most prosperous thought you can reach, and believe. Resonating with abundance through gratefulness of the wonderful things already flowing into your life will attract the increased prosperity you seek. When you focus on prosperity or love, you are going right to the heart of the matter and requesting the feeling, the essence, and the condition of what you really long for deep down.

When you notice and appreciate all the ways prosperity and abundance are showing up in your life, and not only in the form of money, you begin to realize the vastness of prosperity already arriving and growing in your world. This creates more of the richness you desire. Really *feeling* and acknowledging gratitude and appreciation are huge keys in getting the attention of Divinity.

When you desire the essence, any form becomes okay. Any structure that happens to bring abundance or peace is completely suitable, and this opens us up to boundless possibilities. The Universe has many unrestrained ways to fulfill your wishes for prosperity. One winning set of lottery numbers is very narrow in comparison to the Universe's unique and magnificent power to bring you absolute prosperity.

Trust the Universe. When you ask for something specific, you are not only limiting Source's power, but you are probably shortsighted in your own perspective. You may not be aware of the countless ways in which the Universe can respond to your pleas for love, and by limiting your view or request, even unconsciously, you are greatly lessening your chances of receiving what you ask for. The Universe does answer every call, but if it seems otherwise, it is because of the specific forms in your own mind. Openness to the supremacy of Spirit will allow you to notice when anything arrives in its essence, no matter your calculated plea for a certain form.

GROWTH AND LEARNING

By asking for anything, you are opening the doors in your life for change. Be ready for change that the Universe sees fit in order to honor your entreaty. While we cannot know the specifics of what will unfold in our lives because of our desires, requests, and energy work, foresight is an attribute we most assuredly need and should actively investigate. Often we do not realize the power of our supplications or the magnitude of change they will bring. We are *asking* for things to change when we create or manifest something. But we do not need to be afraid.

Keep in mind the varieties of growth that accompany what

we learn and create—and the consequences of our growth. No matter how fabulous your new lease on living may be, no matter how free and bright you feel as you find like-minded others who share your search for healing, a good percentage of folks in your life will be uncomfortable with the speed at which your consciousness is accelerating. We need to understand the practicalities of the effects of our growth spurts on those around us.

We may run into difficulties and misunderstandings when we begin to grow. It is impractical to have meaningful connections with those who are not consciously headed in the same general direction as ourselves. We cannot let the pace of anyone else dictate our own. We can still love and enjoy them; we may just choose to do it differently. Hopefully we begin to find new companions and teachers who see us for who we are and where we are, and who can also help us appreciate our new selves, changes and all. Anyone who can update their picture of us as we change is a great help on paths of growth; otherwise, it is frustrating and shortchanging to be boxed in old outgrown pictures.

Another reason our growth periods may be unnerving is that we may be taking on a growth period that is not ours. When we become caught up in helping others we care for while also integrating our own growth into our daily being, it can be a recipe for disaster. Of course, we can and should be available to lend a shoulder, an ear, and even a warm heart to others in a difficult time, but actively and sometimes unconsciously becoming responsible for another is simply not our place. It is not only in neither of our best interests, but it is also not spiritually feasible.

We have to let others face their agreements and live as they decide to, just as we want for ourselves. We may be able to alleviate their passage with love and kindness, but it will do no service to attempt to help them bypass whatever it is they have chosen to undergo. Many of us are severely empathic and want desperately for others not to hurt. We can offer guidance or direction, and we can certainly give love and understanding, but if we meddle with our righteous knowing or seemingly obvious clues, they may even come to resent us.

I learned very abruptly that people have the lessons they need, and if they do not learn them, they will repeat them in their own time. I had to learn a much-removed role as friend by allowing another her ordeals. I can see more clearly now that I was part of her trials, and that I had my own experiences to gain. I forgot to observe myself in these situations—to clean up my own stuff while letting her have hers.

I can now take a positive yet lovingly detached perspective as I sympathize with pains of loved ones. There is always something to examine about myself when I see another caught up in an active and swirling thrust of accelerated life. It can be turbulent whether we are growing or are part of someone else's change, but as we come out the other side with our unconditional love intact, we know we are all better for it. A little introspection and understanding goes a long way to alleviate any sort of growing pains; we begin to experience that change can be joyous too.

VOID

Ah, the void—the most daunting and misunderstood element of any stage of growth. If we have been through spurts of change and expansion, we may come to loathe and fear the voids in between. We cannot just gather and gather endlessly; be it with wild berries or knowledge, we need time in between to *do something* with what we have acquired.

In the life of spirit and self, the void arrives as a time to process, ponder, understand, utilize, realize, and rest with breath. This is a very good and necessary thing. Although we may intellectually be aware that life works this way, it might help us emotionally to look at what life would really be like if we did not have these respites.

We might think we want to always be experiencing, moving, gaining, and advancing, but that is a scarier thought than we may comprehend. Our voids are gifts. Our down time when we feel lost or aimless is a treasure. I would also like to point out that we do not need to suffer in these places; we do not need to feel we are languishing or losing. We can learn to appreciate the deep and penetrating value of these middle spaces as different, unknown, and as varied as our periods of growth.

We feel elated as we are growing, meeting like-minded others, having new experiences, and rejoicing in profound insights and knowledge. But in order to transform this knowledge into wisdom, we need it to penetrate fully into our minds and lives. This happens in the void. Some voids are deeper and last longer, and some arrive more frequently than we think we can handle, but they all require the exhale of Spirit after breathing in life at its most breathtaking.

The void is referred to by the wise Gary Zukav as "a holy moment." Just when you think you will break or disappear, this is the time that true knowing seeps into our cores and leads us through the darkness with the gained guidance of our hearts. This is the time in which our souls are awakened to completely experience themselves. Whether we enter this space willingly or with gnashing teeth, we blossom through it and are forever changed.

We are programmed to feel more confident and secure when we know what we are doing, where we are going, what goals we are seeking, and what specific steps achieve our ends. When we do not know exactly what will happen, we feel fear or worry. It does not need to be this way. We are being guided and protected at all times. If we listen and get silent, we will realize that Spirit is in the void too.

"If we listen and get silent, we will realize that Spirit is in the void too."

Just because we are asked to move more slowly or methodically does not mean that Divinity has abandoned us. We are not reaping the punishments we feel we might deserve in our dark places. The Universe is still moving through us. It is just asking that we pause, think, or contemplate. It is the winding down of energy, which may then allow us to change direction or see what we have been whizzing by.

And if we listen very intently, we will know that we are on track. Most of us have been trained that we need to be up and doing in order to be fulfilling, but learning to wait is just as important—more so, even, because in the quiet space of the unknown, our possibilities become limitless. When we are unsure of coming events and wants, it is a precious and sacred time to hear, and be led; it is the lull in the revelry that allows you to be directed by higher thoughts. In this space we can reassess and become intimate with our deepest longings and most profound intentions. It is a contribution to our best selves to allow our lives to be reorganized, rejuvenated, realigned, and recharged.

In order to glide more peacefully through any void, we need to find grace, which often requires us to relinquish our demands, manipulations, and even preferences. If we go where the Universe is taking us, we will hit fewer obstacles than if we splash and wail. We are moving from one level—one place of understanding that we have mastered—to another, altogether new, which does not have to be terrifying.

When we acquiesce to Spirit's higher knowing, we can

discover this place that is infinite in its new opportunities. These are usually things we have longed for and requested, and we can be joyously hopeful as we see the Universe lining them up for our greatest good. This is an important time to allow unconditional love to envelope us and our perceived plights.

We will be okay, we will begin to understand what now comes before us, and we will rise again into another active phase of growth; we are assuring our reliable readiness. If we jump through the void with an empty-handed leap before our path is prepared for us, we would have less to catch us and support our beautiful landing into the light. As it is, the light is within us, and as we realize this, it glows brightly enough for us to find our way forward. Breathe, believe, and be patient.

The founder of the Church of Infinite Spirit and the Inner Connection Institute, the adroit Lauren Skye, explained a phase of the void in a riveting sermon that was both humorous and relevant. She described the void as a hallway. You are next to one door, which you just exited, and need to get to the next one. The hallway is pitch black. Blindly, you clutch the door you just left while reaching out with the other hand to feel for the next door. You only feel air.

What you can't see is that the doors are placed just far enough apart that you cannot reach the new one while still holding onto the old. We must, she enlightened us, let go of the door we have just come from and are dearly grasping. That is the only way to reach the other. In between, it may be dark and uncertain—picture walking around while waving your arms in front of yourself—but if you let go, you can begin to go toward and reach the new entrance.

You cannot keep the old door open as you search for the next—choices need to be made, and the outmoded needs to be released before moving elsewhere is possible. It might be nice to waffle in between the old and the new, just to make sure some light or familiar territory is visible. To truly move forward, however, we must let go. And to grow we must trust.

Often the most frightening part of any void is the letting go of the old. We continually get signs that something or someone is not for our highest good, yet we are afraid to be empty for a time, or we forget to have faith that something delightful is on its way. We know in our heart of hearts that our dreams cannot arrive unless there is space for them in our lives, but we resist because we are stuck in insecurity.

In the last two years before we left the pipe band world, Paul and I had plenty of nudges to release it. These turned into shoves as we remained steadfast in our familiar ways. Leaders left, battles ensued, and drumming for hours every day began to take its toll—carpel tunnel and tendonitis in both of my wrists, and then neuropathy up to each elbow. We were not still enough to notice these messages from Spirit.

This happens whether people are releasing an old job that no longer serves them in order to live their true calling, a bad habit that brings about health problems, or a loving relationship that has changed. We stay in relationships because we think we can do more, or we fear we cannot find something different or better. We feel the shoulder taps and eventually surrender to the hits over the head because we have no choice.

I ended up with casts on both arms up to my shoulders, like a mummy, and after another beloved leadership change, we finally allowed ourselves enough solitude to wake up and listen. We lived in that place of fear before finding the faith to let go of the old. Even after we left, we sat there for months in emotional convulsions because it had been our entire lifestyle for decades. Talk about a problem! I remember telling my friend Linda how I liked being an expert in my field and knowing the whole game. She said, "Oh honey, everyone does . . . but sometimes it's more fun to be the learner again."

That beautiful advice stayed with me as I began to center and turn inward for real and divine direction. Our lives changed without the bagpipe band that had become our whole existence. In this absence, we began witnessing our fears: *will I find a career I love, can I feed my family, this is all I have ever known, oh how I miss the music, how will we connect with friends*, and on and on.

After this, we began discovering the important questions, which were a giant step to getting clear about our path. Asking what brings me joy, what qualities I want to envelope, what legacy I want to leave to my family, and what I truly love or value was the way to correct course and live a genuine path. Once we ask these questions, we enter a void where we can be quiet enough to hear the answers. We cannot realize the way of right livelihood, unconditional love, or greater callings if we are running in another direction; this only works in stillness and space.

We can find solace in daily rhythms of familiar acts such as organizing, cooking, reading, journaling, meditating, and exercising while we are waiting for our paths to be lit. The reassurance of getting up and dressed, brushing our teeth, and putting one foot in front of the other will support us in our gray areas. We will use our new habits and our faith in manifesting as small steps to our greater life. Our new calling, new companion, fulfilled dream, or fruition of inspiration is settling into our bones—it just needs us to be still so we may incorporate it fully into the visibility of our souls. Allow this time to integrate experiences and new growth so they stay more evident in our every day.

Wallow in your deep dark for as long as your spirit needs, or pull up the covers and relax into your momentary hibernation. Enjoy it even. The phase of not knowing just yet does not have to bring anxiety; we can unlearn that knee-jerk reaction. The most difficult part might be waiting and wondering once we have chosen to manifest anything new, but wonder also allows childlike fascination and fantasizing.

Rejoice in every varied phase of growing and manifesting, for they each have their unique rewards if we listen and are willing to see. When you are ready to thrust upward again, the time will be right, you will know your way, and Divinity will help take you there!

MEDITATION: MOCK-UPS

- Close your eyes and breathe to relax and set your space.
- Picture a rose in your mind's eye.
- Ground this rose to the earth with any type of cord.
- Place pictures of your desire inside this rose. Take your time.
- Bring light to these pictures, lighting up each layer of your rose.
- Make the picture of your desires happy, and feel your manifestation already here.
- Set in the rose the light of havingness.
- Command that any energy not allowing this mock-up to manifest, whatever it might be, be released down the cord. See it with your intention.
- Place a pink bubble around the rose and cut off the stem.
- Let it go, sending it to the Supreme Being.

CHAPTER TEN

Perspective

Unconditional love is accessible through diligence with our perspectives. If we have faith in others and place trust in goodness, then we will succeed in growing our love endeavor. As we pay attention to our perceptions, we realize they color all we see. Picking out the unpleasing or unsatisfying aspects of others means we cannot see how wonderful and kind they are. By simple choice, we decide to believe the good we want to see, and it is there. We shift our perspectives higher, and we live in finer vibration.

Your perceptions are the eyes through which you experience your world. We see this through manifesting. How we choose to perceive and react dictates which perspectives we validate. Knowing this gives us great power and responsibility. Learning to touch our environment with the discrimination of our desire is moving and mighty. The groundwork and knowledge to acquire what you fancy, what your very soul thirsts for, can freely and immediately be yours.

How wonderful and hopeful that no matter what takes place within the minutes of your life, you can shade it with the wisdom you learn and sustain your happiness, your zest, and your satisfaction with living. Each moment can be glorious, every movement loving, and those with whom you surround yourself will notice the light in your spirit. This reality can be yours.

The power of how we perceive is paramount to how much love we can grow. In this chapter, we learn how perspective is about choosing serenity. We invite release of judgments so we can remember our space of love, because the two cannot exist simultaneously. We find that the truths we believe tell us much about our level of peace.

FAITH DICTATES SERENITY

Luckily, we are not alone on this journey; we all share it. Our journeys lend opportunities to look at faith, trust, belief, and hope, and to be touched by the divine. This faith comes from our attitude and is intertwined with perceptions—how *we* see and what *we* believe. Perceptions color reality, and either allow or disallow peace. *Faith* trusts that when you are on the side of the road changing a tire, you are exactly where you are supposed to be. It believes that everything is unfolding just as it is meant to. *Perception* is how you choose to see things as they are unfolding. It is how you feel or what you think while you are on the side of the road changing the tire.

Between faith and perception is a special space, a blessed living, a sacred choice. The healthy and helpful perception chooses faith in all conditions. Your attitude, as linked with your perception, will either help or hinder you. There is nothing one can do about having the flat and the other inconveniences associated with this "problem," but what you say to yourself about it, both during and after, will procure your level of serenity.

Vanish the negatives. Open your perspective. Be creative with your thoughts. They accurately predict the quality of your life. This flat tire may have saved you from a later accident down the road. It may have made you late enough to avoid running into an angry coworker at work. Even if, God forbid, someone hit you while on the shoulder hiking up the jack, maybe it sent you to the hospital for a minor injury, and resulting x-rays showed a more serious ailment caught by the doctors in time to save your life.

Perhaps you realize the flat was caused by your own neglect, and as you learn better car care, you are led into a more satisfying and lucrative vocation. Your faith in humanity could be restored when another stops to help you. You could even meet your future partner through these "circumstances beyond your control." The possibilities are limitless. It can even be a fun game with your family members to ponder and share just how many ways we can each see a situation.

Why be mad or frustrated when this "problem" was supposed to happen on some level? Nothing can be done to reverse time, so live the following moments, one after another, in a good, meaningful, and uplifting way. We can all choose contrary emotions, but investigating the outcome of such hellish, albeit automatic or unconscious choices helps us seize better perspective. Everything is bad or good depending upon what we choose to see. Let us see and live the good.

The truth is that we almost never know why something is happening in the moment. Trust is part of the divine plan. Have faith in the intelligence of a higher power. Have faith in good if goodness is your intention.

As we explore the varied perspectives introduced in the next example, bring into your mind the importance of different attitudes. Hold the various possibilities of any situation and realize how each interpretation of the same event differently impacts the person and the world.

Ten people stand on a sidewalk waiting for a bus. The bus pulls up and completely soaks and/or splashes mud on eight of them. The circumstances are the same for nearly all of them.

How many will find a lesson, a higher purpose, or a helpful response? How many will accept this event openly, and turn it into light? How many of them will use it as an excuse for compounding negativity?

One of the ten gets angry, mad, and disgusted. He wonders why bad things always happen to him. He takes the unfairness personally. Not only does the splashed mud ruin his day, but while getting on the bus he yells at the driver, ruining his day as well. He gives negativity to whomever he sits next to, who then pass it on to co-workers, and later, family and friends.

Another of the ten gets pissed off and splashes as many people as possible to make others feel bad and himself rectified—again propagating ugliness. This negativity toward a sensitive and suffering soul could be the last straw in his decision that the world is no good and hates him, validating suicidal thoughts. (Please know there is always hope, and many can help you find it. Seek help! The Universe loves you.) The effect of an angry, unkind act is often more wide-reaching than we know. Choose instead to make the world a more beautiful place with healing golden-pink light.

The third of the ten is soaked and smiles, suddenly reminded of the humor of being human. While wearing muddy clothes throughout the workday, he loses any arrogance he had. The experience brings him reality, presence, humility, and amusement.

The fourth person decides to go home and change. On his next bus, he meets someone who shows him wisdom and kindness (and later on, even true love).

The fifth takes it in stride. Later, while driving herself, she takes care to avoid splashing a pedestrian who, unbeknownst to her, has just had a grave personal loss. Noticing this act of consideration, the pedestrian is uplifted beyond her present grief, if even for a moment.

The sixth person laughs aloud about it, then later uses it to break the ice of an uncomfortable silence.

The seventh, a young girl, is so happy the ugly pants her mom made her wear are now covered in mud. She skips home to change, realizing Spirit is on her side.

The eighth, who had been having a hectic morning, goes home to change, and finds she can start the day over. She makes a warm cup of tea and takes a few deep breaths before beginning again, altogether better. It has given her a second chance.

And the two who did not get splashed? The first feels that the others who did get muddy condemn him. Perceiving resentment, he gets upset and wishes he too had been splashed. The second considers himself lucky. He counts his blessings and releases a small amount of victimhood he had been carrying. He later offers to help another who really needs it.

The possibilities are limitless and unknowable. Notice where your reactions might be today and observe other incidents inwardly to create noticeable changes in your attitude and responses. This helps us grow immensely.

IN ANOTHER'S SHOES

Very rarely do we handle every day's situations in the best way for all concerned. Whether because of stress, time, ignorance, or fatigue, life goes on without us, sometimes right past us, and we are not programmed to handle every little thing in a positive way.

This tendency toward the negative is mostly due to conditioning. Look at different examples of any situation that have brought up negative feelings. Delve into the positions of others and see how their action or reaction might have made sense from their perspective. Remember to "walk a mile in the shoes of others," especially when you feel hurt or angry from something you perceive from them or their actions. Trying to understand their viewpoint will allow for peace in situations where you once felt despair.

It is only through listening to the thoughts and differences of another that growth and learning are possible. The question is how intently do we really listen to someone's point of view or position? When you walk a mile in the shoes of someone else, are you not still putting yourself in their shoes as *you* see them? Can we actually drop all defenses of our position, and truly appreciate another's outlook unconditionally? It can be more difficult than we might realize to release all pretenses and understand another's view of reality.

We all believe in our own realities. You may search out a wise sage or someone you admire so as to expand your attitude, but it is still the reality of that person as you understand it, and there are as many realities as there are people. Thus, truly delving into the planes of perception can feel daunting. Begin by realizing none of us have all the answers, and that unconditional love will open with real listening and empathy. This brings acceptance, for us and others, and helps us grow the great life of love we want to live.

PARENTAL PERSPECTIVE

Whether a negative situation is serious, like the loss of a friendship, or a regular occurrence, like someone talking over you, perceive where others might be coming from. Then change your actions accordingly toward giving unconditional love. If you cannot feel love at that moment, at least acknowledge that they are a fellow human in similar circumstances to your own.

Many examples of such "difficult" situations occur as a parent. Take, for example, your eight-year-old child lying to you about having cleaned their room so they may go out and play. While it is more a stretching of truths than an outright hostile lie, any parent knows discovery of such a lie can be either simple or catastrophic depending on the circumstances or mood of parent or child on any given day. Remaining calm and turning the conversation with your child into something positive takes time, energy, knowledge, presence of mind, patience, luck, and a lot of love.

You could both scream and yell about lies, unfairness, "you never let me whatever," slammed doors, and more. Alternatively, you can change the situation with your wisdom, and turn it into a fun room cleaning game, giving the child the extra attention she unwittingly needs. You can utilize this opportunity to talk together about the importance of truth and trust—they only know when we teach them. Not only will a calm conversation bring the two of you together amiably, but you will also have a much better chance of actually cleaning the room.

There are two choices you can make in this or a similar situation: choice one is full of tears, misunderstanding, and angst; choice two involves life lessons and increased love and trust. Make the choice for cheerfulness, fun, love, connection, Divinity, learning, grace, and guidance—and keep adding to this list. You or your child may not know you had it in you, but afterwards, you will both be proud, having bonded in a shared moment of love and understanding. You will have accomplished much for the greater good. Every time we expand the boundaries of perception, we expand our soul's capacity.

We are teaching these malleable beings we call children, and they are learning from what we do and say, whether we mean for them to or not. Every mother, father, friend, and guardian is truly a teacher. Children are very perceptive and are learning more than you think. So make it count. Let them know they are worth the effort of a little thought and energy, that they are worth being listened to, respected, and understood. That extra effort, allowance, or flexibility means a lot to their gentle spirits. They are the future of our world.

TAKE A STEP BACK

Nature offers a plentitude of lessons in perception. Autumn is the perfect teacher. To some it feels like everything is dying, and to others it exudes breathtaking beauty. The turning leaves of the aspens are a definite milestone of time's passing. One may see the leaves on a mountainside as gorgeous colors in thought-provoking jeweled tones. Another walking the mountain trail sees how the individual leaf is rotting, brown spots covering something that used to be pretty, alive, and green. Distance gives you greater perspective both in nature and in personal circumstances.

Time is one type of distance that can shift perspective. The old adage "Time heals all wounds" is true when we allow the passage of time to bring us new insights and a fresh standpoint. You will not feel the same about that fight or loss today as you will in a week or a decade so long as you are consciously opening your perceptions. Time brings growth and opportunity, but you must utilize it. Hindsight is a great example of how growth with examination can instigate positive change.

In one of my favorite quotes that I return to very often, Merle Shain embodies this perspective of hindsight improving trust: "It's hard to tell our bad luck from our good luck sometimes. Hard to tell sometimes for many years to come. And most of us have wept copious tears over someone or something when if we'd understood the situation better we might have celebrated our good fortune instead."

Removing yourself from the perceptions you adhere to and trying to consider a situation neutrally, as best you are able, is another great way to examine them. There are as many perceptions of something as there are perceivers. You are already a step ahead by realizing even this much. You can learn to appreciate why someone acted the way they did, leading you toward, if not necessarily agreement, perhaps at least understanding, compassion, or acceptance, and maybe even inspiration and new, exciting insights unto yourself.

Consider the old man in the following parable by the brilliant Dan Millman, recorded in his book *Way of the Peaceful Warrior*. How did the old man's neutrality affect his perception?

An old man and his son worked on a small farm, with only one horse to pull the plow. One day, the horse ran away.

"How terrible," sympathized the neighbors. "What bad luck."

"Who knows whether it is bad luck or good luck," the farmer replied.

A week later, the horse returned from the mountains, leading five wild mares into the barn.

"What wonderful luck!" said the neighbors.

"Good luck? Bad luck? Who knows?" answered the old man.

The next day, the son, trying to tame one of the horses, fell and broke his leg.

"How terrible. What bad luck!"

The army came to all the farms to take the young men for war. The farmer's son was of no use to them, so he was spared.

"Good? Bad?"

I love the neutrality of this farmer, and his ability to be open and present relieves him of much potential pain. For everything there is a purpose, and we usually do not recognize the use of the experience until later. So keep plugging along, do your best, learn, share your gems, and feel peace in trusting the higher plan. It will be revealed when you have enough distance and perspective. Clarity and Divinity will reign with positive faith and development.

TRUST

We can grow a life of unconditional love more easily as we grow our trust. When we trust that what happens to us comes from a Divinity that knows best, we are freed from worry, pain, frustration, and anxiety. How do we build our trusting perception?

One way I have encouraged my bond, and therefore my trust, with Divinity is through accepting Source's golden light. I have an instinctive and natural communion with nature—the earth, rivers, trees—but I have had to develop my relationship with the Divine. Light helps us feel Source's love, heal, and raise our vibrational energies—all good things that help us trust in its wisdom. The power of light, particularly golden light, is discussed in more detail in Chapter Twenty-Seven.

MEDITATION: DIVINE LIGHT

- Get in a nice, peaceful, and meditative space.
- Call golden light to you, or ask angels to send you light.
- Notice light reacts immediately to your thought of it.
- Fill your aura and body with it.
- Let it glow; let it grow, and really *feel* it.

• Appreciate that this angelic quality is available whenever you need it.

Another approach in developing trust is how we build trust with anything: test and confirmation. Understanding on an intellectual level the importance of trust is not the same as acting on that trust. I too had to build my trust. Constant connection with the numinous led me to many synchronicities, revelations, and eventual deep trust in Divinity and the world at large. I would frequently ask for signs, and I was continually answered. I always found it humorous (and I know Spirit did as well) that I needed so many validations. I would even test my confirmations. The Universe never once let me down. Now I am able to recognize signs and appreciate their divine timing. My entreaties even led me to an angelic visitation, for which I feel special and supremely loved.

FAITH IN THE MOMENT

We can sometimes lose trust when we forget to shift our perspective, and when this happens, we can be comforted by the present moment. If we can reach faith in this moment, it will be enough. If you have never read *Ishmael* by Daniel Quinn, I will not spoil the delicious story for you, but I will urge, for your opening sense of perspective, that you do. I will just share the phenomenon in the beginning of the book where he has his student question how we came to be here. Consider that the story we have been told, whether it explains our existence through evolution or divine creation, might be false or ignorantly believed. Quinn describes that the story of our very existence—and any story for that matter—is always told from someone's perspective.

When you stay with this expanding and mind-blowing

concept, you begin to lose trust in what you have taken for granted about this being *our* earth, and creation ending with, of all things, humans. We can take this leap in perspective a step further and realize that even our ancient texts are the stories of people from people. Remember, the Bible was translated by affluent men across languages—might their perceptions have changed something in the text? Everything we think we know, or have taken on blind faith, is a story created by a human that has made it this far. That is all.

As a concept closer to home that might not scare the stuff out of us—as his enlightened book might—look at the perspective of those who grow up as farmers or doctors because their fathers have. Soon the sons will step into their place as their father's fathers did. This becomes the story for this family, generation after generation. If you grow up and do not feel like becoming that farmer or doctor, you are stepping into an unknown world.

We take many things for granted as being truth or history, but as we peek into the depth of perspective, we can really see that those assumptions could all be made up, false, or worse. When we expand our view of our pasts, and we realize we do not have to believe everything we were told, we can begin to develop a future with limitless possibility.

Since we cannot know or maybe believe that we came from blobs, apes, God, aliens, or whatever story you have taken on as your history, we can reestablish our trust by being present. Now we know a little bit—we've created our current reality. So, after opening your perceptions, let go of the fear and realize that it was all to make you alert to possibilities. This is life. This is this life.

If we look back and cannot know, then perhaps we can be aware that we do not know the future either, which eliminates our boundaries and limits. We can begin to see that perception is powerful and vast. Out of this, we can discover trust for our lives. We are here—we know that much, we think. We can raise our faith that there is some reason and some other power. We can begin to work with this unseen, benevolent force, and know in our hearts that it all means something. If we do not know who we are or where we came from, we will only be occupied with what we can create, see, and do—in the present moment.

"If we look back and cannot know, then perhaps we can be aware that we do not know the future either, which eliminates our boundaries and limits."

I have experienced doubt of the future blossoming into faith in the present, though my children may think of it as watching their mother lose her mind. I had come to trust my husband's appreciation of technology and had moved all my writing to a new computer, which I named Hemingway—Paul's gift of encouragement toward my authorship. Seven months of serious writing later, well into the completion of this book and half into the next, my computer companion died—a close second in tragic Hemingway demises. Not proficient in such technology, I had virtually no hard copy or backup.

I lost it. After my initial meltdown, I was a mess caught in such drama and global destruction that even Paul said he had never seen me in such distress. I was beside myself, and it was not pretty. I forgot everything I knew. After four days of calling tech support, begging favors from kind friends who had computer expertise, and utterly freaking out at "the loss of my life's work," I drowned for a week in my unreserved traumatic loss of perspective.

In my armory of acquaintances with computer know-how was a family member who was on the opposing side of a serious pipe band disagreement discussed in the next chapter. He rode to my rescue with no hesitation and took the laptop to work his magic.

Waiting for my work to be recovered gave me time I did not want but desperately needed. The least of my discoveries during this time was a new awareness for family, and deeper within my life was confirmation of faith and gratitude. It all came back to faith. I began writing down my blessings and all the potential reasons or gifts within this seeming disaster. I realized I was not my work and not to identify my worth in these ways, that even my prized writing was only information, that even life is simply passed on and replaced continually in myriad ways.

I had time to combine thoughts I had recorded and add slips of paper and random ideas to collective books. It allowed me to recommit to my writing, to respect it, realizing its proper place and the importance it held in my life. I found a liberated freedom from its obligations and restrictions as well as reverence for divine expression flowing boundless.

As I began to release my fears and attachments, an amazing experience occurred. As I wrote down lessons and promises, I found faith. I let it trickle through me like light, and it worked. I felt it. Everything I went through in my self-induced devastation, and all the thoughts I entertained, changed when I allowed and pursued faith. I felt grateful and very present. I experienced the sensations of feeling faith, not just going through the motions. The second this relief and trust permeated me, I possessed belief in transformation that all would be well, and that I would either get what I wanted, would for sure get what I needed, or could create the will and fund the power to accept anything as perfection.

I was rewarded for my integration and hope, and all the angst and loss turned ironically celestial. Once I opened to the entire offering of the situation, I was freed. My present moment was joyous as my attitude included the flow and connection of Divinity. I wrote down my realizations and built upon what I was grateful for. I remembered previous awarenesses and was reminded with confirmation to keep my promises to myself and the Universe. I was awarded with unconditional love and assistance required in a timely need from a person I may well have hurt years prior. I had worked through wounds towards love, and he obviously rose with the ability to love and help me. This is perspective. This is growth. This is the spirit of humanity with unconditional love.

CHAPTER ELEVEN

Greater Perspective

While the previous chapter introduced us to the importance of perspective, we now dive into deeper discussions of the concept. By choosing a positive perspective, living aware of the shifts in perspective Spirit is nudging us toward, and finding the truth in a world of people's many perspectives, we continue to grow our capacity to love unconditionally.

FRIENDLY OR HOSTILE

I love the eloquence of Ken Keyes Jr. in expressing one of the most profound and significant realizations of all time: "A loving person lives in a loving world, a hostile person lives in a hostile world. Everyone you meet is your mirror." He is absolutely right. Whether you perceive the world to be friendly or hostile, loving or angry, is one of the most important choices you will ever make—even if you are not aware you are making it.

This friendly/hostile approach may seem cliché, but think about it. Whether you choose to be friendly or hostile dictates how you live among others in this world. We are each able to choose our thoughts exclusive of our surroundings. Your world is what you make of it, and this is the Law of Attraction at its most fundamental. There may be great conflict around you, but you can choose peace and hold your center.

A hostile person sees hostility around every corner. They cause resistance where there is none. Simply by acting as if there is an opposing force, one is created. They may feel paranoid and live in a world in which everyone is out to get them. They will be the first to assume an ulterior motive, come from a place of fear or lack, and might even believe in their own "bad luck" enough to validate it everywhere they look. We create what we believe (The Law of Attraction). We act from the perspective with which we see. If you believe life is painful or the world is working against you, that will be your reality. The rate of our light and vibration determines our reality.

Even if the world was out to attack and stop a friendly person, it would mean very little. All that person would see was friendliness and support. A friendly person takes the life of a hostile person and holds it up to the light of goodness, synchronicity, and love—that friendly person sees the good in the hostile person. Light and love make everything more beautiful.

The choice is yours. Which will help you create the world you want? How will unconditional love serve your desires as compared to turbulence, anger, or conflict? You can experience either, but how do you *want* your life to be? Every possibility is available, so remember that you choose what you see. You choose which thoughts receive attention and therefore power. Sometimes it may prove difficult to get our minds around a specific perception held by another, but by just trying, we are evolving.

FORCED SHIFT

We all know from life experiences—and bumper stickers—

that "shift happens." Usually divine gifts are well wrapped in crisis clothing, and we eventually either get to or have to shift our perceptions. Of course, we can choose to ignore heavenly taps on the shoulder, as Paul and I did in resisting our departure from the pipe band world. But if we are aware and choose to flow with life rather than fight against it, we quietly succumb to whatever happens because we know it is in our best interest.

If we love where we are, no matter up or down, we will not struggle against life. Perceive the good, and release the bad, and love will enter alongside change. The shift does not have to arrive as a beguiling seductress that leads us unknowingly through the dark forest to a secret palace that forbiddingly holds our lessons. We live more consciously by choice, and some of us actually learn to welcome and even relish these big shifts. This is exciting evidence of our growth.

When we do not pay attention to the subtle advice life throws at us—the heads up that newness is heading our way—it may repeat its helpful assistance until impending doom is all that is left. We do not want to learn this way. We are learning to know better than to wait this long. We know we want to live our experiences through joy rather than pain.

Still, it is sometimes difficult to listen to, acknowledge, or even know for sure in which direction we are being led. If we connect with our internal sources, we will have access to more verifiable information. If we listen intently, we will know which way to turn at precisely the right moment. This comes from trusting our intuition, knowing that it has never failed us. When we tap into our light and our center, we are neutral, and we receive clues as to how to go in the direction of wholeness, strength, love, and joy. We go towards peace because we know what we seek.

MEDITATION: CHOOSING DIRECTION

- Get quiet, turn inward, and breathe.
- What life choice or change might you be struggling with?
- If you feel stress or anxiety, that is a giant clue you are on the right topic.
- Create two pictures in your imagination, one of each choice, and place them each in a rose.
- Is one lighter or brighter than the other? Does one rose wilt?
- Note the characteristics and differences of these two pictures, as this is your intuition and Divinity interceding.
- After noticing, let the roses go to the sun and burn up, releasing energy.
- Sit with each choice individually and pay attention to how your body feels.
- Know that as you then act, Divinity aligns you with love, peace, and growth.

It is when we are too tired to try, too stressed to see, and too overwhelmed to understand that life may lead us to a change we may not feel ready for. This may enter us into a void, or it may shake us violently where we stand. This new place or perception may seem too scary, too far away, or just too much. But try to love something within the new situation. Divinity knows the strength and fortitude we possess, even if we have learned to hide it from ourselves. And if we are going through life in unconscious ways that disallow our best good, we may be stopped for that very reason.

For someone who has become seriously ill or has been told they have a limited time left on this planet, they may suddenly choose to live differently. They did not require this illness for their growth, but it was a sure way to insist upon it. Now each day becomes precious. Illusions and small-minded perceptions drop like weights. They recognize what is important and who is of value in their life. They very quickly learn to express love. These are just some treasures afforded by a drastic shift. Where it may have taken lifetimes to learn gratitude, your spirit desired more extreme evolution sooner. May any person in this situation receive blessings of grace and healing for their body and spirit.

The loss of a relationship can push us into self-examination. The inexplicable death of a loved one can force us to shore up our personal strength. But changing our perception need not be brought about by crises. If we learn to precede our lessons with grace, and place our perceptions on real appreciation and growing awareness, we may welcome our true friends as messengers in any disguise. We will discover our courage and the meaning of love all on our own. All the growth in the world may not avert death or certain experiences we agreed to experience as humans, but it will allow us more freedom in missing the crises we do not need undergo.

For many who walk these and other seemingly insurmountable paths, and all those of us who have survived even moments of them, we know there is a series of valuable lessons within what seems like outward horror. Even those who tread along without visions of grandeur know deep down that everything happens for a reason—not to become a saint, but to learn. Millions of people who have been through extreme hardship will attest to its unmistakable teaching. Although some may continue to hate the hand they have been dealt, most inevitably come to soul-changing realizations.

As we willingly permit shifts in our perspectives, we are not engaging the catastrophe of forcing shift as our soul's last resort to unconditionally loving, forgiving, or accepting situations or people. Growth, after all, is by nature full of change, and when we allow flexibility in our perceptions, we can release them more easily than having fate pry them from our hands.

TRUTH AND PERCEPTION

Though we can practice the feelings of love and closely watch our perceptions, our path may get confused when people talk about their own truths. It can be argued that every person's perspective is their truth. This would be an honest statement, but shortsighted within the larger scheme of reality. Many people defend their point of view as the truth, and it may be their truth, but there is a difference between personal perspective and ultimate truth. Who is to say what ultimate truth really is? When we are loving (the highest truth), the specifics no longer matter.

"Our truth and reality are created by the energy we possess."

Our truth and reality are created by the energy we possess. A marked confirmation toward higher truth is if our feelings and thoughts are bringing us peace. A good way to delve into knowing truth is to compare perspectives, and be open to hearing, learning, and revising—or at least accepting. This is unconditional love.

Innocent opposing perspectives in my pipe band resulted in judgment and blame that continue to affect my family to this day. Those several dark years remain a powerful and sad memory, which eventually led me back into the light with more assurance and recognition of my own goodness and love, though others saw only the disgust they chose. It is odd that such turbulent experiences came out of a simple environment of music, but as I have let on before, no simplicity exists in bagpipe bands.

The majority of the people in our band—remember, a pipe band is like a family—expressed that they wanted to try a new leader and climate while still appreciating and respecting the job done by the current leader. The current leader felt attacked and drew a line in the sand, forcing band members to choose him or leave. A quick injunction of perception versus truth here: just because the current leader felt attacked does not mean anyone was attacking him. The leader choosing to play victim was, in the end, catastrophic.

Where does the truth lie between misunderstanding intentions, and trying not to hurt someone you care about? As the group became divided, half were blamed for actions that had never entered their minds, and a war began in the face of what could have just as easily been a situation of listening, understanding, and trying something new to see if it worked.

This single incident taught me unconditional love at its core. Its effects single-handedly led me to write this book. Though I have written hundreds of pages about the experience, here I include only enough for you to taste the consequences.

Months went by with the new leader, barely winning the volatile votes, trying to contain some sense of continuity above the manipulations of nearly half the band who supported the old leader. We tried to love and not condemn those who chose the other side, despite how they sabotaged performances by untuning their instruments or not showing up, leaving a turnout less than promised for the performance fee. We reached out for attempted and repeated reconciliation, but they went out after rehearsals to a separate pub, calculated division that left no chance for communion. An opportunity for unconditional love was lost. Some in my family even chose to go to an impromptu party thrown by one of the band members instead of attending my birthday party. That hurt.

I was grateful for those on both sides who kept their integrity, stood up for what they believed in without personal attack, and really tried to instill love through all the lies and illusions. It was all very sad and shameful but could have been healed by simply sharing concerns out in the open, remaining honest, and allowing for varied perspectives on what made things work. Although I longed to go back and bring the heavens with me to shine unconditional love and truth upon the darkness that ensued, I learned huge lessons in forgiveness, communication, and this intangible force of loving without conditions. I saw wise and good-willed old souls too. I learned what real friends were, and I learned to let go of what I knew to be false, even if it hurt.

Our new leader and his sergeant repeatedly told us that they wanted to ask those causing the trouble to leave. As two of them were family, I pleaded for more time for them to come around, that this band was their life and they had given so much before this. But as their behavior continued to spiral down, I could defend them no more. They were kicked out in what can only be described as an earth-shattering evening. I have never seen an uglier display of adult behavior in all my life. All I could whisper through the yelling as they slammed the door was "Don't go." I received an email that week saying that my husband and I had effectively destroyed thirty years of their work and that they would never make music with us ever again. My mom also said she would always love me as a daughter but no longer liked me as a person. I was, for all intents and purposes, disowned, and we did not speak for most of two years.

Through all this turmoil, I recalled something said to me by my most beloved drumming teacher and friend, Mr. Tim Gladden. At a clinic he taught, we had been agonizing over unfair results and disharmony from mean-spirited competitors. Tim said, "Remember, there are a billion people in China who couldn't give a rat's ass about this ridiculous thing we call pipe band, or about any contest we compete in—a billion people who don't care or even know anything about this world we spend so much time and energy on. Keep this all in perspective."

I learned through pain and distance and would much rather have had it go the way I saw and knew it could have—learning with acceptance and kindness. In my loss of innocence for the world I grew up in, separation from the people I knew and loved my whole life, and in the distance from family, I drew far into myself to explore the very fundamentals of my entire life.

The feelings of being disowned shook my whole world and very foundations. Suddenly everything I thought, learned, or fought for felt like a horrifying, lonely lie. I had to piece myself and my life back together from that moment when I realized my basic premise of being loved and accepted by my mother, no matter what, had been shattered. I was shocked that love was very frighteningly, painfully, and tangibly conditional.

This experience continues to be a solid source of my learning to turn to unconditional love. I learned to empathize with the pain the "other side" must have felt in their perceived rejection. While still unable to reconcile their attacks within my heart, I came to find a beautiful space of understanding them through unconditional love. That devastatingly rich environment for growth experiences is now learned with joy and reflected upon from a distant, more evolved space, though I know those invaluable lessons chose me in that form to make an eternally indelible and unforgettable imprint on my spirit. It certainly did that. It took time, inner work, writing, and healing, but I discovered my constitution, and it could no longer be changed by anyone's approval or disapproval.

To this day, these events along with innumerable insipid details have contaminated many reputations in our old arena of the pipe band realm. Such devastating inaccuracies between perspectives and truth have ruined lots of potential peace and greatness for countless kind-hearted individuals and groups, not to mention—ahh—the music we made. But these are just some of the reasons why we have gratefully walked away from these ancient karmic battles.

I have struggled with wanting to portray these events as the huge lessons of perspective brought to my life with genuinely wanting to let it go and release my family from its pain and memory. We have come so far in our healing and moving forward that I did not want to cause a backslide of that trust or forgiveness, and I omitted much, but I needed to include the basic construct because it was pivotal in my reaching unconditional love. To this, I finally give thanks.

JUDGMENT

When you feel like judging someone, look to love. Forego judgments in favor of new perspectives. Where has your judgment gotten you? Happy? Fulfilled? Loved? Was it meaningful and bettering for anyone in the end? Begin to acknowledge that judgments, created by you, are separate from situations, people, and facts. Each judgment about your feelings or assumptions of another's feelings elicits a layer of perception to cover the truth. Each time we do this, the truth is enveloped in an opaque coating. Imagine how obscured the truth appears when many unchecked judgments cloud its beautiful shine.

All individuals are working through their own fears and blocks, and we need to go forward, with all the strength we can muster, into loving them while working on our own as well. As Sanaya Roman writes in *Spiritual Growth*, "When people are doing something that upsets or hurts you, see it as an opportunity to learn to love them rather than protect yourself."

Awaken from believing that your judgments define anything but your own truth, and place effort in perceiving love in as many ways and places as you can. Make a game of it. Do not get caught in the force that negativity unleashes upon human existence. Stare past appearances, and as our light spirits, instead witness the layers and possibilities within perception, and love.

MEDITATION: LOVE OVER JUDGMENT

- Relax and breathe into a meditative space.
- Remember a judgment someone made of you that did not feel good.
- Place that picture or feeling in a rose, take it to the sun, and explode it.
- Now recall how you really were and would have liked to be seen.
- Ask God or the angels for love and let it grow within.
- Remember a time you judged someone, for anything small or large.
- Imagine two other ways this situation could have been seen.

- Imagine something good that person might have been intending.
- Feel compassion for really not knowing what they might have been going through.
- Grow that love and compassion for all.
- Try to look this way the next time you feel a negative judgment.

If the cycle of judgment consumes us, and we stubbornly insist we are right, we may end up all alone with our justified defenses. This pain is extremely heavy to our spirits. Take emotions out of the equation and look at facts. It might be possible that someone or something was far kinder and more innocent without the personal coloring of circumstances.

On the other side, all of us can recall times when we were wrongly judged, but we may create a world in which we perceive unfairness where there is none. We may have felt wronged, and the other party never had an idea that it happened. The perceived judger may wonder why or how the sequence of events offended you. All angles to this perceptual conundrum are of value and interest in deep self-probing.

Give the gift of allowing for unlimited perspectives without judging others as bad for feeling differently than you might. Their insights will perhaps not only teach you something of great value, but will also benefit the lives of everyone involved instead of creating and strengthening more unnecessary division, hatred, and violence. So many disputes can be shifted at the onset by treasuring thoughtful communication and love without condition. This simply means to allow others their truths and differences without allocating wrongness, blame, or merciless retaliation in any direction. It also means much can be overcome by sitting, speaking, and listening. Trying to be open will light the world millions of times over in comparison to closing down and turning away. We can only find understanding when we are receptive to it.

Before you judge, consider, even for a moment, that your perception may be skewed; you might just be wrong. Consider that things may be different than they seem. Give the benefit of doubt. Realize that it all may appear exactly and innocently opposite to someone else. Always check out gossip or negative information before buying into, or acting upon anger. Sit with that neutrality before judgment.

My experience in pipe band offers yet another personal experience in judgment. I started as a cute nine-year-old girl drummer, and others thought it was adorable when I won so many contests. As I got older and led drum corps, I was called unsightly names for the same successes I had earned as a child. I did not understand how age had turned my skill from cute to selfish. I was great at what I did, I worked hard, and I was fair, kind, and generous with my time and ability. I should add I was one of very few females in that world at that time with high recognized success; it really was the old Scottish man's turf. I endured unfair judgments from random people as I continued to excel in my field.

These judgments peaked when I was honored to become an established and certified adjudicator for the same arena I was raised to play in. Now I was paid to judge the competitions, and while I aimed to always give helpful comments and insightful suggestions, the irony of this title was not lost on me.

Because of all this judging and being judged, I formed some pretty serious barriers to protect myself. I was often blamed for things I did not do and was thought of in ways that were not in accordance with my truth. Because I shared leadership and was always ambitious and successful in my drumming career, a negative reputation spread right past the students that loved and worked hard for me to people I had never met. It was rarely those I sweated hand in hand with that spoke ill words of how much success and strength I had.

From this past place of learned sensitivity, I still have regular occurrences where I wonder if I am being judged, or if I am projecting my old programs onto the situation. I have become so used to being scorned and lashed out upon that when I make a silly comment within a new group of like-minded others, I feel dumb and assume they are thinking I am dumb. Even if they think I am great, I unconsciously place my own fear and familiar perspective onto their actions or thoughts. Fortunately, I have found gentle souls who thrive on healing others, accepting everything, always finding laughter, and not judging anyone or anything as less than their divine potential. What a gift!

I am also learning to be okay in my strength and so stead-fast in knowing myself and my integrity that I can dismiss any judgments upon me from others. I no longer care to listen to others trash me, nor do I take offense. My certainty has grown. When someone wants to judge me, that is their perception, and I do not need to buy their garbage. I can still see love in them—and me! I can look into their ideas and see if it makes me better and more open, or if it does not resonate with my heart and is therefore someone else's illusion to heal.

I am responsible first for my energy space and what I do within it. Then I may be able to help the world. I still sometimes get caught in my own traps of thinking I am being judged, which usually means I am judging myself in some way. And when I judge another, I define them as someone who would be judging me. Crazy how many layers there are to each belief and trait within ourselves!

Let us be clear that my personal story and experience in pipe band is my perspective. These are my judgments, which I continue to look at and unveil. Yes, people walked by me without responding to my hellos; yes, there were years when my mother and I did not talk; yes, one thousand other wounds . . . But we have much to integrate in order to become truly neutral. I am proud that I did not attack out of my fears or judgments (though I did defend myself from lies cast onto me), and that I ceaselessly racked my brain trying to open to other perspectives—with, I can honestly say, much eventual success. But the pain caused to people across the world from those who do act on judgments is breathtaking and needless.

My story is merely an example of how unjust feelings can get out of control when unchecked and untamed. If we had all been looking for love and perceived with more compassion, we could have reached love sooner and better. Had we taken a moment to be in God's space of love, we would have found ways to compromise our differences.

What is true for me may not be for you, and all we have to do is appreciate that fact. No good comes from taking offense or mounting attacks. We are all different for a reason, and we can each honor this in our fellow human spirits. We are here for the higher purpose of understanding, of opening and looking, and of feeling compassion for others in trying to understand them while still evolving our own stuff. Our needless enemies have much to teach us. Some of us may even learn how to receive love. We are here to care for each other, ourselves, and everything on the planet, and we cannot do that if we are rigidly stuck in a quick judgment that we are unwilling to relinquish. Life is about perspective, it is about acceptance, it is about sharing and growing, and it is about our capacity for unconditional love.

MEDITATION: ANGELIC PERCEPTION

- Close your eyes and breathe calmly.

- See a person or situation you felt hurt by.

- Look at this person or situation from an angelic perspective.

- How do this person's angels see them? How does the angelic realm view this situation? They always see someone through unconditional love.

- Take this new perspective to heart.

- Fill this picture and yourself with a pink wave of love.

- Hold it as long as you can.

LIFE AND DEATH

When death stares us in the face, even for a fleeting moment, we can suddenly gain very clear perspective. It is unfortunate we must sometimes be shaken into awakening to love, but it is a gift nonetheless. With respect and hopes of healing, I do not write here of the tragedies and pain of losing someone to heaven, but of my own experience very much involved in living.

A few years after Paul and I had left the world of pipe band, we had enrolled in a psychic school and were learning more about clearing our auras. During an energy healing and reading, given by someone I trusted and respected, I was presented with a choice of my own life or death. Although it was spiritual in aspect it remains my awakening. Though we all have a choice to live or not, it is something quite different to be directly faced with it. It was explained to me that my soul had created a potential "exit point" at this time, for this lifetime, in case things were not going the way my soul had hoped.

It was my spirit's possible doorway out of this lifetime if I had ended up (by my own devices or any others) in an unlearned state of suffering or pain, as had perhaps happened before. A weird concept to be sure, but I am open to all sorts of perspectives as I regularly ask to be enlightened toward the Universe and, this conversation occurred during an in-depth reading and healing by someone very wise.

At first I was stunned, concerned, and even scared. I knew, and it frightened me, that if I chose to stay, to live, I would have to make it count—raise my vibration to a height of previously unseen measures for me, drastically change my life to be a huge positive and moving force. I would need to make a difference.

The idea of leaving was almost refreshing for a time. A history of depression, feeling alone and misunderstood, and suffering my share of attacks, crises, loss, illness, and mystifying pain meant I have spent a lot of time not actually "in" or loving my body. For all these reasons and more, including jokingly counting myself as somewhat of a misanthrope, the notion of "the easy way out" was not such a great leap for me.

It was an interesting and wobbly perspective to believe I had a choice. All of a sudden petty arguments, my past, paying bills, lost friendships, and the like meant very little in the magnitude of choosing my own life or death. Reasons to stay or go flooded my consciousness as I looked at things like having my own children, having found my soul mate so early this time, having lost my beloved best furry friend (and maybe finding him again), accomplishing so much, whether I had even been living, how easy it would seem to go, soul's repercussions, bigger lessons, etc. I had to line up the priorities of my soul and its highest good. It was unbelievably illuminating. For weeks, I felt detached from my loved ones as I genuinely searched inside my soul for many answers.

I talked with the few I could trust who would be able to comprehend this clairvoyant insight and question of choice. My friend Sean suggested it could be a metaphor for abundant or just very big changes in my life, which were surely in progress: I was healing many of my own karmic cycles, and my family was absorbed in talks of moving from my beloved mountains, changing schedules, finding jobs, graduating classes, and many other new cycles.

Another classmate offered that perhaps I changed my assumed trajectory by getting out of the volatile pipe band world two years prior. That by finding the psychic school and learning to heal, own, and clear my space, I had transcended where I might have been, and how I might have felt and lived—enough to make staying worthwhile.

During this decision process, I was stunned when the mother of a friend tragically took her own life. There is nothing like consciously choosing life or death to show our responsibilities and priorities. I chose to stay. The synchronicity of loss of my friend's mother was furthered by my developing ability to converse with passed on souls and to give spiritual healing in all directions to those affected by suicide.

Many angles of suicide have been part of my life—my grandpa's depression and suicide, the death of a high school friend, my own suicidal thoughts as a teenager, my connection to Hemingway and his life and haunting death. I know the action of suicide affects spirits deeply once they have let go of their bodies. The emotions they go through as they come back to their senses after leaving earth in such a manner is soul shattering, the realizations heart-wrenching. Negative side effects of medications, interference in their life by foreign beings, abrupt decisions toward the only way they know to change their consciousness at a critical moment in time— whatever the reason, this way of death has many causes and elicits many judgments.

I am pained when the living believe their beloved victims of suicide are damned to eternal hell. I can honor whatever is one's truth, and I do not know how potential words of God were misinterpreted to cause further pain in this tragic loss. But my truth is that the version of hell some think suicide victims incur is actually a place in heaven where they cannot see heaven around them yet because they are holding their pain, fear, and confusion against themselves. They cannot yet see heaven within themselves. But it is there.

Once they get through the energies of the situation, it unfolds into a coming to their senses and an awakening of the beauty that is before them. They get through this space of not knowing what happened, and then realize one confused desperate act took them off the planet. Once they accept where they are, and the memories come back to them, they go through anger at what they had not until then realized and lost. With certain eventuality they heal and are open to all choices of the Universe once more.

The second they can see, they notice heaven all around them. I have seen no one forsaken. I pray that those still living find solace in these possibilities instead of limiting their friend's healing or potential through further needless con- demnation. These decisions and consequences are phenomen- al to our souls. Any light I can send to the love of those passed on and those left behind is a tiny help toward understanding and moving pain, remaining with our bodies through discomfort, and healing in spirit before our next lifetime where we make different decisions, grow, and are reunited in a return to love with those left behind.

This journey opened my eyes in examining and ordering everything in my life, future and past. Unearthing innate skills to connect with many realms changed my life. I gained new information and wisdom through those I know who have died, as they communicate much with me about their journeys as well as ours here. It helped me move past many of the petty situations of old, like who said what and who believed who. I began to find gratitude and peace for my past, and hope and inspiration for my future. I shared messages from beyond to those who could benefit from them, adding to my healing purpose. I even created enjoyment for my present, and we made plans to embrace a move, a bigger house, and new opportunities.

My ideas about all that had taken place before my present moment evolved, and I saw my "old life" for all it generously taught and gave me. I learned so much from all the close and not-so-close individuals, the band circles, and different ideals. Because of those experiences, I learned about power, leadership, loyalty, and authority, as well as the enjoyment of many people and great fun social situations.

Our perspectives depend upon our light vibration mixed with our soul's core issues; those deep essences we came to work on and evolve; those substances which evoke our emotions. Unconditional love may be one person's truth while another is learning from blame. Both are equal in their growth and value. Sanaya Roman channels this: "Reality and truth depend on your rate of vibration. As you increase your rate of vibration, your truth will expand and the veils of illusion will disappear."

MEDITATION: IF

- Relax, breathe, and close your eyes.
- Think what you would miss if you chose to leave the planet tomorrow. Think of what would be left undone.
- Think what you might do differently if your decision could be reversed.
- Is there a way to add that to your life today, this moment?
- Think of what you would miss if someone you loved, or even were mad at, died. What would be left unsaid?
- Find a way to say it now, even if only in prayer.
- Live not waiting to love until it is too late.

As we contemplate the array of perceptions and their ever-present effect on our lives, I indulge with healing and delight in an opening perspective from Dan Millman's *Way of the Peaceful Warrior.*

There was once a beloved king, whose castle was on a high hill, overlooking his shire. He was so popular that the nearby townspeople sent him gifts daily, and his birthday celebration was enjoyed throughout the kingdom. The people loved him for his renowned wisdom and fair judgments.

One day, tragedy struck the town. The water supply was polluted, and every man, woman, and child went insane. Only the king, who had a private spring, was spared.

Soon after the tragedy, the mad townspeople began speaking of how the king was acting strangely and how his judgments were poor and his wisdom a sham. Many even went so far as to say that the king had gone crazy. His popularity soon vanished. No longer did the people bring him gifts or celebrate his birthday.

The lonely king, high on the hill, had no company at all. One day he decided to leave the hill and pay a visit to the town. It was a warm day, so he drank from the village fountain.

That night there was a great celebration. The people all rejoiced, for their beloved king had "regained his sanity."

This story exemplifies the humor and vastness of the truth. We may never understand some things, but changed sight is invaluable. Appreciating the perceptions of others will greatly increase our pursuit and peace and grow our unconditional love.

CHAPTER TWELVE

Passion, Attachment, and Observation

In this chapter we look at the importance of growing unconditional love through feeling good about how we spend our time. By analyzing and identifying our passions and attachments, and then observing ourselves and our interactions with others, we learn how to grow unconditional love.

FINDING YOUR PASSION

Why are you here—can you put it into words? What are your dreams, goals, and aspirations? What fires you up and gets you going? What do you care about deeply? Living our passions gives us access to unconditional love. The first most pressing question when following your life's passions is have you discovered your inspiration? And second, if you have, do you allow your life to be filled with it? If you do not know yourself well enough to know your inspiration, identifying your passion will be difficult.

Consider what you love, what you are naturally inspired to do. Think about what calls to you, and what you are drawn to. You may feel you have a few different passions. Inspiration levels may ebb and flow as you are enlightened and learning, and then processing and integrating. As you follow a passion, you will find it guides you and gives you light. It brings meaning to why you are here. It is your work, and your inspiration, to deliver and better the world.

When your soul stirs and something enlivens your spirit, are you following it with perseverance and joy? Have you held back because you have let your fears, doubts, or lack direct your life instead? Many of us were taught that we must conform to the patterns of society—get a good and stable job, take over our parent's businesses, keep our feet firmly planted on the ground. But think of someone whom you admire. Look until you find someone who stimulates your highest ambitions. What are they doing with their life and their precious time? I do not just mean what they are doing for a living. I mean how do they spend their time.

PASSIONS ARE EXPRESSIONS OF
UNCONDITIONAL LOVE

Passions for writing or teaching are, deep down, manifestations of a desire for the world to be a friendlier, wiser, and more connected place. Being inspired by art or creating art brings out our longing for beauty and expression in the world around us. Caring for animals or nature, nurturing and growing things, are simply finding companionship, healing, and communication on a deeper level. Whether your passion is counseling children, building structures, or learning about technology, as you pursue that passion, you are healing the world. Whatever grows love is passion.

"Whatever grows love is passion."

Feng Shui is a passion oozing out of me that I cannot cease because of its expanding reaches and capabilities. While it appears to be complicated figures of moving furniture and rearranging elements and flow around someone's space, I know through years of delight and study that it profoundly changes energy by bringing harmony and balance to every area we inhabit.

This passion resonated from within me as I intuitively felt and acted on hunches in sync with Feng Shui as a child. As I have developed greater skill in the art science through much study from professionals, it radiates from me in a manner of excitement that I can help others create blessings and accord with simple conscious transformations. I know it is a deep calling of mine because it comes from me easily and naturally, and when I do it, I feel expansive, spiritual, and of value.

Some of us are born knowing what we want to do, whether or not we can name it. Some of us realize early but suppress it because we believe either the resources are limited or that we just plain do not have enough moxie to pull it off. And who are we to know ourselves so well, to figure we have our own answers, let alone follow our own inklings. We are divine. Our gifts are imperative to the world. No one else is able to give the gifts that are ours alone to give. When you begin to doubt, remember—we are even more powerful and capable than we can imagine, and it is paramount that we find and follow our inspired passions. Our lives and our world depend upon our contributions. There is no time to waste on doubts or judgments.

You can more easily recognize passion by paying attention to *when you're feeling good*, no matter the specific function or structure. Be kind to yourself, employ humor as you set out to achieve greatness, and Divinity will show up as you do. Everything you need will come rushing to your side, and Spirit will applaud as you take each step toward believing in and creating your passion.

EXPANDING PASSION

- Get into your relaxed space of breathing with eyes closed.

- Think of what you are passionate about or something you desire for your life.

- Create success in this picture as if you have achieved it.

- See how glorious it is and really *feel* your excitement.

- Grow this feeling into your whole body and smile. Believe in yourself.

- Add light to this picture. Take a step toward its reality when you gently come out.

MONEY ISN'T EVERYTHING

I always found it illuminating that, when meeting new people, the only inquiry seemed to be about what anyone *did*. My husband was a good man and played along because he had a *real* job. He is a music teacher for children with learning differences. "Oh," they say, "that sounds interesting," or "Bless your heart," or whatever. I, on the other hand, always had difficulty with this line of interrogation because while both of my daughters were little (one right after the other), I stayed home with them while also getting to know myself deeply through introspection, meditation, and inner work.

Before their school years, Paul and I knew we wanted them under our roof. Not just to keep from spending thousands of dollars on what we knew was an under-supported daycare system, but for the promise of nurturing as we chose. I could teach and mold them. I would be responsible for beginning their character and all the beautiful, priceless inadequacies that come along with "just being a mom"—another phrase that does much to undermine this elite, unbounded, and relentless profession.

Paul is very good at functioning in our culture because of his father's overbearing focus on work as what mattered most. He has had to learn to balance the pressing responsibility of providing with his newfound soul's requirement for space and contemplation. He did very well holding a consistent job, even if he hated early mornings and working under time constraints of others. Only recently has he allowed his inspirations to grow into his deeper personal wants.

While it is ingrained and somewhat natural for Paul's passions to be motivated by money and practicality, my ambitions engineered me toward family, creative expression, and spiritual development. I am learning to temper my passion for self-awareness and domesticity with more motivation to be part of the important creation of money as he evolves expression of his spirit. We are very good for each other in these ways.

I always thought it marvelous to spend my time caring for our home and children while appreciating the space to seek out my other desires at my slower, more methodical pace. Different and unexpected epiphanies filled my days with dirty laundry, humorous surprises, huge amounts of unconditional love, and so much learning of important things. I was in heaven growing my soul and theirs.

Of course, it was both a luxury and a constant sacrifice to be in this position. The four of us lived on what our sad society constitutes as a salary for teaching and guiding full classrooms of other people's children, and there was the ever-present notion that I did nothing with my time but sit on the couch eating bonbons. (I have to this very day not found where to purchase these indulgent treats.) It was very difficult to make it on one income, but we are simple, and we all get to choose the priorities that drive our passions, whatever they are. Though our worldly objects and outings are limited compared to folks passionate about travel, we actually believe that hanging out in our backyard forest is a hidden spectacular reward in itself. We felt lucky and grateful for Paul's stable income. We were also very grateful to have family we could lean on in hard times, to whom we owe much.

And so, when posed the question of what exactly I do, there was never a satisfying answer because I did so many things. My "job" as a mother seems lack-luster to some, but family is inspirational to me, and that is enough. I often still feel like the luckiest person on the planet to get to play, teach, laugh, learn, and grow with my children. It is pure enjoyment for me to spend the days of my life with them. I always thought it was quite inspirational to lock eyes with my beautiful toddler and watch how her eyes lit up as she shared stories of squirrels, or thoughts that inspired her.

MEDITATION: CHILD INSPIRATION

- Really listen and engage with children.
- Look at them when they talk.
- They need our attention, and can lead us to find inspiration within their imagination.
- Respond to their silliness with silliness, and feel the lightheartedness of play.
- Validate their wild imaginations and honest expressions.

- Look for a message, for yourself, in the wisdom of babes.
- Let these precious beings know we are seeing them and honoring them.
- Wholly experience this real magic right before your eyes.

There are some days when more alone time would be nice, and when the screeches of a vociferous five-year-old rings in my ears; when I am too tired to be of the value I could be to her works of art, silly games, or repeated actions. But now as my littlest prepares to begin school, I have aches of already missing watching every moment of her experiencing life. With her entrance into school, I'll return to the workforce. It is a double-edged sword to finally make money for our family and gain worth in society's eye. I'm sad that our precious time together shifts and, in a way, ends. No matter what the autumn has in store for me, I still feel immeasurably grateful for the results of our difficult yet rewarding choice. I am to find my new inspirations elsewhere.

Of course, I have already found passions in addition to motherhood. I was a very successful drum sergeant and teacher in the bagpipe band world for twenty-five years. I always wrote and worked on my potential books. I studied metaphysics, read emphatically, communed deeply with nature so as to discover my true self, and passed these gifts of learning along to my children. I took classes on healing, energy, and many other subjects. Though they were my passions and inspirations, none of these jobs were really considered jobs to anyone else because they did not pay money.

My Feng Shui studying resulted in me becoming a certified

consultant—at last, something that paid. And though I did not work forty or more hours a week, I was passionate. I also endeavored to become a clairvoyant energy cleanser and reader, as well as meditation teacher.

I was engrossed in the world of politics and history, always carrying a copy of the beloved Constitution with me, but again, no salary, no worth—except to myself, on which, thank goodness, I learned to place a great deal of significance. In searching for unconditional love I had to hold it for myself. No one else's opinions could dictate what stirred in me. We all have different ideas of what is inspiring, which is what makes the world go round. It is very normal for something we feel passionate about to fall into the cracks of what society deems worthy. We need to try with all our might to put those incessant voices to sleep far away, to follow our hearts, find our passions, and live inspired, as we see fit.

PASSIONS FEEL GOOD

I used to have a great deal of passion for enjoying the perfect sound of a musical group playing together. When the expression is minded, when the embellishments come together with perfect light and shade and everyone is tuned in, there is nothing like the resultant sound or feeling. But, as is often true with life's beauties we delight in, to achieve such an outcome depended greatly on many other people pulling their weight—keeping their instruments in good shape, practicing consistently, engaging with full mind focus. When our passions rely on others, it can be deeply bonding and fulfilling, but also frustrating.

Through experiences working in groups, even with excellent colleagues, we may grow pessimistic of our ability to create our desires. If we look deeper, we can recognize conditions where we can feel empowered, knowing when we can succeed and make a difference.

Although music or sports groups might bring socializing and collective consciousness, there may be an unnoticed reason in your involvement in the group that is your passion. Maybe it's your underlying accolades of teaching or helping another on their path that brings your sense of accomplishment and inspiration. Maybe it is simply the community, social outlet, or human closeness that inspires that particular arrangement. This is simply where you find the love. No matter the venue or form, teaching a skill and sharing your knowledge on any given craft may be what brings you satisfaction at the end of the day. These clues grow love.

I am inspired by thoughts of living in unconditional love, all around and within, from every angle and circumstance. It is not to get my brother to buy into it or my enemies to appreciate me, but I strive to actually exist in this space so love is all I feel and see, irrespective of anything. I endeavor to be in that space of total acceptance and love, feeling no enmity for anyone, not perceiving anyone as against me, not judging any person or action, but expanding the best feelings I have ever been aware of, onto everything, always. As often as I can, I want to be responsible for my surroundings and what comes forth from my actions. I desire to make sure I am adding light and love to whatever encircles me. Though I am not constant with it, the work is passionate, and the goal inspiring.

ATTACHMENT

After identifying your passion, you may notice that much of your time is spent on things you aren't passionate about but feel obligated to—or attached to. Part of living a life of unconditional love is evaluating the depth of your attachments and understanding how to release them. Releasing unhealthy attachments is part of mastering unconditional love, so check in with how heavy your attachment might be to success, approval, chemicals, people, results, stability, and even life. What is the "right" level of attachment to anything in order to grow love?

When you are young, you are linked to your parents to ensure survival. But when is attachment necessary for your wellbeing, and when is it destructive or oppressive? Although some degree of attachment is important, even required, for your development, where does it turn from healthy to unhealthy? When it turns into an addiction it is unhealthy. When it is hurting you or another, or holding you or another back, it is oppressive. When you are not feeling good about it, it is destructive.

Human babies are bound to their guardians for up to eighteen years and sometimes more, while some animals are literally kicked out of the nest or den immediately. This makes humans both the neediest of species as well as the most attached. While animals live from instinct and exhibit qualities of connection differently, our bonding during infancy is paramount to our wholeness, happiness, and functioning as humans.

In the first two years of our lives, the care we receive dictates many of our patterns throughout the rest of our lives— at least, those that are foundational to this present lifetime. How we are responded to, cuddled, and interacted with will tell us much about our ability to love unconditionally later in life, how we cooperate with the world around us in our most intimate relationships, and even our views and beliefs about ourselves.

We find our place in the world based on the feelings we learn when we are first having our needs met. If our attachment process is interrupted during these critical years, either because of abuse, illness, neglect, trauma, or any sort of separation, we will not as easily learn how to trust or find our way to getting our bigger needs met. This isolation or rejection from the parent can be conscious or unconscious, and either way, not having needs met can have far-reaching repercussions of pain, fear, interference, possible mental illness, or even violence as that individual endlessly searches to fill the hole left by the early separation. It is imperative that we attach correctly, consistently, and lovingly while we are babies to ensure our proper, healthy development.

The difficulty herein lies with the fact that as infants we are not in charge of our care. By the time we are responsible for the ways in which we attach or withhold, we are usually acting involuntarily from however our caregiver taught us. If we were picked up and fed when we cried, talked to, looked at, and had our diapers changed, we will have a good start. We will feel more secure in the world and can begin exploring safely, with support. If we were ignored when we cried out for help, we will spend most of our time and energy as we grow in search of one thing: survival. We will be limited in how we experience the world and will act out in myriad ways. Growing unconditional love could seem out of reach—but creating it is possible.

ATTACHMENT ISSUES

Disrupted attachment can manifest outwardly as promiscuous acts, violence, outbursts, and experimentation with drugs. It can also present as a withdrawn child unable to give love, although desiring it desperately, or an inaccessible, misunderstood "I don't care" type of attitude. On the opposite end of the spectrum, some children will become so attached that they are afraid to be separated from their parents at all.

Any disconnection feels to them like the original abandonment issue in their early dependence, which diverted them from the right path. Any way it comes out, if it does in any obvious way at all, it is greatly debilitating to the individual, their family, and their relationships, should they manage to cultivate them.

Many problems with control emerge as these lagging children grow up striving to demand having a say over their boundaries. Even without understanding where an attachment issue comes from or why, they may have created an unquenchable thirst for power because they lack trust in anyone else to provide what they need when they need it. They have been taught that they are alone, that no one else can be counted on, and that they had better figure out how to manipulate their surroundings to fill what they can of this vast and dark void. In essence, they feel it is all up to them.

It is possible to heal the broken heart of a child who grows up without healthy attachment. This can be achieved through deep healing, introspection, and clarity, or involved professional therapy using special techniques. Some of these are presented in *The Love Disorder* by Conrad Boeding, my beloved, wise, and dear father. You can see how this very foundational need, if not met, is a catalyst for all sorts of deficits in love and life.

ASSESSING OUR OWN ATTACHMENTS

Many of us can identify with similar symptoms to those exhibited by neglected children. Even if you had a perfectly good childhood, certain desirable characteristics—like loving unconditionally—may not come naturally to you. Remember it will not help to blame your inability on anyone. Most parents do their best and follow what they were taught themselves. Nearly 90 percent of humans have grown up in what psychologists categorize as dysfunctional homes (and this includes your parents). Your wounded parts are not what define you or make you unique; your specialness is determined by how you repair these paucities, and thus yourself. Your injuries are not your excuses; they are your responsibilities, and your places to heal. This is soul work. Do it lovingly.

"Your wounded parts are not what define you or make you unique; your specialness is determined by how you repair these paucities, and thus yourself."

We all had unmet needs while being formed, and the transformation of these circumstances and their consequences are the very significance of our human existence. Everything that has occurred in our histories has only meant to bring us here, to this moment. In this instant, we can choose for ourselves the directions we dance, the attitudes we allow, and the rewards we receive. If we use our past traumas to justify guilt, blame, scarcity, worry, complacency, or attack, we will be choosing disempowerment instead of the transcendence that is awaiting us. Heal and grow with love.

With these recognitions, and maybe professional help, everyone can see their need and capacity for unconditional love and begin to walk its comforting path. This search for love is a way for each of us to find our own strength, understand our needs—which are the needs of the world at large—and begin to fulfill ourselves. We can then share what we have learned and grown, and these are our gifts.

We have great healing power in unconditional love. Your pain and loss can be undone and turned toward trust and light with the growth of unconditional love and faith. When you are older, you have the power to meet your needs no matter what happened years ago. It is up to you now to release your attachment to how you were attached and to move in the direction of what you want. Believe you have the power, and it will move through you with delightful, healing, gentle force.

MEDITATION: ATTACHMENT

- Close your eyes, breathe, and relax.
- What do you feel so attached to you might die without?
- Breathe through the fear or pain.
- See yourself letting this attachment go, up and away to God.
- Fill in that space with love, knowing you are always okay.
- Fill with the light of divine timing, and see your life always changing, always okay.

OBSERVATION

Where attachment issues formed when we didn't have any control over our surroundings, our powers of observation are in our complete control. We have learned most of what we know about people and our world by observing, and then passing on that information. Travelers found their way by observing the starry skies, and discovered vast knowledge by observing the Universe. By turning our powers of observation inward, we can identify needed changes and growth, making room to grow our love. In examining what is happening around us we can know when to intervene with unconditional love.

Have you ever really watched children play with their whole hearts? Like how kids get totally soaked when they play in a creek or puddle. They do everything fully with confidence and little hesitation until someone teaches them to be careful. Of course staying safe is important, but take an example from the unadulterated joy of children (the pure species), and allow yourself to jump in fully.

When we tune into our surroundings we can accumulate numerous calculations about how humanity unfolds. The possibilities for learning become boundless when we turn this powerful skill onto ourselves. You can know and guide your life by utilizing observation. You can be aware that you might be about to sabotage yourself, and watch the steps set up right before you so you can take a different path.

Live on movement, even slow. Live on optimism and choose to see the good. Choose to learn. You cannot control your world, only your reaction to it, so pay attention to those reactions. Choose peace. Breathe, read something helpful, and enter light into your body. Do not seek understanding in the actions of anyone but yourself. God understands, and may that be enough. Focus on good things, and remind yourself often of how far you have come. Tell yourself good things. Make a list of divine characteristics in you that continue to add to the life you are seeking and creating; *I am smart! I am funny! I am talented! I have given love when before I would have been torn down by certain words. I see hope more often than fear.*

MEDITATION: OBSERVING THE SELF

- Close your eyes and breathe.
- Allow any negative feelings to come up gently.

- Notice where in your body you feel this tension.
- Begin to breathe into and out of that place in your body.
- Allow the tension to release and dissipate.
- Recall some good feelings and let them rise.
- Notice how this makes your body feel.
- Grow good feelings, and add love and light to them in order to hold them longer.

OBSERVING OTHERS

Have you ever thought you had a special talent for recognizing what motivates the outside world? What moves one toward action but another toward defense? You might sense a lot about people, like why they will or will not do what is expected, or how repeated self-sabotage is reflected in their lives. You might recognize simple steps that could improve someone's peace or see the blocks that keep them from succeeding. This knowing may seem egotistical or intrusive, but having powers of awareness to the inner workings of human nature, be they used for good, greatly adds to knowledge and enlightenment.

Having foresight into the motivations of others can open our eyes a great deal and lead us to a better sense of peace and understanding with our world. This knowing people and recognizing patterns and personalities comes from simple observation and evolving intuition. And it is wonderful when we notice love everywhere.

Remember, observation does not mean judgment. To be a true observer you must suspend judgment. We do not necessarily know what anyone needs for his or her best interest or life plan. We can learn to be observant and gain insights from what we witness without opinions, and unless asked for advice we can live and let live. Observation is not a tool for gossip or superiority. You become a silent addition to the situation, peacefully doing your job by yourself. This leads to great realizations as to why and how things are working in the world, and more importantly, to greater consciousness within yourself for your own higher learning. This is the real reason to observe—not to condemn or compare, but to grow.

When observations turn into judgments, and you do not see eye to eye with someone, and they misperceive, project, or blame, it may be time to shift or change the connection. Any negative judgment will limit the clarity with which the relationship can continue. The depth of that relationship becomes restricted in either person's capacity to unconditionally love or see the truth and best in the other.

"Accept someone where they stand instead of judging their deeds."

Accept someone where they stand instead of judging their deeds. Remember the likely possibility that, for instance, if someone lies to you it is not because something in you is unworthy of the truth, but because something inside them is not yet able to do the trusting. Imagine what splendor you will see looking inside when you give compassion in this circumstance. Judgment and misperceptions stunt the deepening to which both people can joyfully grow or remain together. Unconditional love takes judgment out of observing, allows simple awareness to broaden our perceptions, and opens the world we see.

Be aware of the messages brought to you by intently watching your surroundings. Learn great things by taking part in your environment, be it with people, nature, or especially yourself. When in doubt, take time and observe. Spend some time in nature and observe the very constancy of life. Notice the same seedling tree through spring and summer, and witness true growth. Fill your soul by beholding sunlight on tree leaves, the wind breezing by your face, or the same bird flying to the same berry bush each day of a particular season. Becoming immersed in the observations of nature can bring insights and fulfillment of your world within. A good way to learn is simply to look.

OBSERVING OUR INTERACTIONS WITH OTHERS

Observation is also a practical tool that can help you in uncomfortable situations. When you feel out of place, or are not among friends or acquaintances, taking a few moments to observe where others are coming from may indeed ease your ambivalence. Learning what appears to be of interest or disinterest to others and quietly checking out the situation before interacting will lead you to a more intelligent or meaningful conversation. It makes us feel better inside and boosts our own confidence to ease the sometimes difficult task of communicating and connecting with others.

Do you know yourself? Who are you when you are with others? Do you continue as yourself, or do you put on a face for others? Can you be low and unhappy if the situation warrants, or do you feel as if you must always appear together and smart? Are you truly relaxed and centered when in the company of others, or does the presence of another change you? Do you pretend so others might be impressed with you? Do you always have to one-up anyone's stories, wisdom, or even successes to feel important? Look inside, because if you think negative things about another it is more than likely just a mirror of your own illusions.

What we love or dislike in others acts as a barometer of our own characteristics. While we can all be nervous upon encountering new folks or environments, if the anxiety changes us to the point of being exhausted at the front we must portray, we either need new friends or drastic introspection. If we become chameleons more regularly than on a rare occasion of feeling out of place, we should be aware that our personalities are overriding our better, real selves. This trait may stem from a fundamental program that we would not be loved unconditionally as we are, but we are shortchanging the world by withholding our beauty and uniqueness. We are shortchanging our potential by hiding our vulnerabilities. We can exchange our old programs for those that show our truth and magnificence to the world, and ourselves.

"We are shortchanging the world by withholding our beauty and uniqueness."

When we place our gift of observation upon our own feelings and actions while in public, we can learn much about ourselves. Sometimes we have friends who may not love us unconditionally and do not accept us when we are having trouble, being short, or struggling with what might be simple to them. While saying one thing and acting in a completely different way is one obvious form of pretense, this situation of being unaccepted on bad days is not our pretense, but theirs. In our efforts to have integrity in all our connections we need to first place ourselves in the company of trustworthy others who will love us no matter what, and second, we need to hold our centers. Being true to ourselves will resonate outwardly from inner acceptance to being in truth during bigger gatherings, scarier experiences, or more trying circumstances.

Most of us are not lucky enough to always be or encounter enlightened souls in our friendships, family, and daily interactions. We know that dealing with others is a divine opportune source for experiencing and growing, so it often stirs up emotions and questions which may need deep thought in order to understand. While integrity to some is about how you behave when no one is watching, we awaken self-awareness when we turn away from needing to prove our actions worthy and toward the next step of how our interactions are coming across to us where it counts—deep within.

We begin to wonder what will be brought up if we spend time with an old friend compared to a new one. Will so-and-so be loving, or be bringing out stuff in me for maximum growth? Does this friend accept me when I am too tired to offer comfort or assistance to their lives? Do I know and accept myself wholly?

No matter how solid and centered we are inside, certain people arouse different energies to be worked on. When we get down to the heart of the matter, every person and every encounter creates something very different to add to, enhance, or change in order to continue our growing processes. When we forgive the source and integrate the effects, we are healing ourselves through observation. We may finally rise to the level of owning our own space completely independent of outside influence. This begins when we employ this wisdom from Sanaya Roman: "When others don't recognize you for who you are, you have the opportunity to grow by believing in yourself."

How extremely does your personality waver when you engage in or see varying scenarios throughout your day? You may have great integrity in your personality and self-concept and still experience difficulty when near the energy fields of others. You may still wonder what specific interactions are meant to give to your life, or how you may give differently so as to expand love where it languishes. You may wonder why you still leave a conversation feeling dumb or being upset that you did not say something you thought might add to the discussion. These are all authentic longings to improve your exchanges and discover more meaning and love in your daily life.

Having difficulty holding your center when around others does not mean you are not being yourself. It simply shows that you are trying to understand a greater depth to connections and human intimacies. Perhaps your vibrations are rapidly causing your introspection to blossom in seeming turbulence as you shift and evolve right within your entire sphere of relationships. This is an always available and rich forum in which to explore the vast depths of unconditional love, learning, growing, and observation.

SELF-EXPLORATION THROUGH IRRITATION

When you interact with anyone you are opening the doors for all parties to observe and learn. You can only control you, so utilize self-exploration in your responses. Consider others as teachers and messengers. Though a few might be easy to loathe, those who cause the biggest distress are those who may best teach us the most. What someone did to push your buttons is not the issue. Thank them for helping you grow and giving you the opportunity to learn. Get through your hurt and resentment with as much peace and wisdom as possible, then return to compassion.

It is your reaction to them or the situation that has the knowledge or lesson in it. Look past the feelings, evaluate the cause, and extract the importance—the reason for the event. It will show you your shortcomings and insecurities and allow you to change them. It is not always easy, but you can learn tools to help your growth become effortless and even amusing. Life is about learning, growing, and enlightening your soul, unless you choose for it not to be.

See if the next time an entanglement occurs you can even

silently say, "I love you for bringing this valuable information to my attention so I may grow." They are just hitting your buttons and drawing your attention to something that needs addressing, or expanding. Choose self-exploration to discover the real lesson. Why did this bother me? Why does that hit a button? What can I change or control? Find the reason behind the feeling and be proud of great self-responsibility. The Universe will thank you for this in unseen dividends. You will thank yourself in much seen growth and ease. Someday you may be able to say a lot of thank yous.

When you feel upset at the actions of another, remember to look in the mirror. Let them have their stuff. Own yours. Release them, breathe deeply, and blow out. It need not shake you. It is way more exciting to sit in meditation, look at the situation or person, and then look at yourself. Look at their energy and yours. Suddenly you might awaken to the imbalance that rests within. If their action is kind, you react well; if their reaction is awful, you react poorly. It affects you because you are attached to it, and not looking beneath personality into truth.

"Neutrality for the sake of knowledge is priceless."

You become unattached by being centered inside yourself and having something inspiring enough going on in your heart, life, soul, or day that *it* captivates you instead, and you would rather learn than be mad. Neutrality for the sake of knowledge is priceless. It is best to look into our centers and know from where we are coming in order to figure out how best to get where we long to go. It is wise to treat everyone as we want to be treated.

When you request Universal assistance in your personal growth, it races to you. When we shine a light on the recesses of ourselves, and witness life's events as learning steps to peace, we do much for the world. It is nice to be in the sun and light. Focus on your wishes and have renewed hope that positive and great opportunities consistently happen in your life. The Universe rejoices when your heart opens to love.

CHAPTER THIRTEEN

Standard Meditation

The single most effective tool towards enlightenment I have ever found is energy work in meditation! As I look back on my growth, on all my experiences and connections with Divinity that have given me light and perception, I realize that my commitment to meditation was the single biggest mechanism that changed my life. It is a joy and a solace, and it brings amazing and often instantaneous results. Meditation assures growth.

Perhaps the word "meditation" brings up skepticism. You might not imagine growth is possible just by sitting, lighting a candle, and beginning to get quiet. I invite you to see for yourself what meditation is all about. I promise that no matter how you meditate, it will affect your life in wondrous ways. It will change your energy, raise your vibration, and help you manifest the world you desire and deserve to live in.

Everyone will have their personal preferences about which form of meditation suits them best. In order to get into a regular schedule of meditation, it is helpful to have a goal of exactly what you desire from this practice. I use different techniques depending on my needs, and I find even twelve minutes a day makes a difference. I encourage you to look into any formal or non-formal meditation techniques that might spark your interest. This chapter focuses on basic, relaxing meditation techniques; the next chapter offers energy-work meditations that cleanse chakras, change your space, and expand your vibration.

MY MEDIATION EXPERIENCE

Through wonderful varied spiritual studies my parents taught my siblings and I each week, I began meditating at the age of nine, when introduced to Buddhism, as a way to connect with my inner world. But I only realized its potential in my early thirties. I was drawn to find time to continue with consistency even if I felt I was only going through the motions. This helped me to know myself and have a centered place of respite through my teenage years. I witnessed wonderful things and experienced many insights and synchronicities throughout my twenties, but it was not until later that I gave meditation its due recognition and value.

My common practice was to find my sacred nook, or be outside when possible, and simply to visit my imaginary world. I created this world as my first meditative experience, taught to me by my wise and spiritual mother, and although I added and changed parts, it is where I began almost every time.

I imagined a beautiful place with fountains and crystal caves, trees, rainbows, oceans, chakra colors, people I loved, animals, guides, and different places to sit or play, depending on what I was working on. It was my utopia. Once I started learning how to connect with my higher self, or other spiritual lights and energies, I would enter my world, walk through my special areas, lingering where I needed to for however long, and then I would leave by simply going higher into the clouds, finding my desired dimensions of essence, light, love, and guidance. From there, my possibilities became, and remain, infinite.

WAYS TO MEDITATE

There are endless ways to meditate, and choosing one depends on your purpose. You can use it to get quiet, gain concentration, visualize and manifest, release, do energy work, connect with your higher self, or contact spiritual guides. As you continue learning and engaging in meditation practices you will be shown how to do things you never imagined. It is truly infinite in its benefits and has huge cumulative effects. The more you meditate, the better you get, and the more it brings you with greater ease.

"The more you meditate, the better you get, and the more it brings you with greater ease."

When your purpose is focus, a good way to start is a simple candle technique. Sit before a candle, concentrating on just the flame for ten minutes. If you like, mark how many times your mind wanders. Each day you do so, your mind will wander less. This technique calms your energy, and helps you gain clearer focusing ability. This is a good beginning for people who have minds so active they cannot consciously slow them.

A second meditation technique is visualization, and its purpose is relaxation by getting away and also working with your ability to create, which helps manifesting. Close your eyes, and begin to create a visual image of your own utopia or fantasy world to play or relax in. This takes you away from the daily hum-drum and allows you the ease and fun of being childlike. When I was stressed, I employed this often to visualize a better way.

Another calming technique involves sitting with eyes open or closed, simply watching your breathing. Pay attention to your heartbeat, which directs attention inward, quiets the mind, and connects us to our body. We calm down when our awareness is focused on our breath and heart. I still do this whenever I cannot sleep, or during an asthma attack.

These are some of the most basic techniques to get into a meditative space. Meditation can be done during almost any activity. You can wash dishes contemplatively, listen to nature and its endless sounds, and even eat your favorite treat slowly and intentionally. You can do yoga or tai chi for a physical meditation, or you can plant and weed a garden for aesthetic meditation. You can enlist favorite mantras in increasing time increments to manifest, connect with certain gods or goddesses, or induce deep relaxation, thus requiring less REM sleep. Meditation is less about sitting still and more about mindfulness in every action. It is about a state of mind, alert stillness, and conscious awareness.

SPECIFIC MEDITATIONS

The following meditations are guided, but general. The first, Personal Sanctuary, stimulates visualizing and really gets your mind and imagination creating. The second, Present Sense, is all about feeling and noticing in order to bring you present and keep you there when it may not be easy. The third, Communion, is about connecting to something greater than ourselves, as well as noticing messages meant for us, for which we are searching.

Personal Sanctuary builds on the second technique introduced above. It is a simple and individual meditation you can enjoy if you want to quiet your mind, relax your body, or do some creative visualization. Instead of taking you on a specific journey, or taking you to my fantasy sanctuary, I invite you to create and enjoy your own. You can close your eyes, and just escape reality for ten or fifteen minutes while you let your higher mind believe in the wonders of imagination. That is, after all, how we manifest.

GUIDED MEDITATION

Get into your space through a series of deep and slowing breaths or by closing your eyes, and mentally walking upstairs, or through a tunnel—any sort of passage will help you more easily transform your state. You can create places to sit and think, helpers or workers who assist you in healing or doing specific jobs. You can picture cleansing pools, giant lollipops, balloons going up to Divinity full of things you would like to have, or release, or anything your creative juices recommend. You can create a colorful world with rainbows, or use just one or two of your favorites, enjoying the different tints of everything blue.

Call in angels for wisdom or to help heal. Listen to your intuition, and change your palace, cave, or meadow as you grow for optimum enjoyment. Go there whenever you want to get away, and have no expectations or obligations as to what you "have to do" there. Think like a kid, and enjoy your ability to create and delight in the spaces you can conjure in your mind's eye.

There are thousands of recorded or written visualizations if you would like another to guide you to something specific. As with any meditation, some folks like to hear it and be led, or record it themselves and listen. Some like to read and follow, and some like to be all on their own, with themselves and their own stuff. Do what works for you, and enjoy the process of creating, seeing, and most of all, just being!

Present Sense meditation can be helpful for worriers to stay in the here and now, for mind wanderers to stay present, for maintaining connection and relaxation, for relieving insomnia frustration, or for focusing in overwhelming or stressful situations. You can use this in situations where immediate relief or shift is necessary.

Most worriers are in that state due to their focus on times other than the present—be they upsets from the past, or fears of potential futures. It doesn't help to know that thinking about the future will not do anything compared to acting now for what you want. Hurting over the past, albeit the beginning of a path towards healing, can do nothing to change the event. Present Sense, when practiced regularly, can stop the awful cycle of unproductive worrying, giving you a chance to start a fresh moment of better living.

GUIDED MEDITATION

Breathe nice deep breaths. Close your eyes if able. Begin to flow through each sense with as much presence and awareness as possible. You may follow the senses in any path or order you like.

Listen to whatever sounds you can hear all around you. How many different sounds on different levels can you pick up both near and far? Are any of them rhythmic, annoying, or soothing? Can you hear your heart beat? Can you hear the hissing of your blood circulating through your veins? Focus on loud as well as soft sounds. Take your time and pick out as many as you can notice. Do any feel full or heavy, sharp or sustained? Breathe into and from your ears. When you are ready, move to the next sense.

Envision something that makes you feel peaceful.

What do you see in your mind's eye? Can you see or change internal pictures as they appear inside your head? Can you watch them show up and disappear without any attachment to holding or understanding them? Do you interpret meaning in any of the colors or shapes? Can you see the colored light train of your thoughts pass by this space? Can you see and dwell in the spaces between these thoughts—between the train cars? Can you clear your clairvoyant space and create calming or inspiring scenes behind your eyes and between your ears with increasing clarity?

If you would like, begin to look around with open eyes and a soft focus. What colors can you see? How about textures? Notice the difference between close and far away objects. Which colors stand out? Which shapes? Which colors or patterns appeal to you, and which do not? If you gently stare for a minute or so, can you witness the light or aura around the edges of trees or people? Breathe into and out of your eyes and your mind's eye space.

Next, what can you smell, and what can you taste? These senses are closely linked. Although you may not taste much unless eating while meditating, notice the entwining of the tastes in your mouth and anything you can smell; if you are outside, all the better. Does your mouth taste clean or bitter? Is it wet or dry? Is there a metallic or sweet taste?

Smelling is a potent sense memory and leads us to mysterious paths of old. What is the nearest scent to you? Can you differentiate between your personal aroma and others in your environment? Breathe deeply and take in your surroundings through your nose in order to be exactly where your body rests at this moment. Is the air cold or warm as it arrives into your body? Is the air deep and slow, or fast? What do you wish you were smelling right now? Smell something wonderful and notice how its fragrance affects you.

Finally, move onto feeling and touch. Feel your clothes on your body, or the object you are touching or resting on. Feel your feet on the ground, or your muscles in how you are positioned. Feel the temperature around you, and its effects on different places on your skin. Feel your organs, and the comfort or discomfort of each side, limb, and place within as well as on your body. Feel a breeze, a strain, a letdown. Can you feel your heart beat in your chest? Try hearing and feeling your heart beat in many different places within your body. This awareness alone is very powerful, centering, and restorative.

Keep flowing through each sense, and remember to breathe slowly and deeply. Relax, and feel supported by the earth with each breath. Once you finish observing through your senses with ease, you may notice that you are more in your body, you are present and with yourself instead of floating around in thought or confusion. You become clearer and gain serenity as you become senior to what you place your attention upon. Simply enjoy this space, breathe peacefully, and return your awareness to the room when you are ready.

If you need more intense distraction/focus pick up a flower, some dirt, a stick or crystal, and experience the textures of it. Try new things like guessing objects by feel or opening your eyes and searching for colors. Infuse a lovely scent to enhance the room's aroma, or do this exercise outside to pick up many different scents, especially in spring or autumn when the Earth is potent and fertile. Delve deeper, remember to breathe, and if you let in an unpleasant thought, simply let it pass through, come back, and begin again. This can take as much or as little time as you want it to, though as you meditate regularly, you may find that longer periods meditating leave you feeling more refreshed.

This short Present Sense meditation will always work to bring you back to the present, make you aware of the here and now, and let you at least momentarily forget about possible concerns, controllable or otherwise. You will find that some senses are easier to stay with, or are more enjoyable. Mold your Present Sense exercise however it helps you the most. And remember to breathe! Perhaps after doing this, you will be able to release a past feeling a little more, or discover a small action you can take to shape your desired future. Clarity and centering help. But most of all, meditation will teach you to enjoy the present moment. You will gain control, focus, relaxation, and insights to help your presence, and your living.

Communion with Nature, Crystals, and Animal Totems is an easily accessible use of our environment and can transform states of mind with refreshing aliveness. I will continue to encourage, through repeated suggestion, that everyone's lives can be elevated by simply being in nature. To be together with trees, water, flowers, sunshine, breezes, and the earth is a God-given gift paying unseen dividends.

If you would like to connect with the minerals of our planet, find a specimen that speaks to you, from a quartz or river rock outside to a purchased crystal at one of the many lapidaries or rock shops. I find that calcites respond with fervor to human vibrations and give back fantastically with little effort. Read about any specific kind of rock you have chosen in a mineral guidebook (my personal favorites are *Crystal Wisdom* by

Dolphyn and *Love is in the Earth* by Melody) and play with it often to gain from its abundant and bountifully benevolent qualities.

There are no strict guidelines for meditating in or with nature, and truthfully, just allowing it to permeate your space is meditative. Nonetheless, I offer some helpful methods of keeping focus upon our surroundings and benefiting from such interactions. The key to gaining restoration through nature is to be present, aware, still, quiet, and reflective.

GUIDED MEDITATION

Find a safe natural sanctuary, even in a limited space, such as a garden, park, yard, or even better, a forest, desert, body of water, mountain, river, or meadow, and get comfortable. You can look around, and take stock to feel a measure of safety, and create a colored bubble around you for a sense of protection if you need.

Close your eyes, and begin to breathe with the planet. If you can reach out and touch earth or a tree, you can more easily tune into the heartbeat of this energy. Get quiet, still, and open your senses to notice wherever your awareness wants you to follow. By taking deep breaths in fresh air or near ionized water, your spirit will begin to refresh your body.

Let your surroundings envelop you, and just sit within the qualities of time slowed down, of space in healthy, clean condition. Feel the sun or breeze touch your face, and be taken in. Breathe. Let this massive energy clear through you and blanket your personal energy field with the power of the outdoors.

Let your focus follow whatever part of nature grabs your awareness, whether it is a bird flying by, the air,

the colors or sounds around you, the light playing on
the ground, or one beautiful spot that feels familiar.
Breathe it in, rest, and relax. Just be there, in this place
so different from an hour ago, and let it take you past
the clouds, through time, and balanced with the support
of our benevolent planet.

If you would like to connect with a tree and feel its strength and wisdom surge through you, then lean your back against a noble participant and allow yourself to feel and breathe with it. Notice the support emanating from this living creature and appreciate all it does for our world. Look up and delight in the green branches waving above you and see the sky through the canopy with a sense of childlike wonder.

Consider seeing as the tree would, looking out from within, perhaps feeling you leaning gently against it, and ask if it might have a message of ancient wisdom for you. Listen to your intuitive flash, write it down, and believe in and follow it. Leaning against or hugging trees can do much to clear our spines and bodies, and tilting the crowns of our heads against them can clear the seventh chakra like almost nothing else.

If you have a rock or gemstone, hold it, squeeze it, and be mesmerized by its beauty and complex uniqueness. Feel any tingles or vibrations it gives to your touch that might sweep out your aura, ground you, transform negativity, or protect you, and thank it for any information it might offer. Sit with them, charge or clear them in earth, water, sun or moon, and just feel their power. Place it on different parts of your body, and notice healing, connection, or its vibration.

Sit by a river, and while staring let your thoughts be carried away. The sounds of rivers are immensely healing and releasing. Let your body flow, release, and float with the ease of the water. You will feel relaxed immediately by just being next to the steady movement of water.

See the sun reflect and appreciate the beauty and perfection of nature's wonder. When rejuvenation begins to permeate your whole self, bring in unconditional love and turn it inward upon yourself. I often find that doing this near a river connects me to the planet in a magical way, and I begin to lose my boundaries. When nature happens in communion with unconditional love, we can feel an expansion from our spirits outward, and a oneness with the Universe. When this feeling occurs do not chase it and long to hold onto more, but relish in this expansion, for your soul is growing, and your spirit and body are in perfect harmony with our world.

Discovering and working with an animal totem, also referred to as *power animal*, facilitates a much deeper connection with nature's creatures. You can have several at once—one or two that remain with you as well as changing guides correlating with present circumstances. You can determine which animal is offering its wisdom in your current situation by being in nature and noticing which animals you see with repetition or during times of intensity. You can ask to be shown a helpful animal spirit while in a meditative state, or simply notice recurrences of any animal theme popping up around you, whether on television, in books, dreams, from conversations, or from living close to nature.

Have conversations with any animal that comes into your space, including domestic, and learn from their messages. This can be enlightening information and is a huge form of support for you from the earth. Our animal creatures are divine and offer endless means from which to learn about our human habits, cycles, and qualities. If you get close to your totems and enjoy the gifts animal wisdom can bestow, you might want to look into my favorite creature compendium,

Animal Speak by Ted Andrews. One of my first and constant totems is the raven; in today's mystery he leads me to these words:

See the raven and marvel,

Watch the raven and learn,

Talk to the raven and ask,

Hear the raven and understand,

Listen to the raven and know,

Follow the raven and transcend.

Meditation has the ability to transform lives, no matter the structure. Some use techniques for personal transformation, and some seek deep calm. Whatever the need, there is a meditation source that can meet it. All types contain valuable assistance for the varied experiences we have on this earth. Try any method that tickles your fancy or comes recommended by trustworthy others, and then feel free to choose another. Meditation is simply tuning in, focusing, and creating with intention and energy.

CHAPTER FOURTEEN

Energy Work and Active Meditation

Most forms of meditation we hear about in the mainstream fall in the category of creative visualizations. These include going on journeys within, creating a safe haven for sitting still, searching your thoughts or feelings, and many other introspections with guided imagery. These forms of meditation, discussed in the previous chapter, can open our mind and expand our capacity to see and believe more positively. They can also create or manifest dreams we place there with sensation and detail.

We can realize many helpful insights while in this state, and it does much to illuminate and jump-start our imaginations (the essence of learning to trust our intuition). While these are engaging and uplifting, even calming and useful for some revelations, their ability to drastically change our lives is limited. In my experience, the most transformative meditation comes from working with energies.

In the Berkeley Psychic Institute tradition, from where I have received my schooling and certification, each tool builds upon itself. Meditation is cumulative, and we can each go as far and as fast as we want to manage. Its benefits and tremendous gifts are truly inexhaustible, immeasurable, and profound. The idea of active meditation may be easier on our preconceptions because we are "doing" stuff instead just sitting still, clearing our minds, or going blank. This chapter will outline some of the basic tools of active meditation.

A NOTE ON CHOOSING A TEACHER

Learning energy work is often intricate and requires teachers and good classes. Choose to study from masters with high integrity who have been recommended by someone you trust, or who work in schools with proven results. Meditation classes are a dime a dozen, and I would encourage attending those exploring the active meditation methods employed by the Inner Connection Institute, Journey Within, or sister schools in the tradition of the Berkeley Psychic Institute. These practices enable us to ground properly, release effectively, and gain clairvoyant awakening, which allows us to look at and change our own energies and those in our space that are not our own.

ASKING PERMISSION

For many of us it is human instinct to want to assist one we see suffering. It is natural to want to go toward another in pain and help them in any way we can. In the awesome book *Spiritual Growth: Becoming Your Higher Self* by Sanaya Roman, she teaches us about sending love and light to others. Through sending love by imagining waves of light encompassing a place or person, you can change the vibration of a relationship or place, you can heal wounds, and you can create greater harmony, higher vibration, and solid divine connection.

I like to use golden light from Source or the sun, but I also love electric blue. Green is great for healing, and white is pure, like the light of the angels. Though each Archangel connects with their own colors, white is an overall high and pure vibration used for psychic awareness, cleansing, purification, and divine work. But I play with all colors, and suggest you try and see what feels great.

In our work we always ask permission and do no harm. We ask verbally when healees are in front of us, or we heal them remotely because they have asked us. We can also ask mentally for permission, and either go ahead with loving intention when we feel a yes response or send light in loving intention; if they truly do not want it, their spirit will not allow it in.

We also make separation after healing another so spaces remain clean and we maintain integrity and psychic etiquette. When we intrude into someone else's energy, even wanting to give love or healing, we can be subconsciously or psychically whacked by them because we are in their space. We may not be welcome there even if doing good. This is along the lines of knowing we can only control or change ourselves and our reactions, and that we have no power over anyone nor business getting in the way of another.

We each have our own path, and even if we think we would like to help, we truly do not know what lessons that person is undergoing. Interfering with anyone else's energy is paramount to wreaking further karma or damage we may not be aware of. So instead of going toward someone with energy without their permission, it is more helpful and safer for your own bubble if you simply hold a good feeling for them and remain working on your own space.

You can elevate energy between you and another by staying in your own happy place when you think of them and raising your reactions instead of judging that something in them needs to be fixed and believing you are the one to do it. You will appreciate this etiquette in other people respecting

"Mind your own business because you want your mind business to be your own."

and staying out of your space. This also eliminates the worry of having mistakenly overstepped our bounds. Mind your own business because you want your mind business to be your own.

When there is a discrepancy in teaching or understanding, we can always return to pure unconditional love for solid truth and utility. If you wish to help the world heal and evolve, you can make an enormous difference by creating and maintaining a state of unconditional love.

When anything comes to your awareness, such as someone you perceive has hurt you, someone you saw in need, a place that requires assistance, or feelings of pain or anger, you need only to hold thoughts of unconditional love to all the energies to uplift them. Simply see them healed.

You need not go into anyone's space. Just be in that beautiful position of the best feeling you can offer, and that energy surrounding you goes into the Universe. Goethe says it this way: "If each of us sweeps in front of our own steps, the whole world will be clean." If you can do nothing else, stay centered in love, and it will make you better, and then the world better.

ACTIVE MEDITATIONS AND ENERGY WORK

Grounding and running energy, paraphrased here from the teachings of the Inner Connection Institute, which follows the tradition of the Berkley Psychic Institute, is the single most effective beginning to owning our own space, grounding, clearing, and energizing. These meditations are basically living our truth and turning our experiences into soul information and wisdom instead of carrying them with us into our next life as karma.

Learning these simple yet intense and insightful tools will change your life as well as the world you see and begin to claim responsibility for. When you own your space and choose your energy frequencies and capacities, you will see with new eyes, find solace within a personal and secure sphere, and come to understand your life experiences and how these experiences can be manifested with greater skill, clarity, beauty, and ease.

Of all the classes I have attended throughout my life, these first classes on basic active meditation skills are by far the most life changing and transformative. Utilizing these effective techniques on a regular and amusing basis will change your world. If everyone on our planet knew and used them, our Universe would be vastly impacted, comprehensively altered, drastically advanced, and significantly improved.

With the permission of the Inner Connection Institute, which is interested in a healed world for all, I have been graciously allowed to share their wisdom. I share some of the basics in order to expand all who may read this, but this is in no way a replacement for the Institute's in-depth, powerful, and extraordinary teachings.

GROUNDING

Close your eyes and breathe. Feel your body supported by your chair, have your feet flat on the floor, and your palms open upward rested upon your lap. Feel, or simply notice or imagine, your first chakra at the end of your tailbone and at the bottom of your spine. This is where your base chakra is located, and it deals with our physicality, survival, and life force. We can only have a body when we create a first chakra.

From this point, picture a grounding cord growing out and down, as a tail would, toward the center of the earth. This can be a beam of light, a tree trunk, plant stem, or any hollow type of tube. You can also play with this and make different and interesting tubes, such as a waterfall or spout of chocolate.

Feel or picture your grounding cord growing into the center of the planet, deep, deep down. When it reaches the center, whatever the center of the planet looks like to you (a molten ball, a field of lavender, a lake, etc.) attach your cord to it. Make sure the cord is strongly attached to both your first chakra and the center of the earth. Feel connected to the earth.

Make your grounding cord as wide as your hips. Take a breath, and let it expand to whatever width feels comfortable for you now. Connect it securely on its top to your base chakra and on its bottom to the center of the planet. Somewhere on this trash chute of release write the date in gold letters to bring it into present time, and write your name on it so it is for you only. Place a lever on this tube near the top and put it on full release to begin clearing out all the energies in your space that are not yours or that you do not want. Simply intend, and allow the release. See everything yucky or heavy leaving, and have all foreign energies slide down to be recycled by our wonderful earth. Feel the release and relief.

The grounding cord is the preliminary energy tool to transformation because without releasing the old, outmoded, foreign, or negative, there is little space to refill with your own desired energies. It is often the tool that, when used, brings people on board to loving energy work. It is simple and extremely effective. If you experience any critical or overwhelming situation, get that grounding cord on.

It is this first skill that powerfully convinces most on this spiritual path that we have found something tremendous and that our lives will never be the same. Lots of books help us on our path, but a main ability to release first is missing from some doctrines. This grounding cord and release mechanism is one of the first ways many of us awaken to clearing out all the garbage we have picked up, can feel, or know surrounds us. It is amazing and powerful how we can change our lives once we let go of that which does not serve us.

Sometimes others attach to our cords as a way of getting grounded themselves, or to suck our energy, even unconsciously, because it is easier than doing the work themselves. If others are in this space or cording into your cord, then completely release the tube into the center of the earth to disintegrate, and create a new one.

I replace my grounding cord several times a day, and sometimes more often depending on the intensity of my work or environment. Never worry that you are over-releasing; you cannot. You cannot release loving connections or important thoughts unless you want to, and if something needs further processing it will return again and again until it is worked out.

It is great to play with this supportive and clearing tool, and it will become a solid friend in your quest for healing, balance, and clearing. Notice when you are out in the world walking around surrounded by millions of energies, and then notice the grounding you feel when you do this same activity with a grounding cord on, connected, working, and on full release. This connection to the earth is stabilizing.

You may find it difficult to ground if others are interfering in your space, and this is a good awareness. Just keep working with it and releasing all you can. Mentally ask others to politely leave your space, and show them the way out if needed. It causes no harm to use your grounding cord to release the energy of someone who is in your space. Throw their energy down the chute so you can have your energy, and they can have theirs back. Once you are proficient in use of your grounding cord you are well on your way to owning your own space. Play with its effects in differing circumstances.

Take time to focus on and master this first tool before moving on to the others. They do grow upon each other, so competence with this first and most important tool will impact the benefits you are able to receive from the other energy techniques. Your grounding cord will always be the first, basic, and most important tool to utilize.

No matter the class I am currently in, or to what realms I may be traveling, I always begin by grounding. Many will not begin their day or get out of bed until the grounding cord is securely fastened. I will let you find the importance of this energy tool on your own, for nothing will help you believe me like personal use and realization.

Center of Head: After your grounding cord is on and working, we turn to our sixth chakra. This is sometimes referred to as our third eye, but it resides deeper within our heads, behind our eyes and between our ears. This is our clairvoyant space, and from where our psychic seeing is developed. We expand and use this space, known as our neutral space, simply by noticing it, or placing our awareness there.

Everyone has a center of head, and it is simply a matter of seeing there. One can allow the images to flow unfiltered and believe them, or one can block them out completely. The level of filter is your choice. Our teachers often say psychics simply choose less filters, and anyone can learn to do this by looking and believing.

As we close our eyes, and place our attention here, we open our center of head space, eventually unlocking vast insight and seeing. It is a beautiful and peaceful space and can be enhanced over time to become your own command center from where all your best living is determined by your clearest and highest authority.

This is the chakra that holds our spiritual sight, where we learn to see pictures, and to be neutral. Neutrality here is important so we are not coming from the judgmental or analyzing part of the mind. Sometimes just throwing purple onto our images clarifies our head space as neutral; otherwise, we just intend neutrality, and discriminations cease. As we progress, the space we create here is limitless with limitless other chakras lying within its vastness. We expand this space as we enlarge our psychic awareness and increase trust in our clairvoyance and intuition.

No one else is welcome in this chakra; it is our own space, our own control station. No other person should technically be in any of our chakras, of which our greatest work is to clear in this lifetime. But as we come to learn, others are often found in our chakras, and it is in claiming this center of head space that we begin owning and being responsible for all our other areas. This is where we become senior to all energies. Breathe from this place. Choose to live and decide from this neutral and clear place. Soon it opens doorways into the Universe.

At first it is simply a calm place. It may first look like a dark empty space, but we can then place a chair there, and soon create a whole room or sacred place in which to sit alone. Begin to command your energy work, and even decisions, from this sacred space.

Watch your grounding cord being created here and see

from this place as you learn to run your energy or just check in throughout the day. Simply bring your focus here, deep inside your head. Relax and enjoy the clear darkness.

Watch from this space, and perhaps you will come to see colors and energies passing through your awareness. This is your place of calm, and from here you can create spiritually and visually. Intend to clear the energies that pop up in your mind's eye, but also enjoy the inner watching and believe what you see.

When we are caught up in emotions or analyzing, it makes a huge difference to bring our awareness back to our sixth chakra. This is our neutral space, and when we make choices and act from this unpolluted center we remain balanced. In this center, our lives and decisions can unfold with more Divinity and neutrality than when we are stuck in feeling or thinking. This place of clarity is neither thinking obsessively nor feeling and being caught in emotional states. We can remain here for clear insights on how to proceed, and eventually it expands in space and depth, offering us great information and connection to seeing as well as certain knowing.

When we cannot act from clarity, or we find confusion or instability around us or bubbling out from within us, we can come back to this center by remembering to bring our focus back to this vast, non-judgmental, neutral space. When we live from our center of head space, we will notice a clear and peaceful difference in our awareness and experience. When an entire room sits down together to find and focus on their center of heads, a unique and peaceful feeling enters the room—it is quite something to behold. Be in this space as often and as consistently as possible for yourself.

Running earth energy: After you are grounded and have your awareness in your center of head space, feel your feet flat on the floor. Picture or imagine your feet chakras, right in the middle of the bottom of your feet, opening and closing a few times just to become aware of them. Simply place your awareness there and use your imagination. Allow them to open to whatever percentage is comfortable. Play with different amounts of earth energy at different times.

From the center of your head look down to the center of the earth and say hello to the center of the planet. Call whatever color you would like to run up to the bottom of your feet chakras as earth energy. I mentally say: "Blue earth energy please come up to my awaiting feet chakras." Feel it cleanse your feet chakras with the light like a good wash. You may want to play with the speed and width of these channels, as well as the colors you choose.

After filling your feet and even toes with this color vibration, which clears your feet chakras, begin to bring the earth energy up your ankles slowly, really feeling and seeing the surge, then through your calves and into your knees. Allow it to really cleanse and fill the knees as this is a place that holds much past life energy that sometimes gets stuck.

Continue to run the earth energy up your leg channels through your thighs, into your hips, and fill in your first chakra at the base of your spine. Let that vibrant energy circulate and give your first chakra—and even your whole pelvis—a good cleansing. Then send it down your grounding cord back to the earth to be recycled.

Bring it up again to your first chakra, forming an earth energy loop by running it up and down several times, and really enjoy the magnificent feeling of earth energy. Feel it as it moves. It can stimulate and revitalize your energy quickly and effectively, and I think it is better than drugs! Notice a difference between running browns and blues to running fluorescent pinks, golds, or brighter colors.

Running your energy helps support the first chakra by

keeping it healthy, clearing blockages, and bringing support from the earth. It also keeps our grounding cords functioning, flowing, and clear. It helps us to be more in our bodies and to live our truth as the earth energy automatically kicks out lies and negativity from our space.

Whether you feel a delightful tingling or a subtler sensation as you run earth energy, the beneficial effects of this tool are immense and incredible. When I focus on feeling or seeing it fill each part of my leg channels instead of just going through the motions, it is my favorite feeling of these basic tools. It has done much to support and heal me, and has set each day on the right path for me.

Running cosmic energy: After grounding, getting neutral in your sixth chakra, and running your earth energy, close your eyes and look from the center of your head up to the Universe. Pick out the color you would like to run for your cosmic energy this moment and say hello to it way out there. Pulse open and closed your crown chakra (at the top of your head) and palm chakras just to notice and open them to whatever percentage you would like.

Bring your chosen color down from the Universe, through the atmosphere and sky and into the top of your head or crown chakra. Let the crown drink in all the cosmic energy it likes, really cleansing it, then bring it down your two cosmic channels in the back of your head. Let it fill the back of your sixth chakra and continue down the back of the neck into the fifth chakra in the throat. At the shoulders, the energy breaks into four channels, two along the inner lines of your spine, and two along the outside edges of your back. Make sure each line is running inside your body.

Bring the colored energy light through your fourth or heart chakra, down the back through the third or solar plexus—the second chakra, below the belly button—and into the first chakra to mix with your earth energy. See the colors mix however they mix for you; sometimes they create a new color, sometimes patterns, and anything that works for you is great. See the mixture of earth and cosmic energy really clear and spin the first chakra.

Send about ten to fifteen percent of your cosmic energy down your grounding cord to the center of the earth and pick up about ten to fifteen percent earth energy. It does not have to be complicated, just let it go however it likes. Begin to bring this mixture up your front chakra channels, really cleansing each area and gently spinning each chakra as it passes. If your chakras are out of balance or off center then they may not be spinning, and if a chakra is not spinning, it is unable to release or function properly.

Bring the mixed energy up through your belly, clearing and spinning the second chakra, then into your solar plexus at the bottom of your rib cage to clear and spin the third, up the front cosmic channels into your chest clearing and spinning your fourth or heart chakra, and into your throat clearing and spinning the fifth. Visualize or feel it as best you can, and do not worry; the energy is doing its work.

At the fifth, allow some of the mixture energy to break off and go down each arm, down your creative channels, and out your powerful palm chakras. See the energy fill your aura bubble. Continue to send the rest of the energy up the front of your face clearing and spinning your sixth, and then up through your seventh chakra to fountain out your crown and spill into your aura bubble. This is your cosmic energy path. Run it several times, and feel free to use different colors and various speeds and widths.

Running your earth and cosmic energy (with a grounding cord and from the center of your head) will change your life. It clears foreign energies from your space without you needing to understand what anything is specifically. It will energize and heal your body, and it will allow you to own your space and have seniority over your life and certainty over your spiritual tools.

These energy cycles will help keep you in your truth as they kick out any lies in your space. They also energize you dynamically. They are an unbeatable skill for enhancing your power and light—words cannot describe their potential capacity for greatness and magic. Enjoy this enlightenment courtesy of the Inner Connection Institute in the Berkley Psychic Institute tradition. Your life will never be the same, and utilizing these energies will allow your soul to create and release all it came here to change, taking with it wisdom and experience and leaving behind integrated karma and old lessons.

Beyond running energies inside our bodies, paying attention to what energies are present outside our bodies is also important. We now look at the aura bubble and how to maintain the health of the energy around us. The closest aura layer to your body corresponds to the first or physical chakra. The next few inches out corresponds to your second chakra and layer, which holds emotions, creativity, and female energy, etc. This layering continues outward, one layer for each chakra, until an arm's length around you connects to your seventh and spiritual chakra. This is our energy culmination that we show to the world.

Aura bubble: Once your grounding cord is established, you are in the center of your head, and your earth and cosmic energies are running, turn to the bubble around your physical self. Sometimes referred to as your personal bubble, this really is *your* space—a sphere encompassing your aura.

Picture all around you an egg or soap-type bubble of color extending about three feet in every direction—above, behind, below, and in front of your body. Color this bubble any color that suits you for today or for this instant. If you have difficulties assuring that your bubble is colored behind you, simply paint the front and keep spinning and painting until you are surrounded by your own energy, your own protective layer. Tuck the bottom of your bubble into your grounding cord for maximum support and release. You can release a lot of energy from your bubble and down your grounding cord this way.

Although your aura has a layer for each chakra—from physical and close to your body, to spiritual and reaching out arm's length—all you need to do is focus on the circumference of the bubble. Sometimes we tend to pull our auras closer to our bodies as a protective measure, or we allow it to fade out and disperse as we are affected by energies we accidentally pick up from others (remember to release these foreign energies as an aid to securing your border). Painting your aura with your chosen color helps create your boundaries and delineate what is really your space to own.

One of my favorite realizations, explained by my teachers, is that this aura bubble and what lies inside it is the only space we are responsible for in the world. I love this. It is a relief to me. There is a distinct and euphoric feeling that encompasses an entire room when everyone has sealed up their own bubbles. Only this circle around us is ours to be concerned with.

Chakras spinning and healthy send out vibrations to complete your spherical bubble. A lot of energies flow through this bubble, but do not get overwhelmed, for this is what comprises your aura; your memories of all time. Just focus on doing what you need to in order to feel good in it. Repair tears if you see them, and make it a light and bouncy bubble.

Golden suns are the way we fill the spaces we have cleared through all this previous energy work. They are an easy and satisfying way to refill our spaces, bringing back all the energy we have left in other places and times, and to create desired qualities coursing through us. It is the perfect finish to simple or intense energy work and release. And once we have focused on releasing, it is always good to fill back up so we are full of the energy and light we choose.

GUIDED MEDIATION

Eyes closed and energy set, picture a golden sun or big golden ball above your head. Either choose a quality you would like to have more of in your life, and write that word across the sun, or intend that quality to fill it up. Infuse this golden sun with whatever quality you have chosen, and see it filling with this vibration using your imagination. You can ask your guides, angels, or Supreme Being to help saturate it as well.

When it is as full as you can have it, and it is heavy and ready to overflow, mentally reach up and poke a hole in it so you can begin to bring it in. Feel and see (while in your neutral space) it coming into and filling your crown chakra like honey. Let your crown drink in all the sun it can, and then have it fill your sixth chakra. As it pours down through you, coating and filling all of you, picture it nourishing all your chakras—your fifth in your throat area, your fourth or heart center, your third and solar plexus chakra, your second just below your belly button, and your first at the base of your spine.

After your chakras are all full and plump, allow the golden sun energy to overflow into your body. Make sure to fill all the way to your fingertips and toes. A wonderful addition is to have the golden sun quality permeate every cell in your physical body as well as fill up in between each cell. This is dramatically healing.

When your physical body is full, continue bringing in more golden sun energy overflowing and spilling out into your aura. Fill your entire aura bubble including behind you and below. You can even let a little golden sun go down your grounding if you like. Use as many suns as you need to feel the way you want. When you are all filled up—and take your time—then bend over, stretch, breathe, open your eyes, and come out of meditation exuberant, clear, healed, and recharged.

Congratulations, you did it! This is setting your space. What you have just learned is offered over intense and lengthy classes, and is priceless knowledge for any earthly journey.

It is fun to play with the size of these golden suns to see how much you can truly allow yourself to "have." You can bring in several suns, one right after another if you have released a lot of energy, or simply would like to add more wonderful qualities. Some of my favorite qualities to fill the suns with are ease and amusement, just to ensure that I am not getting too serious or effortful in my expanding. I also enjoy being filled with prosperity, health, peace, and love. Such qualities help us refresh and vibrate to the qualities we want in our lives.

The other work that is really helped by golden suns is to reclaim our own energy. Every thought, place we go, and interaction we have takes a bit of us and leaves a bit of it. Our spirits imprint a bit of energy in every experience. When we are ready to have our energy back from a place, person, time, or event we place a magnet inside the golden sun that looks like us or has our name on it, or we use our intention, and we call back our energy.

This sun gathers all our energy from wherever we have left it and simply fills us with any of our energy that has been dispersed. We do not need to know from where it arrives, though we may. When it is full, we pop it and bring it in just like other golden suns. I find I leave more energy with specific people or experiences in my life, for myriad reasons, and when I look, it is from those people and places that I need to consistently reclaim my essence. After filling from these suns, my teachers like to tell me that I am "full of myself"; amusement is always helpful in spiritual work.

Send quick thanks (mentally, psychically, or otherwise) to the Inner Connection Institute for these marvelous and extraordinary tools. Take some classes there, virtually or at their sister centers, or attend public healing fairs, and bask in the knowledge their brilliance and awareness has afforded you. They also have meditations on CD, and sound files recording a skilled teacher running you through the exercises, so all you have to do is deal with your energy. These skills will truly change your life—enjoy!

CHAPTER FIFTEEN

Chakra Healing

Now that we are awakened to the profundities of energy work, we can take a look at specific chakra healing. It is perhaps the most engaging and direct energy work we can do when seeking monumental benefits. Our chakras (Sanskrit for "wheel") are energy centers within our bodies that hold libraries of information from all our lifetimes and experiences that are then carried within our souls. All encounters and incidents (if integrated) are currency for the soul, and all experiences affect our energy centers, leaving imprints upon our spirit as well as present body. Every thought we have is expressed somewhere within the body. Read that again because it is important.

"Every thought we have is expressed somewhere within the body."

These active and dynamic spheres of our experiences range from information on our body's survival, emotions and creativity, power and will, to our pictures of ourselves, our capacity to love, express, create, see spiritually, utilize insights, and understand or know consciousness and divine unity. The main seven chakras run from the first chakra at the base of the tailbone, upward along the spine, through the belly, solar plexus, heart, throat, and third eye, to our crown or halo chakra. We can also affect great streams of energy flowing through our hand and feet chakras. Although we have many points of energy, these are the main centers we usually work with and are common to any chakra balancing or practice.

HOLDERS OF EXPERIENCE

Whether inside the chakra specific to the quality, or where something occurred physically, all thoughts take residence in our bodies. Experiences that are integrated, learned, and released are contained as wisdom, growth, and light. Experiences that are not recognized or reconciled become the karma we hold against ourselves. Working directly with our chakras can produce immeasurable results in our lives and is a powerful method of transforming our energy at the heart of our matter.

When we look at and shift the energy in our chakras we come in contact with the source of our evolution—everything that has ever happened to us. Here we create the changes we desire, over time, with consistency, and often instantaneously. Magic appears to happen as we focus directly on these centers of power and clear them out, learn what information is being stored there, and then diametrically fill them with preferred qualities. This is healing.

Working directly with our chakras can open our knowing to what we have previously learned or can further glean from this library of information, which is always shifting. It allows us to cleanse our space of old experiences in order to keep only what is currently valuable, which keeps us in present time. We can really look at and increase the degree to which we are owning and creating our space. Only then can we have clean energy agreements, transactions, and awakenings.

You can study endless texts on chakras in order to learn more about what information is held or stored where. Some of my favorites are *The Truth about Chakras* by Anodea Judith, *The Chakras* by C.W. Leadbeater, and *Spiritual Amnesia: A wake Up Call to What You Really Are* by Lauren Skye. Some information varies, as do most spiritual wisdoms, but the basics are clear and can guide you with knowledge on your way to personal freedom and power. The way to meditate with your chakras includes different forms of energy work that are simply more locally focused. This is growth through foundational healing and opens us to unconditional love.

You can clear and learn from your chakras either as part of energy work enhanced after your energy has run, which would be most effective, or separate as its own focus. You can draw your attention to the chakra or place on your body that is calling to you, you can work diametrically on your entire chakra body, or you can choose systematically by learning some basic chakra information and attending to that which you feel needs the most or immediate attention based on qualities or difficulties.

ENLIGHTENMENT

When our energy meridians are in true alignment, we are enlightened, even for a moment. When we are focusing outside ourselves for approval or getting caught in energies from other people, we are out of alignment. When we carry around foreign energies or more ingrained energy known as programs, which we have picked up and that no longer serve us, we are out of alignment and operating from an unwanted, automatic response. When we place our personal worth upon any object or person, our energy pours out of the affected chakra to that point outside ourselves and causes misalignment.

Enlightenment, or true balance, occurs at the very instant

in which our chakras are lined up from earth grounding, and a straight flow of energy can pass through each one and out our crowns, through our own knowing to Divinity, with our point of awareness placed within this flow of energy. Very few humans are in their truth all the time, but many realize moments of this feeling here and there, and it is great.

We have all felt times when we are on our path, following our truth, owning our space, and knowing what we know. We have also all felt thrown off by an intense emotion or because we do not feel in tune with ourselves. Working directly with our chakras and learning to both clear and align them is our highest functioning goal as humans. This is my truth and understanding. When we look at an experience and integrate its information, we are evolving our souls and carrying that wisdom with us when we leave. When we do not have an awareness of the information being offered—the lesson potential—then we carry that piece with us to our next life as karma—an experience we allow again in order to realize.

HEALING

We actually cannot arrive on earth without creating a first chakra; this is what separates us from non-physical beings. Most humans today are primarily focused on the lower three chakras—survival, emotions and creation, as well as will and power—but as the paradigm of consciousness shifts, more of us are learning to live from our higher centers. It is important to have our first few chakras in order before we can really keep our attention higher; we cannot attend to our spirituality if our basic needs are not met or our emotions are totally out of whack, but any chakra work can bring relief and healing benefits. We can work on and heal our lower chakras, moving upward only to have each slip back out of alignment at different times; this is the human experience. Different areas need assorted help at different times and through varying experiences.

Our heart chakra is the connecting link between our higher and lower selves, and focusing unconditional love in this hermetic center can be life-altering. Expanding love in all directions from the fourth chakra fills our being with love.

Know that all physical problems are the manifestation of energy blocks. Even cancer is the result of some energy unable to flow through the body with ease. That is all any pain ever is. Working the corresponding chakra to any ailment is healing on the originating level. It is no coincidence that many people have heart attacks after losing someone or suffering grief, for those are all heart energy matters. When something from the past rears its ugly head, it often causes pain in the knees, for that is where we store much past life energy. So work the spiritual energetic facet of any physical issue and create sweeping healing results. Get your energy moving . . . flow to grow.

"Working the corresponding chakra to any ailment is healing on the originating level."

Also employ loving affection to grow the health of your chakras. It is not only by energy work that we can affect these meridians; human connection also stimulates and heals our energy. When I hug someone, I usually send love from my heart chakra to theirs. I believe this connects us on a deeper and more joyful level. When we smile at others, we heal our fifth chakras with kind communication. When we hold hands or touch, we exchange powerful vibrations. When we kiss, we share vulnerable truths. All this is the reason and the way to expand love through us into the world.

Our spiritual "church" gives free energy healings each

Sunday after the "sermon." In the first year of our attendance, receiving these energy waves and clearings was amazing. I learned about the programs each of us learn to live or process through by believing something we witness or feel as a young being and then buying into it as a truth. I look through my programs to see what assists me and what gets in the way of my greatest good or was sometimes put there unconsciously by a well-meaning parent or intimate.

Once certified, we engaged in daily personal practice and got to be part of the healing team every week. I work with my clairvoyant space and tap into what is blocked, healing psychic whacks that have been put in someone's space. I see or intuit and then share visual images of problems or energies that surround them as I heal. Other times I heal silently and am all about moving energy through their space in ways that will help them in their own work to release the outdated or unwanted and bring in the new qualities they desire. We are increasing our potential to help the world, one space at a time.

It is truly amazing stuff, and whether you learn to do it or just receive it, it is the very best non-invasive, tangible form of healing I know of that can heal both your immediate space as well as clear out the past, and core matter. Healers usually live within the highest of integrity, and want to help, with permission, everyone they can. We find neutrality before beginning, and we can even heal remotely. Often we cry when we release.

As you release and integrate the symbols and messages you pick up, you can continue with more healings, and eventually become responsible for your own space and health (which is a tremendous gift to each of us, and our world). You can learn quickly to eliminate unwanted energy, name exactly what is going on within your body, mind, and spirit, and you can sit within a circle of only what you choose to be inside your experience. The best tools I have ever learned!

FIND A TEACHER

We do not want to open all our chakras as wide as possible. Of far more importance is to look at, cleanse, spin, and refill. We are healing with activation. We can get out of control very quickly if we focus only on opening these centers. We open and close lower chakras depending on need or utilization of our psychic and clairvoyant space. We actually have degrees we allow our lower chakras to close when we are focusing our work in the higher planes, as closing some chakras causes others to open more easily. But this is work for a specific skill set.

There are more involved techniques of clearing and releasing foreign energies from chakras than what I introduced in the previous chapter. If you are interested in these more advanced uses of chakras, I suggest you take a class on this topic, which would involve a discussion too in depth for inclusion in a book on general healing. Be sure to seek guidance from professionals who know how far you are ready to go and in what time.

Whether an aura clearing, an energy cleansing, chakra balancing, or energetic healing—if you can find a trustworthy place or person qualified in this power then I urge you to do it soon and often. Through classes, my husband and I have both learned to connect with our healing master, a loving guide who enjoys helping others heal with energy. This is like connecting with our guardian angel. He or she helps us heal through our hand chakras and also in undirected ways. We learn to move energy around the body, releasing blocks, clearing out what does not belong to a particular person, as well as many other fascinating and invaluable skills.

I saw this done once at a metaphysical fair and was in awe at how the healer worked and knew what she knew. I was a young girl, and I remember wanting so badly to know how to do it. I thought it was magical and intangible, that one sort of had to be born with this great rare gift. Years later I was led to learn the same ability.

I recently ran the pure, magnificent energy of unconditional love in a loop from placing my point of awareness inside my fourth chakra, and then through my arms and hands touching gently. This was in a class led by Master Teacher Paul Miller, and weeks later I was still processing the ramifications. Because my teacher believed in my ability, glorious were the eventual results.

As unconditional love consciously runs in this specific and advanced loop, it loosens and releases, and then replaces its counterparts, such as sadness. Unconditional love kicks out what is unlike itself, and those lower emotions need a place to go, an outlet of release. When you fill with unconditional love fully, nothing else can exist in it, and all the lesser stuff comes out—consciously if you let it, or unconsciously through outburst or illness if you do not.

"Take your energy work at a speed that is right for you."

Directly after this intensive exercise and for weeks later, I opened to tears and crying. This deeper work is intensely transforming and, even with unconditional love, is not for the faint of heart. Take your energy work at a speed that is right for you. Release can be healing, and transformation is great, but follow a level that will not interfere too much with functioning daily. Massive energy release creates growth periods, and requires processing.

CHAKRA COLORS

Many studies present each chakra with its own color of the rainbow. This is most commonly from the bottom up: red for the first chakra, orange for the second, and so on with yellow, green, blue, indigo, violet. My teachers have explained that this is mainly for practical explanation and application, and that a healthy second chakra, for instance, does not necessarily resonate orange. You may use this color guide if you like, while noticing what colors you actually see in each space, but it is more important that the energy center is spinning, bright, and clear.

Colors "vibrate" to certain frequencies, like wave lengths in prisms, and even respond to notes or sounds. It is these vibrational frequencies that more likely explain the visual colors we assign to them. We can also come to know our chakra colors intimately and notice that any color held within them that deviates from our original is foreign energy needing to be released.

Auras and chakras are very often not one color, and within these combinations are colors not really known in our world. One of the first auras I saw clearly as an adult while spacing out in high school psychology class was a mixture of green, brown, and orange, but together was an unexplainable color and pattern I had never seen on earth.

CHAKRA HEALING

Sit and relax, breathe, and close your eyes. Run your energy or set your space first if you can. Focus your awareness on whichever chakra you have chosen to look at today, and simply be aware of that place in your body. Be aware of the entire layer throughout your auric body corresponding with that chakra, even if you do not know exactly where it is or what it looks like.

Look within your mind's eye at the aura layer or chakra you have chosen, or that which corresponds to any physical area you need help with. Note any intuitive images, feelings, or words brought to you. This is valuable information that can open your knowing into how to best heal this space.

If you like, mentally ask what this chakra needs in order to be healed. You may ask what type of foreign energy may be blocking it, or you may see a current or past life picture of injury. Sit and listen to your inner knowing for these answers. This wisdom may be impressed upon you at this time, or anytime later after having worked on a particular area. If you are not ready to release, experience understanding, or move energy, then you may not consciously allow your spirit to bring in the information just yet. It may also be a matter of learning spiritual interpretation. But you can still heal. Be patient, each layer helps.

The three best ways to work with your chakras are through awareness, breath, and different colored energies or light. Notice and listen to this area, and realize that just focusing on any space will help bring healing. Breathe into and from this chakra, nice and slow, to clear and release it. Bring your powerful presence to it.

You can release anything unwanted down your grounding cord. Then bring golden light to the area, and see it as healthy, spinning, and gently functioning. Or you can create a rose, fill it with stuff to release, and then take it to the sun and explode it. Run different

colors of energetic light through the entire space of
the chakra, see, and feel it being healed. Let go of old
energies that no longer serve you, and fill up with colors
and qualities that you prefer for your present self.

MEDITATION CONCLUSIONS

The previous three chapters provide a basic outline of different forms of meditation. Meditation will change your life. Chakra work will heal you at your core level. If you only receive one idea for living life in a lovelier light, let it be the significance of meditation. Energy work grows us toward the perfection of love. Any form—some more than others—will enhance your human experiences. Begin, and you will notice the change of magnificence when you look back.

You can run through the motions to get things set and going, or you can focus slow and steady for penetrating results. Some days I spend two minutes, which is good, but when I choose an hour of my time devoted to looking at, healing, and moving energy I feel the difference. It is tremendous. Have gratitude for any time you give to your own highest good with no guilt on the ebbing days.

You may come to observe your life in two distinct components: before you brought meditation into your daily life and after. In my understanding we have come into this life to awaken to two larger comprehensions: the first is to recognize all interactions and agreements for the matching pictures and feelings they bring into our awareness. The second is to find a way to integrate the information from those awarenesses and experiences into our souls so their lower energies may be released. Their higher knowledge may then and only then be carried with our spirits as eternal and increasing wisdom,

> "We can better assimilate the core of what we came here to remember through the the infinite uses of meditation."

and then shared for the betterment of our world.

Meditation is the best way of accomplishing these objectives. Whatever the experience, feeling, thought, or issue brought by living and connecting, our main goal here is to come to a far better sense of ourselves. We begin to live and grow in a state of meditation, realizing what is at the heart of each occurrence, then transcending it into soul currency. Although there are varying degrees to which we may observe or integrate the forms of our daily phenomenon, we can recognize the emotions and energies for what they are while gaining the deeper meanings. We can better assimilate the core of what we came here to remember through the infinite uses of meditation. Love will then be all we know.

CHAPTER SIXTEEN

Nature

In the deep realm of the Faerie forest
Where the sunlight reaches the earth,
Autumnal jewels fill my senses
And it is there I will find myself.
Focused intently on the sounds from above
Wind, and leaves, and fresh breezes,
The loveliness of life all around, everywhere,
Is too potent to collect.
Warm sun and our clear sky
Touches me perfectly,
As I am whisked into another feeling space.
Breathing the damp earth,
Sensing full visual spectrums,
I may understand heavenly vibrations
For many moments at once.
Life melts into my surroundings
And grace expands in spirit.
Eternity is felt, and realization occurs
As Love brings knowledge from beneath its shadows.
Cosmic life glides gently upon my skin,
What I hear and see and know
Cannot be real.

But I stay with it and follow
For this understanding of beauty is rare.
Today God knew me, and I knew God,
And every breath,
Each thought,
Graced by nature
Held celestial magic in my being.

Ah . . . the natural beauteous world that God literally laid at our feet. How lucky we are to live on this rich planet, and how often do we not only take it for granted but ignore the healing qualities it offers every cell of our bodies and spirits. If ever you are in doubt, feel lost and confused, or are languishing in any way, get into nature. Our outside world of trees, flowers, birds, and bees heals us without effort. It is always waiting, always ready, and its medicinal qualities abound far beyond our senses.

The natural world of earth is the best, most perfect example anywhere of unconditional love. We have been given everything we need within our environment to rebalance, reconnect, and rejuvenate to our very cores. All we need do is sit quietly, and breathe it in. And just as nature is perpetually in growth, as we attune to its beauty, we will find the best in ourselves—unconditional love—growing as well.

APPRECIATE NATURE

If we want to maximize the uses of nature, then interaction with any part of it will exponentially increase its curative properties. Nature's healing is gentle, pervasive, and all-encompassing. Use it as it was intended and as it was given to wholly bless our lives. The wonder of the mountains and rivers, deserts and oceans, are just one of God's genius plans to offset the turbulence of being human. But if it goes unnoticed, untouched, or unappreciated, then you are missing something you were generously handed—something that can change your place in this world.

In my very humble opinion but consistent experience, nature contains within it a more vast capacity for healing than has been acknowledged. It is the most overlooked and undervalued physician there ever was. The spiritual growth, emotional connection, and physical healing it bestows is incomparable.

While being totally unattached to any results or manipulations, it is continuously rebirthing and creating. Its loveliness enriches any path we walk, and its source of offering never dries up. It cradles us in its arms, and teaches us very well about here and now presence.

The gifts that come from nature may change with the seasons, but it always gives if you are able to see. Our entire environment supports itself and everything around it, asking nothing in return while continuously generating whatever life it can. Our nature wants to heal us. Our nature always loves us. The sun enlivens and energizes us while the flowing water cleanses. The earth itself stabilizes us. Anywhere you connect with nature, there exists limitless therapeutic and restorative energy ready to be given to anyone enlightened enough to simply reach out for it.

No one needs to be extra special in any particular way to be enhanced by our life-giving planet—one only needs to notice it, and be. How lucky we are for these gifts and for the real acceptance our surroundings teach. Do not underestimate how our human energies can be touched and purified by the cycles of nature. Even on the worst day, nature can transform our attitude one hundred and eighty degrees.

As the beloved John Denver invites, "Can you see yourself

reflected in the seasons? Can you understand the need to carry on?" He states eloquently in his music more than a thousand reasons and benefits for getting closer to nature. When we spend time outside in rural environments, our relationship to the world changes. We begin to flow with it.

We tap into our natural rhythms by witnessing and relating with outdoor beauty. The Native Americans were connected with the earth in the exquisite extreme. The Japanese have lived in deep connection with our planet for thousands of years, healing through Shinrin Yoku, or forest bathing. Now, most of us live with the opposite extreme, and experience very little cooperation with our surroundings.

Embracing or just enjoying your environment may take some minor effort on your part, but it is necessary to our souls. I am an admitted and proud tree hugger, and living in the high country of Colorado, we position our lives around nature. The harsh winters mean it does take some effort on my part to contact nature. When the wind is howling, blowing snow sideways, I sometimes balk at making the effort. But as my husband is very good at taking the time to properly prepare and reassuring me of its benefit, he is always right, and it is always worth it. Wonderful snowsuits are made for a reason.

Few have any excuse not to utilize nature's power—even for the city dweller, some form of nature is usually a short drive or walk away. Do it. You will feel so different after a few moments, and if you are lucky enough to experience silence, its effects will be monumental within mere minutes.

Appreciating nature is more about learning unconditional appreciation for it and treasuring its unique giving qualities. Nature will enrich you on a deeply feeling level without having to give much back, although respect goes a long way. Each season and every element has vast and varying rewards for you. Learn to recognize what these are and capitalize on how they can recover your being to a cellular level.

THE SEASONS

The seasons and cycles of our planet were planned for a reason. It is no simple coincidence that the Earth grows, changes, decays, rests, and is reborn every single year. It mirrors our passage as human beings and can tell us much about the paths we walk, if we notice. Our planet was bestowed as a prize for anyone who realizes this. It contains all the healing we can imagine, including herbs, so utilize them—you will thank yourself and God's brilliant insight for this guaranteed rejuvenation.

The seasons were given to us as a gift of rhythm. They are wisely constructed for maximum introspection, learning, joy, and peace. They all bring great pleasures and specific lessons. The subject of true presence is among its largest teachings, for as each season gives way to the next, nothing is mourned or lusty. If you long for spring flowers in winter, you will miss that season's contributions of peace, silence, and blanketed beauty. It does not judge itself that one season is better than another, but gently continues its cycle of growth and release. We can learn much from its natural rhythms.

I find that I am usually ready for the coming season just as it arrives, even if I may feel temporary anxiety over any anticipated changes. At the end of summer, I miss when our children return to school, but when it actually happens I realize I am ready. I wonder about the flowers leaving, the arrival of snow, and the rejoicing once again to be outside with new life, but I have finally learned to enjoy each moment as it is before me, and to appreciate them all. Nature has taught me wisely about my own presence and acceptance.

Consider your favorite season. Why is it your favorite?

Perhaps the season includes special holidays, fond memories, cycles of society we love, comfortable temperament, or even when or where we were born. My favorite has always been winter! I love Christmas lights peeking from beneath new snow, and my birthday just happens to be on the winter solstice. Observing your favorite season might tell you a lot about yourself or your needs. Winter turns us inward, and brings contentment, joy, and beauty. As for autumn . . . ah, autumn is for the poets.

Spring, the first season of cycles, invigorates our soul and can revitalize our examples of unconditional love and growth. No matter what the earth has been through, it begins again with full faith. It has no fear or memory of loss; it simply gives as it can, unconditionally. The sun shines a little more each day, and with growing light, the plants and trees open up to receive. They become beautiful and fruitful. Spring inspires and delights us with growing life.

Everything works together and depends upon the unconditional giving of the other. The water feeds the earth, the ground grows flowers in the sun, the bees pollinate with luscious nectar, berries fill the birds, and so on. No one is stingy or withholding, and they all thrive effortlessly, without knowing to call this unconditional love. What a sweet scent and beauteous sight to behold in our greening hearts. A shining example of the best life has to give, over and over, without fail, and for no particular reason, is spring.

Abundance, fruit, fun, heat, freedom, life, and joy: these are the delicious delights of summer. In the luscious mountains, we avoid the sweltering heat and find friendly shade everywhere. We lie among the wild flowers, and watch the billowy clouds pass overhead. Where there were the beginnings of seedlings in spring, we watch all the flowers come out in their turn, first yellows and whites, then reds and purples.

Summer reassures us with abundance, freedom and satisfaction. We give thanks for summer break, free flowing days, warm starlit evenings, and a liberated spirit. We are emancipated from the seasons of indoors and heavy clothing, and we rejoice at the vibrance of life all around. Everywhere we turn we see existence confirmed, and we feel bountiful feasts for our senses and souls. We catch a breath of relief as life takes on moments in no time or space. We live for the feelings of aliveness that stroll through the lengthening days with more light, more fun, and more freedom and adventure as we fulfill our states of mind with reckless abandon. We dance in the radiance of the sun and wonder at the luminescence of the moon with increasing access to the outdoors and nature's reward.

The jeweled tones of the sky and turning leaves are the breathtaking contrast of autumn. The fertile smell of pine needles and aspen leaves blanketing the forest floor. The pink salmons, burnt oranges, coppers, and yellow-greens; the fire glowing golds and crimson reds of the leaves against the evergreen pine, and bright fluorescents of trees transforming. Lit with the backdrop of clear, cobalt, and mesmerizing blue so potent it engulfs your spirit from the sky, I think we listen and love more in autumn. For it cries out with colors, *Notice me! Breathe me; let us be one.*

Listen to the secrets it has to offer in each breeze. There is an angel in every cloud waiting to give its messages and a contemplation to every leaf as it falls. You have so much beauty and prosperity in your life; recognize what that is, and treasure it. For it is precious and passes with the seasons. These are the messages we receive in fall, and pass on to those we love.

The gifts of winter are quiet, and deep. Step outside as the full moon glows its bluish hue on a snow-covered mountainside; there you will know loveliness and grace. There you may see your reflection, and watch it with the guidance of divine love as it leads you upon your true path. Soon the world will burst with life and light, color and movement, but in this iridescent electric blue of winter's evenings, fire light and life is as it should be. You can know solitude without loneliness, and you can find the self you forgot to remember.

Only in this special glow and this sacred silence are you afforded such an opportunity to look within your own spirit while soaring toward celebrations. This season is blessed with the consecration of inner worth and knowing, but it is only for those who realize its essential meaning is veiled. Its secrets walk hand in hand, gently concealed for only those with the ability to discern the unknown powers of magic. Unearth your dreams; embrace your increasing ability to love. Sit with love, feel it, and sigh deeply as you allow it in. Winter remains something you can feel rather than distinctly place as the most similar seasonal sensation we know to unconditional love.

Go outside and feel this poem as you read it. Follow the animals and breezes, and notice if your soul feels more visible. As this chapter comes together with love in your life, notice what effect nature has upon you when you really experience it.

NATURE'S SOUL

When the ravens gather in the end of September,
Through golden leaves in the rushing wind,
Rolling over you, from thunder into stillness, your soul
becomes visible.
As falling leaves blanket the wooded earth
And sunlight traces the raven's wing,
Peace descends.
Fertile aroma brought with earthly grounding

Helps you find your center.
True solitude,
Tremendous connection.
As whispering leaves dance through the autumn-toned
Universe with delight
Knowing knowledge, Feeling splendor,
Soaring in the cobalt ocean past tree tops,
You are with them.
Observing with gratitude,
Internal light shines,
And numinous love encompasses the soul.

MEDITATION: HEAL WITH NATURE

- Find a lovely spot outside, and take many deep, slow breaths.
- Look around at the colors and listen to all the sounds.
- Take note of how you feel as you just sit still, being with the planet.
- When you breathe out, release tension.
- Run your earth energy while outside for dynamic cleansing.
- Run your cosmic energy from the sky, and let the sun fill you.
- Feel a deep connection with this wondrous planet.
- Do this every day to grow your unconditional love.

CHAPTER SEVENTEEN

Deeper with Nature

Follow me as I run down the forest path of nature's guidance, deeper into the wood of discovery. In this chapter, we examine what the details in nature—water, trees, minerals, and crystals—communicate to our soul as it grows unconditional love.

WATER

This water refreshes me,
It flows through my body and purifies my blood.
It brings clear nutrients through my organs
And helps my skin to be smooth and clean.
Water removes toxins, washes away impurities,
And keeps me healthy, energetic, and clear.
Water cleanses and sustains the earth, bathes the world,
Nourishes every living thing on our planet,
And replenishes all life.

So too does love refresh me,
Flow through me and purify.
It brings clarity to my Self,
And it cleanses any toxins within my life.
Love keeps us together and healthy, and sustains the earth.

It holds the Universe in place,
And replenishes all of life.

When we are in a space of unconditional love, we are like water. Besides light, the element of water most closely resembles love's gentleness and encompassing. When we love, we are temperate and yielding, touching everything, and pouring everywhere. We do not judge where we go or what we come in contact with; we simply flow to the available space and fill it. Even though rocks may be blocks that keep us from seeing what is in front of us, water caresses, wearing them down to soft edges and smooth textures.

What were obstacles to one's path become another mineral with which we flow and share space. Moving water carries much downstream to new surroundings. It may dam up barriers to protect others beneath it, or may rest as an animal's home, or precious watering hole past its mirage. It changes scenery, and soothes our weary selves with its continuous movement. It drowns out the noisy bustle of the world and it shows us the way of least resistance and release. We can reach in, touch it, and become one with it. It cares not if we stand in it or redirect it toward our needs; it still ionizes the air for us to breathe. It invites us to partake of its clarity and replenishment. It gladly grows our world and awaits, as does love.

We are made mostly of water, just as we are made from love. Water affects everything around it, just as love does. It can only be contained by something larger and more open than itself, but it can be enjoyed by all. It is forgiving and all-encircling. Both water and love have a healing and cleansing effect, transforming what they meet. We could not live without either element. Water falls from the sky, absorbs deeply into the earth, and surrounds the very foundation of our land masses, which we consider to be stable and solid. Love is everywhere, fluid, and useful without condition. One might need to dig a bit to find and reach it, but it is there, hidden but flowing, just waiting to bubble up and fill.

Water represents the grace of life energy—chi—and it carries the movement of prosperity to us, keeping it constant in our lives. Where there is water there is health and riches. The current of water represents the flow of all life. It illuminates the epitome of abundance and love. It enables us the ability to thrive, and without it we would perish. Fill and surround your body with it often.

HUG A TREE

Even though it may sound trite, watching, communing, and connecting with nature transforms our energy and our humanness. It is immensely healing. So, get in nature. Especially if you are feeling blue, blocked, bored, or bad, get where there is warm sunshine, growing flowers, green grass and trees, a cool, gently blowing breeze, moving water, or stillness and quietude. Relax and breathe it in, deeply. This should do much to soothe and restore you.

And when no one is looking—or in front of the whole world—find a tree that needs a hug. You can bet that tree saw you needed one too and was hoping with all its might that you would choose it for love. It will give to you and refresh you. If you want to appear inconspicuous, lean your back against it while pretending to read or gaze skyward. You will feel its power coursing through your spine, tingling your entire body.

Trees are a pure form of energy. Wood is one of our planet's most prominent growing elements. Sharing space with and receiving from a good tree is not like being near a person, where numerous, different, and not necessarily positive energies are being shared, transferred, or subconsciously picked up or taken in. That kind of interaction leads to necessary clearing out, aware noticing, and conscious, sometimes repeated, releasing. With trees, it is all good, it is all innocent, and it is pure in its love and gentle healing for everyone.

When we hug a tree, and benefit from its coursing, energizing strength, we also do well for the tree. We must look to notice that the tree loved our love, and it dances in the breeze as it too receives. We support each other, and we need each other, not just for birdie and squirrel homes, or shade, oxygen, and beauty, but also for life, power, and liveliness.

Support the Arbor Day Foundation by any means, as they know and defend the importance of all trees everywhere. Increasing the number of trees is paramount to our thriving. In a recent survey sent to me by the Foundation, they shared that not only are trees good for beauty and the brightly colored autumn leaves, but they provide us with clean air, soil, and water. Trees combat global warming by absorbing carbon dioxide, cooling our neighborhoods so we use less energy, and creating homes for millions of species that are integral parts of the ecosystems of our planet. I love that the Foundation sends mail awakening people to the fact that trees are priceless. Find a tree and give it thanks. Plant trees on Earth Day (April 22nd) or care for trees and enjoy them anywhere they can be found.

If you can find a tree to swing from or climb and sit in, all the better for both of you. I did not grow up around many great climbing trees and am now mostly surrounded by aspens and pines, but I dream of those places. The children's stories of tree houses and swings are all very exciting, and if you are lucky enough to live in one of those places, utilize the added support of being *in* a tree. Safely. What a great and wonderful treat! I do have a special tree in my mediations that I call my writing tree. I climb it often in my imagination because it gives me wisdom, comfort, and perspective. We are never too old for imaginary friends or trees, and getting perspective is always good.

In the early 2000s, all over the West, the pine beetle began its plunder of my precious forests. I tried to reconcile the need for the huge purification of some of my closest friends with my deep sorrow and loss. I soothed some of the trees and let them know I loved them. They seemed okay with what was happening, as if it were a preconceived agreement of circumstance—necessary pruning for rebirth. It is another thing I love about these great sages: they do not mourn their own change or fret over something they do not essentially wish to change. Trees simply are. They are great at being trees and hold so strong to detachment and presence that they are always at peace.

Nevertheless, I distinctly remember the day when tree beetle claimed its first life on the land we owned. It was devastating. Within weeks, the tree turned from noticeably sick to completely brown. I watched my trees closely and went out every week to talk with and touch my beloveds. By the time I noticed this one had been ravaged, I found out the eggs had been laid there years prior. I cried many tears at my helplessness to change what was an awful and hasty deterioration right before my eyes. But I had to give in and let it go, as the tree knew I loved it, and convinced me that it simply was the way it was. Great unconditional love.

In the Lord of the Rings novel *The Two Towers*, I cringe at the part where the evil wizard has destroyed the forests, and the grand Ent (a shepherd of the forest in tree form) has just come to realize that not only should a wizard know better, but that those destroyed were some of his oldest friends. It is touching to me that this show of affection is so human, and it is a relief that although they do feel, these feelings are wholly different from the whims of us. This brings some small measure of okayness as I watch streaks of brown dying trees race up our mountain sides, wondering what will be in store for the world when so many have gone.

When I once stood in front of a town meeting during the debate over the potential ski resort, in tears I professed that trees are people too. I sometimes feel embarrassed about this plea, but many who knew what I meant supported me. I am glad they are wiser and more flexible than others.

It hurts to drive by and see anyone cutting a grand life short. Many people come up our roads to cut Christmas trees, even though it is illegal to do so. The irony of this act never fails to startle and horrify me. I am proud that my young daughter has learned the love of the forests. When she sees a truck with a bleeding tree lying helplessly in the back, she quietly admonishes, "Tree murderer." The apple does not fall far. I adore watching my children run up and hug trees. It is endearing and brilliant. There is magicalness in nature that teaches and cures with potency.

These breaths of life are our dear friends, and none of us would be here without them. If you have ever seen the changing of the aspens from a satellite perspective, it is amazingly breathtaking. To pass on information I have received, trees love being lit up at Christmas time with pretty and colorful lights as they stand in the ground where they have planted. It is a truly beautiful sight to see living trees with lights.

MEDITATION: TREES

- Go outside and silently or boldly thank a tree near you.
- Try not to take for granted any small token of life.

- If you listen closely, you will sense its thankfulness.
- Put your arms around it and hug it.
- Feel its great energy and the strength available to you.
- Look up while hugging and notice the great entity.
- Place your spine against it and feel the coursing energy.
- Put your crown chakra against the tree trunk and feel the dynamic cleansing.
- Wave to trees when driving and notice them waving in return—they always do.

Meditate with trees, brush against them, squeeze them for strength, and say hello. Sit with them or admire them. With trust and delight in your imagination you can often drive by forests and see them waving. Sometimes trees just want you to notice them individually. I like to wave back in acknowledgement, and their response never fails to please me.

If you want to see the effects of the love you give, learning to see auras will bring validation. One gets lighter and emits a rosy glow when in the presence of unconditional love. When humans first work to see auras, trees are a great place to start. At dusk, watch the edge of a tree and notice the circle of light around it. This is an aura, and after thirty seconds of staring, you will usually see it. Trees teach us many things.

Visiting the redwoods was a lifelong dream of mine, and we went as a family in 2009. The reverence of these forests, albeit with a devastating history, is truly immeasurable as some of the oldest and greatest beings on our planet epitomize nobility. They bring grace to even the biggest cynic. I remember as we were buying provisions for our trip, we checked out with a depressed, quiet clerk. When I asked if she had ever been to the redwoods, she perked up and smiled. Where before she had been distant and dragging, she suddenly became alive at her memories, and we had an exciting and enlivening conversation. She told us how much we would love it, how majestic and incredible it all was. I confirmed her enthusiasm with the most glorious summer we have ever spent as a family. These giants are quite something to behold, and you will never forget the awe in all your life.

From *The Giving Tree*—a book that makes me cry just thinking about it—who gladly gives its apples and most of itself, to the grouchy tree in *The Wizard of Oz* who does not, many stories speak of talking trees. Most myths are based on folklore, which comes from the passing of information through ancestors and millennia of generations. Animals and trees can speak and offer valuable information with simple connection. Words of a beautiful song by John Denver, who knew the truth, sang of speaking with trees, and how some could not know that trees spoke simply because they had never spoken to them. I know they speak to me. If they have not yet to you, we can change this by simply loving and tuning in.

MINERALS AND CRYSTALS

The profundity of our planet is offered in tangible form through minerals and crystals of every kind. No matter how, when, or where they were created, they hold gifts for our benefit, and are valuable friends always available for our use. Each different rock brings to life different qualities, whether for healing, stabilizing, releasing, cleansing, or pure magic. The minerals holding our planet together and furthering the continuum of life are hands-on unconditional love. Their beauty and vibrations are small parts of their monumental abilities and gifts for us. As trees heal and sustain us on the surface of our planet, rocks bless us from within our foundations with unconditional love.

I began my beloved crystal collection more than thirty years ago, not long in the life of a crystal, and I am now lucky enough to have thousands of rocks—bought, found, or gifted—in my home, one or two usually in my pocket. No matter your choice of rock, their uses are innumerable and unmatched by most unnatural objects, and their blessings are beyond comparison. Appreciating these specimens points our way to higher, unattached love.

Beyond geology lies a deeper, more spiritual study of minerals and their significance. Some information has been channeled through and studied from love of rocks or geology, and other information is believed to have been left within the rocks themselves for us to discover. The phenomenal rocks of this planet have been here for millions of years, and their exclusive purpose is to give assistance. Thus, they hold clues to the vibrations both found and needed to thrive here. There are numerous books I employ for my rock research, but I will only mention two here. Melody's *Love is in the Earth: A Kaleidoscope of Crystals* is a fantastic monster compendium noting typical size, formation, and colors, as well as spiritual qualities of crystals. Melody's work is the encyclopedia of rocks, containing detailed information from all angles. It is equally geological and spiritual. *Crystal Wisdom* channeled by Dolphyn is a profoundly spiritual approach to crystals and minerals and remains my favorite source because of its personal touch on the mystical connection with the spirits of the rocks themselves, much like nature divas. This book contains little geological information, but it is thorough in its explanation of the gifts bestowed by each friend in rock form.

Schools of thought may vary slightly as to what the uses of each mineral are, but the first and most important characteristic is how it feels when you touch it. Always ask permission, of course, if it belongs to another—this is crystal etiquette. Most rocks as well as transmuting energies can pick up and hold energies within their fields until consciously cleared, and are usually special to the carrier as well.

When we tune into the sensitivities around us, we notice much more about life and love, and it is no different with rocks. They usually first appeal to our sense of sight—is it pretty, is it the right size for its applicable use, is it a brilliant color or one of my preference? Does it shine or glow or reflect rainbows in the light? After all these questions are satisfied, usually with haste and little conscious probing, we can hopefully pick it up and feel what sensations it brings. Some give off very noticeable vibrations and some are more subtle, but whether you feel tingles or an energy surge or nothing, you will know early on if you are a match.

If it is the right rock for you, there will often be a moment of friendly recognition. The feeling may be as strong as "meant to be," "pick me up," or if a true enthusiast, "I have to have this one." A familiar feeling of a long-lost, even if small, and sometimes not so small, old companion. Some crystals just do not get along with certain compositions, and this will be different for each human-rock contact. To this day, I cannot hold a big wulfenite belonging to my husband without feeling nauseous. That wulfenite is his and only his.

Whether you are an explorer of rock formations and mineral study, have a fondness for crystals, or just think their appearance is pleasing, they are helpful servers for all humankind. You may have experiences like mine where you pick up a certain rock and know immediately what healing it brings, or you may consider keeping simple quartz, the all-encompassing of the clan, just for good measure. Clear quartz covers the basics of all the other minerals and is inclusive of the general magic. It regulates energies around it, which is why they have long been used in watches. It is also known that where one finds ample quartz on the ground, ample gold is very near. Always a good thing, especially if you have a shovel.

I have had hundreds of instances where, upon picking up or seeing a rock, I have instantly recognized and needed it. This is the usual routine for any crystal hunt and subsequent purchase. While some are sticklers for whether it is a mineral, crystal, or rock, I care more for the spiritual qualities, and therefore use the terms interchangeably. I know the rocks themselves appreciate my attention, no matter how it comes.

The study of the spiritual aspects of minerals can be learned as the love of rocks grows. After introducing a good friend of mine, Luna, to our favorite rock shop many years ago, she ended up working there and has now opened her own store, Luna's Mandala, where she carries raw minerals and fossils, and makes jewelry and Earth Guardians out of various beautiful gemstones and crystals. She meditates with crystals and from that creates angel-like statues matching certain rocks and qualities until something healing or magical is created.

Luna has learned information over the years on both the spiritual and geological forms of numerous rocks. She is a wealth of knowledge on this subject, which is one of her higher callings this lifetime. I love wearing her rock jewelry, bringing both style and support, fashion and function, ascetics and assistance. Brilliant! As lovers of rocks, it is tantalizing for us both to see others delight in their connection.

About two decades ago I eyed a large blue calcite—throw

pillow size, which is by any measure a big rock. This old haunt, Eggers Lapidary, had the best prices before being sold to a new owner, and upon the final installment of purchasing my calcite—it had been an extended courtship—I was beyond excited to get it home. While I was holding and squeezing it, making introductions, and welcoming this beauty into my life, I felt a surge of energy pulse through me in a wave.

I bought this guy based on the attraction and sensation rather than based on research into its characteristics, so I was unfamiliar with its gifts. I put it down on the table in my home to prove to my husband that I was feeling dynamic vibrations from our new friend, and as we proceeded pushing on it while having the other sit and feel, the findings were amazing and irrefutable. We looked it up in "the purple book"—Melody's *Kaleidoscope*. To my excitement, it spoke of blue calcite having an electrical pulsing effect, exponentially equal to the force applied to it, causing a sweeping sensation clearing the auric field—the exact sensations I encountered.

These occurrences are the norm for rock hunting, and it is always entertaining to get to know each other. My beautiful big blue calcite remains my favorite buddy to this day, which I would not dare say aloud around my numerous other companions.

Paraphrasing from rock books, I eagerly share just some qualities of my favorites. Hematite, a silvery iron ore, is next in order of my loves. Hematite is always grounding and agrees with my makeup profoundly. Its presence is stabilizing and helps us gain the substance of situations. If in doubt, I always have a hematite near. It has a soothing effect when I hold it and was the first crystal given to me by my Beloved in our early courting days.

Malachite, a bright green-banded gemstone, is also among my handful of allies. It is an excellent stone for general healing, growth, and love, promotes peace and balance, and always comes through for my wellness.

Amethyst, a well-known crystal in arrays of purple, is for me the spiritual master of stones, enhancing meditative and psychic abilities and promoting altered states of consciousness. As one of the oldest rocks on the earth, she transforms negative energy into positive and guides healing on personal and planetary scales.

Kyanite is a gorgeous blue with striking features and has led me on numerous journeys in search of it, as it used to be difficult to find. Most crystals need regular cleaning and energizing, but this loyalty stone is self-cleansing—always handy.

Rose quartz is the stone of unconditional love—need I say more? It helps heal all forms of love, from kindness and nurturing to self-love and romantic. While it is powerful, its soft pink quality is gentle, and this combination creates both opening and comfort.

I am also partial to tourmalines, tiger's eye, citrine, garnets, sodalite, celestite, selenite, topaz, and Shiva lingams; said to hold one of the loftiest vibrations on our planet, among other thousands.

MEDITATION: CRYSTALS

- Find a pretty rock outside or at a rock shop.
- Look it up or ask about its spiritual characteristics.
- Close your eyes and feel its sensations.
- Ask questions of this friend, and its dynamic energy will answer you.

Ignore crystals and let them just be peaceful and beautiful, or hang out with whichever one calls to you. Carry or wear gemstones with you for support through your day, for protection, healing, soothing, etc. Set them around your space to help anchor, cleanse, or energize. Squeeze them for potent energy and healing. Use them in meditation, or create meditations around them. Meditating on their energy illuminates their blessings, and gives knowledge. This can be done simply, and any way you like without training. You can learn the laying on of stones, or pay professionals to assist.

Each crystal corresponds to a different major chakra, by color, and can be used directly in healing specific areas or ailments. They are excellent energizers when used with some knowledge of their personal talents. I have an azurite/malachite mix that heals sore throats and asthmatic illnesses. It alleviates much of the tension that comes with and causes blocks in these chakras. Your favorites or most powerful helpers will always be different than another's, just as connections to animals and pets are unique.

I almost never leave home without wearing, in some form, a semi-precious stone. I have bracelets that protect and rings that imbue peace or confidence. I utilize their gifts whole heartedly. Before going out into the world, I peruse my friends and ask for helpers. Tiger's eye is my favorite protector, malachite my favorite healer, and rose quartz my favorite lover and calmer. While topaz helps good fortune and luck, I also employ rocks like lapis or even diamonds, which help cure some Feng Shui time afflictions (challenging energies that flow in a time cycle between heaven and earth). I come to rely on them as constant supporters in my life, and even when they are lost, we know they are doing their job, or finding a new friend to help.

As said before, crystals ask nothing in return for their

unconditional healing and energy, but do work better when they are taken care of. Activate them in the light of the full moon, or cleanse in the earth, water, and sun. If we use them a lot, or release a lot of energy, then it helps their energy remain clear if we allow them cleansing and replenishing. It is fascinating when some even break in times of high need or stress. I used to hike up the steep side of a mountain we called Peace Rock and leave my favorite amethyst hidden in a cave for the winter so it could return to the earth for a respite. It was always so potent when I returned to claim it as a helper friend.

You can ask your crystal what it would like, but some simple procedures just utilize nature. I like to let mine sit in a flowing river while I play or meditate, and then let it take a sun bath to energize. If they need more profound clearing, they can be buried in the earth or salt, then bathed in a river and sunned, or they can sit overnight absorbing the light of the full moon, which energizes magical instruments. Anything that works for you and your friend will be sufficient.

That I only express my common favorites here is of no song to the numerous others I adore, and use every day. I encourage everyone to explore rock shops, the ground, and crystal books to replace just a little of what we sometimes feel is missing inside us. Rocks can help us find and create ourselves with electricity, calmness, and magic. If we ask and look, they will guide the way. There is no end to how minerals can assist us, and small amounts of cherishing the gifts being offered by them is a step up in our higher vibration and connectedness.

I cannot over emphasize the abilities and energies that crystals can bestow to help us heal, cleanse, open, balance, and transform. They are a tangible form of unconditional love, and are nature's doctors from heaven and earth. It is like having a wise friend with you at all times, but transportable, and magical. They will speak to you, guide you, and sweepingly affect your essence if you ask. Even a river rock thrown in your pocket brings rewards and communion with the earth; try it, you will be grateful and glad you did. And so will they.

PART THREE

Keeping Love through Living

"Love is the doorway to enlightenment."
— Sanaya Roman

Keeping love through life's challenges is the essence of part three. We look at some of the many circumstances we endure regularly and contemplate allowing their unfolding with peace and insight. We keep in mind our growth of love thus far instead of getting caught in the common swirls of hypersensitivity. We keep our wits about us instead of reacting the way we once did. We keep love in our hearts through it all, and then we have love to give.

Keeping love through loss can be daunting, but we vow to remember. Turning to the importance of loving our bodies, and even our distractions, we promise to try. Retaining the healing we are processing and the maintenance of release begins to direct our way to love. We hold our centers, and as we sustain treasures every day, we keep love in the forefront of our lives.

CHAPTER EIGHTEEN

Healing

We all need healing in some way, and as such it has been touched on in each part of this book. Usually we need it in many ways, and it is in seeking this wholeness that we come to realize much about ourselves, our finite time in this body, and the Universe to which we belong. Whether your ailment is emotional trauma, past psychological issues, physical wounds, or illness, we have come to this planet for very specific lessons and insights on creating health. The wholeness of health is different to each of us, and keeping it means many things.

"We are fortunate that care and recovery exists in as many forms as our sicknesses appear."

We are fortunate that care and recovery exists in as many forms as our sicknesses appear. Something can help each of us achieve whatever remedy we are looking for, and to keep it, even be it peace of mind. We can better give unconditional love when we feel good. As an addition to the discussion on joy through struggle in Part One and energy cleansings discussed in Part

Two, this chapter and the next explore more ways by which to heal common mental, physical, and spiritual ailments.

OVERCOMING STRESS

If I am buried in stress, or overwhelmed by pressure or anxiety, my functioning begins to shut down. I am caught in my mind, obsessively contemplating, addicted to thought, and reacting quite involuntarily. I experience emotional outbursts and hear myself yelling before I am even aware of it. I realize this is my cue to find myself. These are some of the first signs that we are holding stress in our space, and if we do nothing to release or ground it, we will continue to snowball into further trouble. Stress affects everyone in different ways, and being alert to its presence and utilizing tools to free ourselves from it is invaluable. We should contact professional healers and doctors for help when we need it, but we can also do much to restore by reducing or eliminated the effects of stress. Whatever it takes, your job is to restore your body to its healthy original state with every choice, thought, and action.

We are not to feel guilty if we have something we cannot instantly heal; we have all sorts of soul and body agreements to fulfill. Some ailments arrive as lessons in perspective, or jolts of awakening, but we can do much all on our own to mitigate pain, anger, hopelessness, limitations, and resignation. These all cause physical imbalances, and over a lifetime can accumulate like sludge in our cells. We cannot keep love in our lives like this.

I was quite sick as a child, and my life was constrained on a short leash around severe asthma, which included colds knocking me down for weeks at a time to collapsed lungs with helicopter rides, and various other related problems that must have been loads of fun for my parents. I had sixty plus stitches from trying to stop our dogs and cats from fighting, as well as several falls, broken bones, and various surgeries.

I realized as an adult that I got sick when I needed extra rest, care, and downtime. I suspect this is true for many of us. Now I precede my needs with TLC. The gift of allowing ourselves pause so we may retain our well-being is a priceless contribution to a healthier world, albeit sometimes difficult within today's compulsive society. If we admit it to ourselves, most of our daily life *is* a choice, and if we lose our health we will wish we made better ones.

Self-nurturance is the first place to expand healing awareness. Notice warning signs in time to repair minor problems. If you are in need of a tonic, put yourself on the top of your priority list, and search for the help you require. Your life will not work to your potential if you are constantly ill. A chronic illness may require some adjustments in your perspective and choices, but suffering over avoidable problems is needless. Simple procedures for caring for our bodies, minds, and spirits can heal most minor ailments. Get in tune and follow your instincts before you require more drastic measures.

Some tips for self-nurturance include the following:

- Clear your space of the calamities of others through releasing.
- Engage in small personal pampering, perhaps by taking a bath or nap.
- Drink tea, and water, and take vitamins.
- Get into nature and breathe, listen to, and receive energy from plants, trees, and sun.
- Eat well and allow your body to sweat out toxins.
- Find reasons to smile and be happy.

- Read, sing, dance, laugh, and connect with trustworthy others.

- Be grateful, and envelope yourself in feelings of appreciation.

Follow your inner nudges for renewal. Done on a daily basis, our small tending makes a difference to the whole of our lives. What is your equilibrium restoring ritual when you get home from a difficult day? Do you cuddle your pets, call a friend, or sit down and take off your shoes and all the clothing that pulls and tugs? How do you heal yourself in common but private, sacred, and simple ways? Becoming aware of these familiar and consistent routines in which we refresh our harried hearts will lead us to live more nurturing lives, both in giving and receiving.

Just noticing specific parts of our bodies through our breath can initiate healing. We have this simply powerful ability to heal just by seeing health in our minds eye while feeling it deeply into ourselves. By placing our attention on and working with our physical sensations, we can activate clearing with love and light energy. By directing our focus wherever our intuition leads us, we simply breathe into that area with relaxation, or bring in colored light which then heals. We picture and feel it healed and re-charged. This allows us to know and change our inner essence.

By interacting with ourselves in intimate knowing, feeling, and awareness, healing occurs on all levels, and to all chakras. Once we are connected to any issue inside our bodies or space, we can use positive transformative imaging to clear, energize, and re-balance our systems. It is valuable, and easy to relate and cooperate with our bodies in this way. You will be surprised by the potential magnitude of just noticing, watching, and sitting with yourself quietly in order to breathe change into any area with your focused energy.

RELEASING

When we look at all the avenues of healing, whether conventional or alternative, it can seem overwhelming. We know we "should" eat better, meditate, and move our bodies regularly—all that common sense stuff—but when we need a cure, small or large, it may be difficult to know where to turn for easiest or immediate benefit. While we visit with doctors, read books on health, look online for answers, or even learn to work with our own energy, we can take heart in one tool that will not fail.

The skill of releasing is effective and accessible. Releasing can be done anywhere at any time, as much as one likes, and it will sustain our equilibrium, granting relief even in the midst of a crowd. Releasing returns us to love.

We release by imagining or image-creating a hollow cord growing from our first or base chakra at the bottom of our spine to the center of the earth. This is the foundation of our support system, and release mechanism. Using the grounding cord meditation in Chapter Fourteen, you can notice energy in your space that you might not want to stay with you, or that does not belong to you. Feel or picture it going out through your aura and down through your open grounding tube to the earth to be recycled by our gifted Mother Earth, or Gaia. We also release by blowing up energy we feel does not belong.

MEDITATION: BLOW A ROSE

- When you feel stuck or mired within, close your eyes and breathe.
- Picture a ball or rose before you.

- Intend all energy you do not want filling this ball, rose, or other symbol.
- When it is full, take it out of your space, far away.
- Send it to an ocean or mountain top, or even the sun.
- Imagine it blowing up, like an explosion. This explosion will return the energy to its own realm.
- Do this energetically as many times as needed to clear your space.

This tool is effective for expelling all sorts of yucky stuff within our space and is complementary to our grounding cord. When we clear our space and release masses of energy by blowing it up, we need to replace that energy with something else, and we may bring on a period of growth due to the space we have just created.

Grounding and release is one truth, and I employ it as a long-sought answer because it includes recognition of the energy passing through before it leaves. Use whatever techniques have proven effective for you. There are a growing number of books, centers, and gurus that can lead you to the great skills of caring for your space.

When we manifest or release our energetic and spiritual potentials, we may have many concerns about how to do it "right," what repercussions may occur, or just how much can be influenced. These concerns are reasons to take a basic class or seek a guide, but don't undervalue your own intuition. By using your imagination and staying lighthearted and childlike, as if we were in kindergarten, you will learn the best ways to work on your own body. There is no wrong way. Listen to your truth.

Some may worry about severing a bond with a person when releasing the energy of that person. You cannot harm bonds by clearing your space. Some may wonder if releasing is just trying to neglect further responsibility of working through issues or relationships. In reality, releasing allows us to look at our stuff and is the opposite of ignoring.

When we start to look at and deal with what is holding us back, numerous daunting ideas or old programs may surface that cause hesitation, fear, or retreat. As we integrate and release, another layer of the onion is removed. It is no longer baggage we carry, and it is no longer a heavy burden—it is currency for our soul.

You may be wondering how the Law of Attraction applies here. If you're constantly releasing negative energy, which requires you to think about the negative, will those negative thoughts manifest as negative circumstances around us? No. When we look at and then release something, even negative, it has no power over us. We can immediately replace it with something we do want. By filling the empty spaces, left by that which we released, with unconditional love, we won't get caught up in each thought or feeling.

It is important to understand what each experience offers, but it is even more crucial to be able to let go of what no longer serves our paths. We can do both without burying or hiding important matters from ourselves or the light. We do not need to incessantly hold pain in order to be sure we are working through it. Consciously bring up feelings, look at their affects so they can be integrated, and then set them free according to your own time and comfort level.

Releasing also allows others to have their energy back from us. We all know people who hold grudges, and more than that live in the grips of their anger or grief. When something small causes an extreme outburst, issues of old are resurfacing. It is difficult to progress in life when we are stuck in another time or place because of unresolved thoughts or stale mindsets.

How do people who do not implement these tools release? Many don't. Most of us have, a time or two, suppressed feelings of dissatisfaction with life by swallowing chocolate cake or other delicious and grounding foods, but we know this is temporary, and hopefully we grow toward more healthy outlets. Some run, exercise, bathe, or scream and pound pillows. Although some of these may provide temporary relief from anger or that dull feeling that something is amiss, they only provide a physical release.

When we deal with each experience and feeling as it arises and then let it roll away, we are utilizing the power of our awareness along with spiritual release and forward movement. We then have more space in which to bring back ourselves. Learn from every emotion, thought, and stress, and when done with its offerings, release it because continuing is useless and even harmful.

"Radiate the essence of joy to keep healing with love."

To see repressed emotions or old heavy feelings within someone's aura who has come to me for clearing is very telling. Often it literally looks like heavy gray clouds above the person are pushing down, and when I begin healing, I can see and feel the relief as burdens are lightened by the release. One can actually breathe deeper with sighs of reprieve. Then we fill up the space made within the energy field, and the sun follows them with a lift in their step.

MY PAST LIFE OF HEALING PAIN

Of all my spiritual practices, receiving aura and past-life readings creates the most valuable insights. While these tools are not necessary for evolving the pain of our past, I urge each person to seek this wisdom, as it lights a clear map to inner understanding of our most daunting blocks. My personal past-life readings have aided my path to healing tremendously. Lynne Burrows, a trance medium channel, spiritual minister, healer, and one of the wisest women I have ever had the treasure of knowing, has shown me that from past lives, I have energetic garment after habit after vestment of old pain absorbed in trying to take on the ills of others in order to heal them. This was done both consciously and unconsciously.

In ancient times, healers cured maladies by taking on the sicknesses of others and then transmuting it. This has become an outmoded practice to our present times. Our species has evolved to a point where we can be responsible for ourselves instead of giving our power to the gods or others as our ancestors did. The old ways of transforming energies has turned into new, healthier forms of allowing someone to be healed without an individual absorbing the ailment.

Lynne let me know that as compassionate, gracious, and empathetic as my soul might well be, taking on the pain of others to heal was clearly no longer serving me. I felt honored that this was part of my past and was endeared to hear of my kind soul, but that was only the newest irony of my challenges.

The way she explained the state to which I should aspire was a beautiful metaphor. She said I was to be a waterfall of love, so that others may drink of it. That I was to learn to witness those in pain, or even dying, and to not go *to* them or need to fix them. Instead of taking responsibility for them, I was just to be a reservoir of pure love from which they could partake if they so chose.

I needed to release these cloaks of pain I had dragged with me, some for thousands of years, so I could discover my own inspirations. I had lived so incessantly in feeling the pains of others and taking on their torments out of a desire to heal and help that I had become burdened by what I had been unable to transmute or release, lifetime after lifetime.

Part of my teaching in healing now is to make the world more beautiful and whole by taking care of myself, enabling me to be present and available for others. This is a different concept for my soul. It first felt selfish, but I loved her ideas that real healing is about being the healing essence from which someone can draw light and love, if they choose to. It is good to be gracious and kind to be caring, but it serves no one to be caught up in illusion or drama.

While my ancient "stuck" cloaks of pain may be similar to the energies of Mary Magdalene absorbing the loss and pain for Jesus, Lynne assured me that His path was about a larger lesson of resurrection, openness, and unconditional love, and was not meant to captivate loyal caretakers in a constant mode of hurting for the crucifixion. He never hoped anyone would suffer. Now, because of these past-life readings, I consider myself spiritually free, and focus my life on unconditional love instead of specific doctrines while still respecting their value.

Although many of us experience deep empathy for others and genuinely care and long to heal them, we are not necessarily taking on another's pain consciously. We are not as apt in releasing or transmuting as the Native American shamans or rage dancers of Cuba, who are specifically called to such a task. The effects for us laymen are therefore more dangerous and detrimental because we unknowingly absorb pain or loss without the skills to alter and discharge it. Lynne assured me that what people really needed from me was simply to be in the presence of my joy. I loved her words—radiate the essence of joy to keep healing with love.

PAIN AS A PRIVILEGE

Part of being human is experiencing the pain game, or distinct feelings accompanied by our growth and learning process. But feeling our pain, being aware of our pain body layer, and moving pain out is quite different than taking on pain from others. When we watch television and burst into tears, we may notice that our empathy is out of control because we are allowing in the feelings of others. Our second chakras have fallen open if we feel tremendous emotional pain while nothing is happening directly to us.

My phenomenal and compassionate minister Margaret speaks of pain as a privilege to take part in because it tells us we are growing and changing. Pain is not a sensation felt by those in spirit without a body who are living as light. She assures us that we can transcend our pain by staying present. We can keep our centers through love.

"Instead of putting our pain in the future, having marked the next twenty years full of the darkness we are feeling now, or holding the pain from the past, we acknowledge that today may hurt, but tomorrow might just be different; this allows for infinite possibilities for the miracles we all need and often receive." In our exploring of what we are feeling, and from when or where in our lives (or past lives) it actually occurred, we can learn very much about letting go to make space for something, anything different, as well as the broadening perspective that the definition of life *is* change.

Margaret goes on to teach, "If we accept our feelings, stay present, and continue having dreams or hopes, pain may pass far sooner and with greater ease than if we blindly succumb to the agonizing emotions we feel in this moment and might sink into as the new way our life will be forever." These steps, along with awareness of what we are carrying with us, arm us with great gifts toward enabling our private internal freedom *through* our pain. After all, the only way through it is through.

While caring so deeply about others is honorable and healing others is a noble calling, we must be careful of the positions in which we place ourselves. We may not even mean to or be trying to heal someone, and may just be so sensitive that our tears are touched by seeing, feeling, or sensing sadness. These are beautiful traits. But for the same reason children need rules and discipline, boundaries for all of us are healthy. If you hurt when others hurt, know that your joy will expand others also, but use some energy delineation to secure your space, and keep your second chakra in check.

I implore that we all seek to replace our vulnerability with unconditional love. Instead of being sent crashing on the waves of emotional disturbances from our past or others, we can become the waterfall of love and joy from which anyone can be healed. We remain safe, open to neutrality and truth, and we learn to hold our space and maintain our strength as we give. Unconditional love heals all of us, everywhere, from inside out. We can desire health and wholeness for others while keeping our space and lending our best qualities responsibly.

MEDITATION: HEALING OTHERS

- If someone you care about needs healing, first set your space.
- When you feel certain your space is your own, simply spend time with them. Just by being in their presence, you will be offering healing.
- Ask the angels to care for this someone. Archangel Raphael is a great healer with emerald light.
- Think of them with love, light, joy, and healing, and their spirits will receive.

- See them healed and add light to that picture.
- Encourage them to learn energy techniques of heal-ing or receive from a professional.
- Learn healing techniques from trustworthy others to aptly heal, and remain clear.

THE SACREDNESS OF DIS-EASE

Pain is our body's unmistakable signal that a shift needs to occur. We have wonderful mechanisms that alert us when any part of us experiences imbalance. When we listen to these clues, we can take immediate action to undo or change our disparities, and when we ignore them, our natural internal response is to make the problems more noticeable until they can no longer be disregarded.

Whether we are in a state of negativity, have stomach pains because we ate something bad for us, or are dealing with a severe or chronic illness, there is a gift in our awareness of these ailments. Our attention is brought to focus like a laser beam when we have no other choice but to slow down and listen to the signs that something is not right. Inside this state are two wonderful opportunities: the chance to gain understanding and communication with the change our body or life requires, and limitless levels of knowledge brought forth from it that could not be recognized through any other form.

This knowledge is great as it shows us true paths we may have been missing and grants us immediate clarity we rarely know. What is meaningful in our lives, and what priorities are for the higher good of our purposes? These are blessed insights brought in disguise.

In doing so much for others, we often forget to place as

much care on our own needs. In searching for ways to give unconditional love to those we treasure, we forget to treasure ourselves with the same love. This is when we get a cold, a sore throat, or something worse. It is not for lack of good intentions or kindness—it is usually the opposite.

Inside every damaging feeling is a lesson. We must now look at what this dysfunction is telling us. This is the sacredness of any illness. We cease fighting against (vibrating with) what we do not want, or playing the victim, and we ask instead why it has come to us and what vibration attracted it. Regardless of how sick you are or for how long, it is the result of something trying to get your attention.

When we discover what brought us to this point and what changes we desire to make and will follow, we then receive our holy moment of the circumstance. It will present itself to us the instant we open to the experience and allow the lesson. Even if we are not meant to or able to make everything better, when we absorb the truth and fullness of this message, we will come to the shift in our illness. We recognize the program and disperse the stuck energy. This is the day we see our reflection with acceptance or wake up from a long illness finally feeling better—energy restored, breathing clear, and a new gratefulness just to be well. This is when what remains becomes valuable, and when immeasurable love can finally take precedent.

Gratitude is an excellent cure for any dis-ease, small or large. It may be the single most important insight to keeping us healthy and loving. Even when we are in the midst of something bigger and scarier than a cold, a sense of appreciation for the little things can bring us holiness within the experience. Obviously, we were missing something or living out something, and Spirit reassures our support system when we see what that is.

In the middle of years of long frustration and worry over my dad's heart problems, his devastating knee injury from college reared up and blew out several times. He had it repeatedly emptied of fluid and reconstructed in rare surgeries. As he was laid up for eight weeks at a time, several times throughout a couple years, he searched for answers. Why did this keep happening? What was he supposed to "learn"?

This physical disability brought him opportunities for delving and clarity. How could he find any enjoyment for living when he could not get up, move around, and accomplish simple tasks he usually took for granted? The lesson could be as simple as recognizing gratitude for simple living, or something more convoluted like past emotional traumas not yet attended to, or even past life issues come to be resolved. (Knees tend to hold lots of past life energies.) It is not about punishment or deserving, only awareness, insights, growth, and love.

My dear father-in-law was diagnosed with lung cancer in 2008. I struggled to find the sacredness in this illness. He is a generous doting grandfather to our young girls and is an involved and very engaging presence and helper in all of our lives. From making us breakfast and watching our girls while we take care of healings and errands, Richard was suddenly looking at a limited span of life, and we were counting the years—or, God forbid, months—we had with him.

We wondered if our youngest would be old enough to remember him and their special and unbreakable bond. We walked around in a daze, still in shock. We cried and tried to communicate our feelings, but we felt something was torn away from us, even though we knew Spirit lived on and that we all had our agreements. Our spiritual teachings and realizations do not prepare us for or save us from this inevitable devastation.

Where will holiness in these moments show itself as we count everything he does as potentially the last time? How do we reconcile jumping into the future in our minds, and feeling such sadness at the impending funeral? We talked with our friend and minister Lynne, and she helped us through this path she knows so well.

"It takes a lot sometimes for people to learn to open their hearts," she began as we started the long road of chemotherapy. Richard usually showed his love by sending us home with his delicious food, taking our girls shopping for coats and shoes, helping us financially when goodness knows we needed it, and various wonderful acts such as these, but affection and warmth weren't openly expressed.

I was astonished as Lynne reassured us that "you never know how this will change someone," and she was right. Richard suddenly reached out to his son and lovingly connected with him. It was so sad that it took a cancer diagnosis, and while I am sure there are numerous other levels changing and being learned from this terrible ordeal, I see a bit of beauty brought about by it. We try to accept that things progress as they are always meant, and we desperately look for a way to understand and shift this feeling of tragic loss.

In writing on healing, I am today left with mostly questions. Why do people do things they know are not good for them? How can cigarettes still be sold and consumed so voraciously? Why, with all my study and learning, am I still afraid of losing others to death? How can my confusion and frightened worried feelings ever help anyone who dares to read this book for some sort of inspiration or hope? Why am I wallowing . . . digressing . . . and on and on.

This much I know: we are mortal. Instead of fear of limitations, our bodies can bring significance to our present. I have a perfect example of "not sweating the small stuff" right before me—a sentiment I have worked towards for years but which has, until now, felt a bit intangible. I find our family closer this week, just being with each other and enjoying it. I suddenly feel grateful just to see my husband walk through the door at the end of the day, and I pause when we kiss to really take it in. I don't feel a wave of anxiety as an insignificant cold or flu passes around like I usually would.

I remember the times I was sick so often as a child, feeling pure contentment in the hushed surroundings of my humming vaporizer, soft lighting, and pleasant music. I hope Richard too will feel that peace. I see a stronger importance accompanying us as we get with the grandparents for mundane meetings. Everything with them, and our children especially, has taken on greater meaning. I share with Paul as he looks into himself deeply and begins to ask his own consecrated questions. I make sure to verbally appreciate Richard for much that is overlooked as we carry on our busy lives, and I validate humor in his joking about death, which was not funny but was his way of accepting the evil.

It is strange to go to sleep at the end of each day wondering what it has meant, and for what reason we were allowed another day when some are not. I wonder if I am fulfilling my highest purpose. In all my musings, something bewildering hits me; I sense penetratingly what Lynne was speaking about as far as this experience opening hearts, and I realize that she was not just talking about the one with cancer. I see clearly that it has also, and quite unexpectedly, opened mine.

CHAPTER NINETEEN

Love Your Body Unconditionally

We may be aware that seeking harmony in relationships brings peace in our lives. We may know that higher knowledge gives us secrets to live with grace and abundance. But as we strive to keep unconditional love in our lives, we need to include our bodies. We cannot search for ways of healing our energy, honoring our great purposes, and making awesome differences in the world while we are at war with the very flesh and bones that hold our existence. We cannot reach enlightenment while we battle with ourselves in any way, and this most definitely includes our bodies.

The body is an under-appreciated gift. We devalue our vessels when we should treat them gratefully, and worse, too many of us take them for granted. Though we are more than our bodies, I invite you to look at how you treat your body, and how you can care for it more lovingly. Negative thoughts can affect our health, and we learn that healing can only come when we are at peace with our bodies, for we cannot keep love in our lives without them. As we learn unconditional love for those around us, we need to learn to accept and love our own makeup.

THE AMAZING BODY

Our physical body is what separates us from amounting to just energy, as are all other beings. It is our form. The body is what allows our experience here. It is amazing in its internal structure, its ability to heal itself, and in its pure and whole uniqueness. We can heal our body by simply listening to what it needs and following through.

Our bodies do so much without being asked. Sometimes they respond to our cries for protection by allowing a little more weight and security. They work every minute of every hour of every day to keep us alive. We are carefully constructed to handle infinite processes at once that configure our thoughts, feelings, sensations, digestion, nervous and immune systems, muscular and skeletal systems, respiratory functioning, memory, responses, and much more.

Our bodies really are phenomenal, from the way we use energy, to how we move and release, how we are stimulated, how we know, and how we fight all the foreign chemicals, substances, and environments we expose ourselves to. It is astonishing just how much our body loves us no matter how we treat it, and when we do take care of it we can be awed by its extraordinary potential.

Striving to love every part of our own body leads us to appreciate the efficiency and beauty of all shapes and sizes. You may grunt and say "yeah right" as you may desire a more healthful and vibrant figure, but at least seek to affirm some appreciation for all it does for you today, and then take a healthy step to appreciate it.

CARING FOR THIS BODY

It may seem innocuous as we scowl at our puffy red face in the mirror or turn sideways and sigh as we walk away, discouraged at our profile. It may appear harmless to hold in our stomachs and wish for the flatness of our youth, or groan at the back of our thighs as they resemble anything but smoothness, but we know through our feelings that these thoughts and actions are an affront to our miraculous bodies. We simply cannot think and feel negativity or disregard toward any part of our bodies and not have it affect us. When we judge our bodies, we are not loving them. Every single thought we have is expressed somewhere within the body. Really think about this. This truth means guarding our thoughts is a significant responsibility.

"Every single thought we have is expressed somewhere within the body."

Our physical body gets our attention very well when it is in discomfort or crisis, but short of responding to em- ergencies, most of the human race does not highly esteem these treasures that house our souls. And for some of us who have a difficult time reconciling changes in appearance or who never found true appreciation for our physicality, we might not only disregard its importance, but sink to loathing it, even unconsciously. This attitude will not help our spirit achieve a higher vibration or keep unconditional love strong. Such unkindness is not what was intended as we forego the substance of the physical for the spiritual or anything else. We are one with our bodies, and we are in this together. Without our bodies, we, being so powerful, could not progress.

It is an astonishing phenomenon to get caught up in life, forgetting about your body more or less, and then to realize your body did not fare so well in that time, especially having been slim, and having not appreciated it while it lasted. It hits like a brick wall, with accompanying feelings of shame, betrayal, and hopelessness. This is not much fun. This does not help us keep unconditional love in our hearts.

Besides time, a lot changed for me after leaving the world of dancing and having kids. Suddenly I was raising my own family even though I still felt like a child myself—though a look in the mirror revealed the truth. When you still feel like a child but do not resemble the self you thought you would see in the mirror, it can be startling. Every day I feel like that young adult of skin and bones, able to wear anything without thinking about it—until I look down or into that betraying mirror. Tough stuff.

The main things I try to remember now are that I got myself to this place, whether it was conscious or not, and that I need to love myself in order to have a happy body now. I can be disappointed in my choices, mad at myself, and overwhelmed by the load of work and miracles it might seem I need to return to a healthy figure. Yet if I choose to love my body, all the facets are manageable. Feeling good about me is one healthy choice away, one meditation, one half hour of movement. It is better to focus on how I can love my body today than to expect myself to start working out two hours a day or to cut out all sugar. Just today. How can I care for this body today? What choice will I make to love it right now? This is important because it is an acceptable frame to control what overwhelms us.

I am trying to work, in little bits, on my love for sugar and fats. I do love eating healthy natural foods, which are optimal though not advertised as voraciously in our society. Recognize that the road to health may not have been made easy for us, thanks to incessant TV commercials, magazine ads, and whatever other reasons. No blame or self-condemnation is needed. Just be easy with yourself and turn to solutions.

Our regular grocery visit, and cooking is now pretty well geared to high fiber foods, whole grain, natural, and fresh or organic choices, without most sugars, syrups, and chemicals. But with all these good habits we still find disappointment in some of our numbers. Obviously, the less empty calories you ingest, and the more natural and vitamin filled, the better. We need to look at the convoluted side of consumption, as well as how often we move our bodies. When we do this with love we get much further.

Learn not to take out your disappointments on your physical being. The body asks for very little—to be fed and watered, sheltered and rested. If you skip eating when your body asks for nourishment, you are hurting your body. When you learn to ignore how thirsty you are because you can't be bothered to get up and get a drink of water, you are disregarding your body.

Some people hurt themselves purposely because they feel torment in their souls and anguish in their hearts. Such action keeps us in an internal battle, disallowing peace. Find help to express pain in a healthier way. We cannot hold love while harming and hating ourselves. Even if taking your body for granted has been an unconscious choice, it is time for us all to become friends with our whole being, to care for our bodies, and to be pleased every day at the very life it enables us.

"We can only completely heal and love when we are at peace with our bodies."

We can only completely heal and love when we are at peace with our bodies, as they are the beginning to the rest of us. Take some time to love and be kind to your body. Find good things about it every day.

HOW I LEARNED TO LOVE MY BODY

Though I danced for hours every day in my youth, the epitome of svelte health, I have not, through maturity, welcomed my body as the friend it has always been. I do not look the way I used to—I am not slender, I have red marks and dots on my face and arms, my hair is graying. I weigh more than television commercials suggest I should to fit into great jeans, and my weight fluctuates depending on how well I eat or how often I exercise. I skip meals when I get into my writing and do not drink enough water while loving sugar and chocolate.

I am trying to shift these habits. I have changed from coffee to herbal tea and golden milk, and I have lessened my intake of high fructose or hydrogenated anything, but I know that I rarely take care of my body as I would someone who I am trying to love unconditionally.

I used to blame my body for many things and withhold nutrients because I was too tired, too addicted, or too lazy. I hated being sick and finding bathrooms when in public for the two years after giving birth. I was blameful of my breathing frustrations with asthma, which caused long illnesses. I hated looking in the mirror and feeling quietly disgusted about myself and my choices. The sad thing is that I still thought this way when I was young and skinny. What a giant clue that it never really had to do with how I looked. I carry all these emotions and thoughts in my energy field, which tells my healers I am not truly loving my body.

Only recently have I realized that I was keeping happiness at bay with this internal struggle. I truly cannot be in a space of unconditional love if I am loathing any small thing about myself. I have only now begun to acknowledge all it does, ceaselessly, to allow me to continue on my path.

It has taken care of me all these years despite my neglect, abuse, and subtle revenge. I am cultivating a better understanding and kinder relationship to my constitution—my flesh, bones, and everything else. It is not the fault of my body if I carry extra flabby, sagging parts or anything else that I have finally come to view as acceptable, even loving, changes of growing up. Some parts maybe glow less and wrinkle more, but I can either spend a fortune on trying to change what's "wrong," or learn to love it. It is I, and I am it.

I do a lot right. I exercise and watch my portions, I try to speak nice things about my appearance, but I also know I can achieve greater consistency with keeping fit, eating healthier, and affirming appreciation. It is little consolation now to acknowledge in hindsight that I should have appreciated what I had—but I can start, and you can start, today.

WHAT YOU CAN DO

Do what you can today to forgive your body, to love it, and to be kind to it. We are, of course, not just our bodies. We are not our poor or great bone structure, our weight, height, or any other function of our body. We do not need to classify ourselves based on an illness, disorder, or any ailment we might carry within our bodies. Those are just symptoms or organized categories we have bought into as a label. We are not these changes we view as problems—and if you are still here reading this then there are at least some parts of your body that are working and healthy. There is something you can find to be grateful for in that.

Here I offer a variety of ways in which you can begin to love your body and love your efforts to be healthier. See which ideas resonate with you and the health you are trying to achieve.

Do not make it work overtime to get rid of toxins when you could feed it proper nutrients. Try not to contaminate or consciously pollute it. Eat organic to limit pesticides and hormones that mess with keeping your health. Limit caffeine intake so you are not robbing energy from your future. Caffeine also lowers your baseline mood, thus becoming addictive in order to maintain even normal equilibrium.

Watch the documentary *Fed Up* to learn about the American food industry. Limit sugar, or eliminate it if you can. This includes empty carbs like white flour and rice containing no fiber. Sugar destroys your precious microbiome, which is responsible for your gut health, mood health, heart health, immune system, and more. Cutting out this one poison in what you drink and eat changes everything. Nothing could make a larger contribution to your physical wellness. On a personal note, it was only when Paul and I gave up sugar that pounds finally started coming off naturally.

Take in deep breaths to restore your body and nourish it well in the correct amounts. Rest and relax your muscles. Energize them with inspired action and movement. Get a massage or make love to a sweetheart to expand your body's beauty, warmth, and magnetism. Drink water and bathe in it. Stay away from chemicals and environments you know do not add to your overall health. Feel your energy coursing through the cells of your being and observe the capacity of that energy when it is focused on, enhanced, and healed.

Learn to meditate and release so you can bring in the vibrations, colors, and light that you crave physically. Just acknowledging parts of our bodies allows them to be loved, and therefore stronger and more vibrant. Smile and feel your chemistry change. Laugh and notice the penetrating force and aliveness that is inside you. Befriend your body for life, and when its job is done, graciously let go. Until that day, which will come for each of us, show it respect and care for all the miracles it unconditionally gives us each and every day.

MEDITATION: LOVE YOUR BODY

- Take a quiet moment with your body to really feel it.

- Bring in love and forgive your body and yourself.

- Feed and water it well, limiting toxins of all kinds.

- Breathe, rest, and move your wonderful body.

- Move your joints—circle your wrists and ankles, lift your shoulders to your ears and then push them down as far as you can in a rotating circle. Make sure to breathe deeply.

- Meditate to clear your space and your body.

- Focus light and breathe into any area that feels off.

- Smile at yourself in the mirror, and say nice things about your body every day.

CHAPTER TWENTY

Every Day a Holiday

To overcome letdown from post-holiday fervor, and to revive the spirit of a holiday, treat every day as special, each moment worth celebrating. When we keep every day extraordinary, we keep our connection to unconditional love at the forefront of our living. Find joy in each day instead of placing pressure on holidays with high expectation. This way we will not be let down and disappointed by their brevity or imperfection.

We often forget love at these times too. We spend money we maybe didn't have, and feel saddened when a tradition, gift, or quality time spent with loved ones doesn't bring the fulfillment we expected. We mistakenly thought the special day would make everything better or satisfy us in some grand way. We may even have put so much effort into the occasion that our letdown may result in minor illness as our bodies play catch up and release pent-up stress.

HOLIDAY HANGOVER

No matter what you celebrate, how you decorate (or not) for any holiday, or how special a particular day is to you, the sense of discouragement as a holiday ends is accompanied by the weight of the world. The obligation to see family may be a major stress for you, and your desire to avoid certain family members may keep you from spending time with any family. If you do get together with family, you might act politely while feeling pain at the emotional distance between you and those who you should feel closest with. These engagements force us to deal with much, no matter the event.

We are bombarded by obligations on every side and neglect our private rituals because the normal routine has been foregone for the requirements of the holiday. It is no wonder that we often end up emotionally bereft and even sick after attending to all the social hoopla of any big day. We overdraw from our personal accounts as we try to live up to the collective ideas of how to celebrate. Putting personal life aside for these unusual days means we rarely observe them in the way we might truly wish.

We also sometimes hope that these vacations, or breaks, will reset our lives, and somehow bring back the balance we have been lacking. Whether we are anticipating a new job, the beginning or end of school, another big birthday, or even the warmth of Valentine's Day to make everything feel sweeter, the event often falls short of our needs and hopes. Those milestone days of the year are filled with heavy expectations that, when not met, weigh us down, and the current social structure does not allow the majority of folks time to take off and recuperate.

We try to fit all we need into these special celebrations, but it is difficult with so little time. We take out our good china to create festive feasts. Yet even with bursts of laughter and fond friends, we whimper when it is all over, suddenly left with the messes, bills, and lingering emptiness. Packing everything in does not work for the necessary renewal.

The reason this letdown occurs at the end of every long-anticipated occasion is because, as the saying goes, we have put all our eggs into one basket. We have, once again, without awareness, placed too much importance on the qualities of one day, all the while maybe forgetting to keep love in our hearts. We celebrate because it feels good to participate in the delight of a special time, and it arrives as a respite, an excuse to break from our ordinary daily existence. With so much significance placed here, it is no wonder we often feel disillusioned and disheartened when it fails to meet our needs. How do we value and keep love woven through every day?

CELEBRATE EVERY DAY

When we expect any one day or event to fulfill us and create magic, we are discounting the value of every other day we live. It is too much to expect any holiday to satisfy all we long for. We need to learn through daily practice and priorities how to assure our happiness every twenty-four hours. We need to set aside time for ourselves and those we love without special reason. We need to check in more often and know that we are doing what we want to be doing. We need to chase our desires and dreams in an ongoing and consistent fashion, and find what works for us, so that holidays are one day, one hope of a pleasant decorated dinner or gathering, and not the end all of perfection.

> "When we expect any one day or event to fulfill us and create magic, we are discounting the value of every other day we live."

As we raise the worth of each moment we live, and the promise of every single sunrise or sunset, we will not be wasting time looking forward to whatever we think will make it all right. If you need a rest, take one. Whatever you think all these specific days will bring into your life, that is what you need to consciously create on a regular basis. Do not lose this present by waiting until something changes for you to celebrate, rejoice, or relax.

Though holidays are meant to be special, you can allow more peace in them while taking a step back along with several deep breaths and making sure you are noticing and enjoying the day in your own little ways as it passes. Make sure to do whatever has meaning for you in your private space or with those you love. Take moments throughout the special day with your thoughts to make certain you are creating and receiving what you most need. If you need space at a gathering, visit the bathroom for a few minutes, breathe, and count five blessings. Enjoy where you are, and what you are doing, but glance at tomorrow with hope and also gratitude for what this day brought to the rest of your life.

By looking for something special in every day, we will create spaces in which to enjoy our holidays with more depth. If we cannot find a special moment, we can make one, and consecrate our being alive and well in daily rituals of gratitude and splendor. Use your good china if you like to look at it, cook wonderful meals for yourself and any person who wants to eat with you. Decorate with pleasing colors and exciting seasonal beauties every month if you like.

Find magical experiences in this day right now so your mind learns to see them more frequently in unassuming places. Take in the surroundings of your outdoors to relish in, and pause the present time to feel the moment. Smile, and allow the day and season to pass as it will. Be a part of life as it moves without condition to your wellbeing. Appreciate your increased flow and ability to watch for sacredness. Breathe as you experience love in this day, and know it is a measurable step.

Make changes now, little by little, and fill up your wellspring as you require. No day, no person, and no event can provide everything you think you need. Create a safety net. Find what you are searching for by doing it, every day you can, and live that. Hinging any contentment or joy on decorations, gifts, gatherings, and dates is a dangerous and unfulfilling way to serve our highest potential.

Every day is a holiday if we know what to look for and how to approach it. Everything we are a part of is important and should be treated as such so that we do not feel imbalanced or in need of some change that will allow us to be happy. Do not put off seeing those you love. Do not wait to acknowledge the specialness someone brings to your own meaning until the arrival of a society-ordained "special day." Live in splendor every minute, by gratitude.

"Spend our days the way we want our lives spent."

We can impart value more often, more consistently, and spend our days the way we want our lives spent. We are worth exceptional acts in our daily round, and living that way reminds us to keep to the path of unconditional love. When we instill this significance into every day, then not only will the rest of the year feel more sacred, but we will be relieved with the coming and going of holidays as we no longer need to hang our hearts upon their effects.

MEDITATION: CELEBRATE EVERY DAY

- Close your eyes, breathe, and know this time is important for you.

- Choose one way you could make today feel more special, perhaps by connecting with someone you love, setting pretty place settings when you eat, lighting candles to create nurturing ambiance, moving furniture, or changing decorations to bring a feeling of freshness.

- During busy holidays take several quiet moments alone, ponder, and be grateful.
- Commit to do this one thing to make today special.
- Well up unconditional love within you. Let it overflow your heart into the rest of your body.
- Keep that feeling with you as long as you can.

CHAPTER TWENTY-ONE

Distractions

Distractions of varying degrees and personas fill our lives. We can seek out distraction when we are under enormous stress to find relief. We can welcome distraction when we are stuck in mountains of grief or despair to calm and soothe our wounds. We can sometimes utilize distraction as a way to quiet an obsessed addiction, or to ease the mind when it has grabbed an emotion like a pit-bull, unwilling to let go.

Distractions are helpful when we are overwhelmed or immobilized. And while distractions in all of these cases are therapeutic for a time, it is when we live our lives within distraction's chaos or employ it constantly with unconsciousness that we are abusing its benefits and distorting its usefulness. Don't let anything distract you from keeping unconditional love.

MODERN-DAY DISTRACTIONS

When we live amid obstructions on a consistent basis, we are living inside of distraction as a shield from truth, reality, and discovery. We create diversions so we do not have to look at our lives, our selves, or our higher purposes. Our inner workings are sometimes hard to look at. Escape seems easier. Who could expect us to be meditating when we are so very busy that we cannot prioritize twelve minutes for inner searching? Who can blame us for unsolved personal issues when every minute of every day is taken by outside activities or obligations?

Might we line these up in our favor to cope, unconsciously? When we are running around incessantly quieting the wants, who even realizes there is another way? In that state no one can focus on bringing peace, knowing awareness, or the great promise of presence.

Subconsciously or not, our continued life of busyness enables us to avoid those dark and questionable places within ourselves. Whether or not we are aware of our distractions— and how much time they take—they are usually just excuses. If you want to change, how can you not find time to meditate? It may take some sincere honesty to look at the role we have all secretly yet willingly allowed distractions to play within our lives. It may take the strength of inner seeing and transparency before we understand what our daily turning to drugs, alcohol, or work might really mean we are running away from. Distractions may be unconscious, but their effects remain harmful.

We run to the office or obsess over work to escape the home front. We smoke or drink so we do not have to feel the turmoil of what is seething beneath the surface. We eat because we are "bored." We turn on the television to avoid relationships or the communication that can become painful because it stands ignored and unresolved week after week. We hide from abuse. We lose time and focus innocently, but we lose it nonetheless.

We create all this stuff, leaving no space in which to reconcile from a place of quiet and peace. We fill and fill our lives until we no longer know or, even worse, desire solitude. We are now spending even more moments of our days with gadgets that disallow the capacity for us to talk with one another while holding eye contact or actively listening. Many children and adults have so much going on that they are far away from the ways of "the good old days." Some would never be able to recognize what they need, even if it was right in front of them on the screen of the latest electronic device.

SLOWER-PACED PAST

And what of the good old days, we might ask? What is so great about a time when there was little indoor plumbing, no extra freezers full of food in the garage or basement, and even a car or garage was rare? When we get past the survival issues folks had to contend with and we add the growing light and lust for spirituality of today, we get an idea of a world that was much more beautiful, real, and whole than present day reality allows with constantly mounting global distractions.

The slower pace was apt to our capacity as humans. It allowed more time to contemplate love. People knew each other then. They knew themselves, and they knew their neighbors. Entire towns combined their efforts and provisions to raise barns or add rooms upon news of a coming addition to a family. People baked pies for those who lived near them, and they shared afternoon tea as they spoke of all the goings-on within their close-knit communities.

Television did not reign supreme in the family room—or every room—to keep intimacies at bay. There were no video games or fixating trinkets to numb the minds of children and kill millions of brain cells while teaching players to completely ignore their physical surroundings and sit for hours on end. There was no constant access to correspondence or need to know what people were doing each minute of the day. One could not be found without reaching out.

There were, however, lots of books, conversations, and quiet—actual quiet time alone in which to contemplate, listen, connect, and learn. The values of peoples' lives were placed on matters of importance instead of on fashion, appearance, status, or gluttony. People worked hard and enjoyed their families and children—all they had earned, they cherished.

No one had to get busier making enough money to satisfy more requirements. The never-ending wants and gimmies have inadvertently passed on to posterity. Family units were close, and friends on your own street were aplenty. Everyone shared in the misfortune or celebration of all who were near because they were bound together by circumstances, knew those circumstances of others, and came to care for all concerned. They were not distracted from empathy. This was actually a beautiful life. Gratitude was prevalent, and people were intimately connected. It had to be all for one and one for all—this is how to keep love prevalent.

REMOVING MY DISTRACTIONS

We have steadily moved our family west over the last twenty years, from the city toward our beloved mountains, then bigger, further mountains and more sparsely populated areas. We have found, through specific searching, more natural environments in which to find ourselves, as well as the beauty and pace of the life for which we longed. Over the years of moving and not having much close at hand, we weaned ourselves from convenience store trips when feeling the urge. We learned to prepare for grocery trips and make do with what we had, but it was not always easy. Nearly an hour round trip just for milk took some getting used to.

At one point we did have a coffee shop fifteen minutes away, but with so few in the community, it did not make it for long, despite our best efforts. From three minutes walking for yummy treats to a thirty-five-minute walk just to our mailbox and back, our lives, by choice, drastically changed. No one really had any idea the extremes we went through for what others considered normal or took for granted. It was our willing choice, but the point is how the pace of our living has changed, and what glory has come with it.

I remember when we first moved to our St. Mary's glacier mountainous location; it was so desperately quiet, even compared to our previous mountain residence, that the silence was truly deafening. The darkness outside was so dark my husband would not go out far, and the eleven-thousand-foot altitude gave us headaches and fatigue for the first month. Of course, these minor adjustments were small compared to the coming winter—it surprised us much like the advent of parenting; something no one could prepare you for if they tried.

What we afforded ourselves in this slower, more peaceful environment was the ability to eliminate distractions, and discover unknown secrets. We drove further to everything but unearthed many mysteries of life simply because there was not much else to keep us company way up there. We were not bothered by the hustle and bustle of others around us, and outside noise no longer interfered with our thoughts. This continues to be the case at our current mountain residence.

It was somewhat shocking at first to be left to our own devices in such a severe climate, but it has become a glorious tranquility, a path nowhere else found. We appreciate the simple things like reading before a fire or gathering for a meal, and we know ourselves deeper than most can imagine. Our children choose to play with trees, sticks, rivers, and mud, much like I did as a youngster in poverty. This gives them appreciation for nature, as well as for toys. We have only three or four channels of television depending on the wind or snow; we have no satellite or cable, fast Internet, or other such fancy distractions. It is truly liberating. We choose where we spend our time and are not obligated by our possessions.

Our entire life is beautiful, albeit difficult in winter. We have changed our priorities, and learned with discernment, sometimes by force, what we can live without. While we cherish electricity and public sewer systems, we have been without amenities many times each year due to weather, and we have found gratitude for things otherwise disregarded.

We are by no means simpletons and could live more like naturalists than we do, but because of all this "volunteered simplicity," we have come to adore life, the pleasures of love, and the unbidden which grows up all around us. We have limited distractions in our sacred home and forest and have created the space in which to search the songs of our hearts.

LIFE OF FOCUS

I have a friend who moved from her busy life as an accountant for a law firm in Denver to the sticks on the other side of the state—the side no one hears from. She is now in a small town, a rural environment, and a state of mental confusion. While there is always something to do, there is not much going on after the sidewalk rolls up at dinner time. Those things to do differ greatly from nightclubs, noise, and life familiar on city blocks. For the first time in a very long time, she is surrounded by people who all know everyone, or by no people at all.

As she shares in our spiritual passions and meditates at our church when she returns for visits, she is discombobulated by both her newfound peace and open space, and by the disturbance it has brought in its aloneness. She suddenly realized she had much to figure out, and she had no choice but to do that in her limiting yet enabling freedom. She thought she knew herself, but we are all different when isolated. She had been focused on energy healing and inner sight but was shocked at what this new pace brought to surface. Wisely and profoundly, she looked in the mirror of realization at how many distractions she had unknowingly been living. What a gift!

You too can create a new life focused on your soul's desires. Sit in the cool, dark quietude of your environment, assuming you have created such a place, and search your soul for the answers—or for your reluctance in answering the following questions.

What are you hiding from? Why are you running in this direction, and why so fast? Can you stop? Can you remember the last time you walked with Spirit in each assured step instead of living unwittingly? Why do you say you want something yet act against it? Do you know what you want, and are you truly deciding every day to go toward it? Are you afraid of what you will discover about yourself or the world if you sit in clarity, in stillness, or completely within silence? Do you need to always be moving or doing in order to feel productive, and does that mean you haven't a second to catch your breath and take a good look at yourself?

Is your life honest—does it feel good? Do you know your inner longings? Do you even want to know yourself? Is there a single moment in which you have consciously given or received unconditional love? If you sit still, what will happen to you? If you look discerningly at yourself, your environment, your relationships, what will you see? What will you realize about your life if you begin to meditate or talk with God or the trees?

If you truly rely on your inner fortitude, and you recognize your greatest potential, are you frightened by your own strength and power? Does anyone know you? Do you give to yourself? What is really important? Where do you want your sacred heart energy to go, or to what would you like your life to amount? How much of your life is consumed by distractions, and do you even know or care? Ask yourself questions to unveil truths. Write down answers and consider.

With only some effort we can all turn away from what media insists is important, and we can turn within, as did our ancestors who had only time and faith. They fought generations ago for our freedom, their posterity, and it was not so we could have phones, video games, or compacted schedules. It was for the purpose of having enough of our survival needs met that we could instead focus on living in liberty and pursuing happiness. They fought for our ability to keep our focus on love.

Can you imagine our ancestors believing that in a time not so distant, people's lives would be so easy they would not get enough exercise for their bodies only by their means of survival, and would instead have to buy equipment to stay fit? Take progress for its gifts of longevity and time, but do not let the goings-on distract you from living love, simply. Use the extra time our society has now created for the higher good of introspection and love.

When we are focused instead of distracted, we can answer all our questions, and learn what will keep us fulfilled. We can follow our hidden yet compelling desires for clean and quiet air as well as time and space in natural surroundings. We can receive what our spirits yearn for, and we can live through unconditional love because there will be no greater opportunity near us.

No longer will things keep us from self-discovery, self-love, or self-healing. We can utilize distractions when we need a break or change of pace, but don't need them in order to feel fulfilled. We have no excuse to shorten our gifts of knowledge or decrease our potentials for serenity and centering. Created all around us, we can become responsible and aware of the supreme power of our focus, attentiveness, and capacity to live the conscious lives our ancestors lived, with greater gifts and ease.

MEDITATION: ELIMINATING DISTRACTIONS

- Set your space, and focus on one body part you feel needs healing.
- In your mind's eye send healing light to that area, and breathe it in with your breath.
- If anything passes into your awareness, put it in a bubble, take it out, and explode it.
- Get lost in your breath. Do this for every thought that is not healing light in your body, with your breath.
- When you feel some sense of relief, think about a life goal you wish to achieve. If several come to mind, see which one keeps your attention the longest.
- Think about that goal. If a stray thought comes to distract you from visualizing that goal, put it in a bubble, take it out, and explode it.
- Choose two things (or more) that have kept you from making this dream come true.
- Release them down your grounding cord.
- Bring in light to fill the empty space.
- Consider two practical steps toward your goal.
- Hold your visions in your mind with light, release distractions, and act.

CHAPTER TWENTY-TWO

Loss

We all have times in our lives when things seem to be falling apart. During circumstances of extreme stress, things repeatedly going awry, emotional or financial tension, or relationship difficulties, a common underlying theme is loss. Loss impales our lives in various ways—injury, failure, grief, death, or defeat—and to varying degrees. An announcement of a terminal illness in the family or among friends activates these feelings of being trounced upon even before the bereaving occurs. Losing friends, jobs, connections, dreams, a beloved home, or special place—all these and so much more constitute loss. And it is no one's judgment but our own as to exactly what counts as a loss for us, or how deeply it is felt for how long.

In experiencing loss we can all be bound by the familiarities we share, and this shared experience will cultivate unconditional love in you for other humans. Loss can bring us together with others, deeper toward our highest priorities, and closer to the understanding and knowledge of unconditional love, because we have all experienced both loss and love. We share pain, the need for healing, and the new wholeness that will inevitably come.

THE SCOPE OF LOSS

My father, a wise psychotherapist, acknowledges that ninety percent of his clients seek his help after suffering a loss. This singular subject is the most common theme in human pain and suffering. The scope of loss is vast and individual. We can lose possessions, recognition, privacy, ambition, creativity, or our edge. We can lose control, understanding, our position, authority, and our sense of self. We can lose a loved one, our hopes, dreams, foundation, trust, companionship, or relationships of all kinds. We can lose our familiarity, our ability for movement, our reputation, health, comfort, sleep, money, support, means, opportunity, our dwellings, or space, faith, justice, freedom, ease, or even humor.

We can lose through theft, illness, competition, indecision, death, attrition, fatigue, and misunderstanding. The specific process of losing matters little compared to its effects. To that which anyone places importance or value, we can feel sorrow and endure anguish when it disappears. We humans fear change, and this is just human nature.

Any loss is terrible. An endless barrage of losses can leave us with little ability to cope. "When it rains, it pours" seems to be the common thread of this growth cycle of turbulence. It does not help to hear, "It's always darkest before the dawn."

When we are caught up in grieving for one aspect of our lives, or someone we loved and miss tremendously, and something else occurs with negative effects, our circumstances feel unbearable. It does not serve us to look at the Universe with punishing eyes or to wonder what we did to deserve this. As we've all witnessed and likely experienced, bad things happen to good people. Eventually, we realize that we do not yet know the gift within the opportunity; which sounds trite, but, as they say, we cannot always see the forest through the trees.

MY EXPERIENCE WITH LOSSES

How can we understand what is happening in our lives until we have hindsight? How do we heal if we find no space in which we are left alone from the evils of the world? We wonder if we are reaping old karma. We wonder why bad things keep happening. When we have been trying to be good—vibrating to the positive energies we want to attract, volunteering, working hard, and so much more—it does not seem fair.

When significant loss reared its very ugly head in our lives, I wished to hell I had those answers. I had been meditating and delving within to get centered so I could seek solutions and understanding. I found little solace. We were on our eleventh trauma in eight weeks . . . and, I feared, counting. It was hard not to collapse into pessimism, or even just pull the covers over my head and become immobilized as I cried, swirling in a tornado of despair.

The only thing I discovered was that the answers were not the answer. I may not have been privy to the whys and hows of all the horrible incidents happening to us and those we love. I do know that I perceived them as horrible, although that perception may not have been shared by the Universes or another more enlightened. The main thing I realized was to shift my attention from the reasons, or the punishment and deserving, and begin to look elsewhere for my peace, because surely it was not there in front of me—or at least I could not see it.

I went back to gratitude, appreciating the one fact that I felt better than I did the day before and that both my children were healthy. Lots of hugs and cuddling were going around in our little family of four, and that helped as well. I tried to focus on simple routines of balancing the checkbook or cleaning up the kitchen, but everything I handled seemed touched by our calamities, so even the simple was difficult and full of emotion.

Each situation provoked fear and worry as present concerns absorbed me. I needed to have a healthy distraction, a warm bath, if even for just a moment, to see that life continued around us. It insulted my sensitivities that life kept moving all over the world while my Beloved Paul was in the hospital, my father-in-law was losing his fight with cancer, and our power, water, and sewer stopped working at the very moment we took them for granted. So much for the warm bath to rejuvenate even my flesh. How could the world continue spinning when my life was going through all of this?

It had been a bad two months if ever I had experienced them. And because the first incident was the loss of my sweet best doggie friend, I felt even more alone in my heartache and devastation. Without him as a constant and joyful reminder of the present, I more easily lost myself in my traumatic perceptions. I missed his love, cuddling, and companionship. I felt alone, though I know I was not—in theory.

I began to worry that as my shoulders drooped and I could not stop crying, perhaps I was attracting more of this into my life because that was where I was vibrating. Suddenly the pressure to feel good frightened me because I just could not figure out how. I needed to stop swirling in my own juices and suffering over my suffering. I realized millions of others faced such hardships, or worse, with far more grace than I could seem to muster. Such thoughts only added to my sobbing and guilt. I sensed this devastation would last forever because perhaps I deserved it. I was ready to abandon ship, throw in the towel, run away, give up, and so many other cliché statements. *STOP!*

SURVIVING LOSS

None of this will help. It is not the day we quit. It is not the straw that breaks us. Without the big answers and a visit from God or the angels (which we could also implore), we must turn to what we can know and reach. We know that calling a good friend will help. They may have wonderful insights and sacred memories for our re-focus. They might help us laugh, if even for an instant, and they sure as heck can open our perspective beyond our frail manipulations. We know to pamper ourselves and take it easy, if we can create the space for such, and we try to make sure we arrange things so we actually will. We can pick up a good book or ten, and see what ancient sages have to say to assist our dark loneliness. We can go for a hike in nature or sit by a fire. We should breathe fresh air and take a nap. And we need to know that it is all right to cry.

"This too shall pass," Paul Hamilton Hayes assures us, and he is right. Even the worst times will transform eventually. Hold onto one hopeful thought; the sun will rise again. It may not be better today or this week, but utilizing our support system—or realizing we need to find or create one—will bring a semblance of comfort.

Hard days come for all of us, and it is okay to acknowledge that it stinks. Be honest with yourself and allow the time for pain to penetrate and be felt, so it can be seen and willingly moved. Neglecting or denying terribleness will only bind it to us. Try to flow with the goodness of the Universe, because it is still there. Rely on Divine connection because it will be close, even if you have lost some of your senses to notice it.

There are no huge answers, but all professionals will tell you going through this is common, and it cannot last forever. Grieve and wallow and allow yourself the space to sit with what is happening around and within you. No one can tell you when it will be time to get up and go again, but you will know when the wing of an angel brushes your soul and whispers words of encouragement. Little by little you will find things that make you smile and restore your faith.

We all lose people or pets that we love dearly. We all have things in our lives that come undone. We all feel alone at some moment in our relationships. If nothing else, see that you are not alone. Take care of yourself and your beloveds as best you can, and permit some grieving, tears, naps, and contemplation. Without answers, we can continue to ask questions, and wait. If we can find and express more questions, the Universe will eventually provide more answers. This is our breath, for the heavens want us to breathe and take time to look around.

PERMANENT LOSS

Some of us take for granted familiar people, their voices, their routines, and the unfolding of the expected hours of day-to-day life. We go along unaware of what could be around the corner. Suddenly, one of the familiar voices is taken away, and everything is difficult and different. My dear father-in-law Richard passed away only months after his diagnosis with cancer, and the ramifications felt earth-shattering, especially to his two innocent granddaughters.

It all happened so fast we had no idea what was hitting us. Today it seems like an instant ago, or a hundred years ago—we cannot discern. Time cheats us, and we spin trying to grasp anything we can believe in or hold onto. We look for solace when all we can really do is wait for the wound to heal, slowly, if ever.

Though death is a shock, it is not shocking in the way it awakens us. It often seems like a bad dream we rise from with groggy eyes and fuzzy vision. Perhaps daily events are not immediately changed because we are used to the loved one's absence in some temporary form—a business trip, inconsistent communicate due to distance, or any number of reasons. It is when we realize they are not coming back; they are not gone temporarily, that we begin to miss the most simple of actions and connections. It will never be the same as it was, and those feelings and memories will begin to fade as we move forward, as required by the ticking of time. It is insulting to recognize the world continuing, and not seeing us or our pain.

The force and speed with which life has to go on is insidious to our grief. We wish to stand still and feel the moment before life was changed. We long for one real minute of how it all was just a few days or weeks ago, but we cannot get it back. The world does not care that we cannot put feet forward today, or that our entire life has just been turned upside down and will not come back together as it was. We can spend only small afternoons of sadness remembering, crying, and aching to our very depths. When we look up again, the world has pushed on.

Life cannot be abandoned for long because we all have so much to do. We have a few days off from work if we lose a "close" relative in which to orchestrate funeral plans, finances, people to call—not to mention the physical constraints of eating, washing clothes, and taking care of the children. So wrong is our society that preaches the sooner we can forget the pain and forget the person the better off we are. It is reprehensible to our souls, the sense that we too will be left behind if we don't wipe away the confusion, forget what we have lost, and simply make a new way in the world. Little time sits at our feet for us to stare and hurt and mourn. In our grief we cannot even remember how to breathe, let alone function.

Every action we perform is different now, appallingly so, and it appears that no one understands this. It is new, all new, and there are no templates left to get us through the most menial of tasks. We must learn how to live again, even though each step is changed. No one around us and no one in the world notices that we need more time and space than is allowed.

When the smallest incident sets us off, we apologize for the show of emotions unwelcome in sensible circles. We have not gotten through what we are told we were supposed to have gotten through, and we are not "over" anything at all. So we stumble around as if in fog, bumping into the world at large, and we never really receive or find the healing we so desperately require.

How can this happen to thousands of people every day, and not one person has figured out a better way or a satisfying answer? It feels like it happens only to us, and it often does because those we lean on have their own duties and obligations that congest their time. People may offer help or a shoulder, but few can come through in the ways that are needed, and it is a lot to ask for in such a weakened position of fear and bewilderment. We may already feel guilty for the help we have asked for and the time we have taken.

As we slowly move forward and try not to look back because we are already behind in work and life, guilt arises because the soul that was lost to us, even with spiritual perspective, seems an unreachable distance, and an inconvenient rawness. How much time can we spend talking about this loved one who has passed on when there are other, more pressing issues facing us directly? What time is wasted in remembering who they were? Society has little forgiveness for such unproductivity. And then we too will be gone, as will all those we still have today, and all will be for naught—this love, these labors.

Eventually you find other distractions or people to fill up your time, although not fully, and you are prompted by the relief of others to appear "better." Everyone wants you to be fixed, and most are uncomfortable around your sadness because they do not know how to heal it, not that you ever expected them to. It is easiest to step out of your surreal state in order to assume your expected life positions of responsibility and joviality, even if you cannot remember how. It is insulting to your memories to forget what or whom you have lost, but it is impractical to keep remembering, and life is very practical, even if death is not.

It becomes rare to even cry because we may feel we have no right as time increases the distance from the event itself, or because we are afraid we may be unable to stop if we allow ourselves to start. Pain is pushed around and hidden in order to cope or function. As an energy healer I can see why so many humans have so many levels of unresolved issues and torments carried within their soul layers.

LOVE AND LOSS

I wonder if those in heaven feel betrayed at our eagerness to move forward and are disconnected by our forced, for-our-own-good detachment. Perhaps they know and understand with the light as their guide, and they actually intercede on our behalf with approval and encouragement of letting go and moving on. Not forgotten, but unbearable in constant remembering—some thanks for the entirety of a life.

Perhaps if we anchor a quiet part of our life and our hearts, we can keep the love; little else stabilizes us during this thing we call life. Does it all come down to the love we gave and received? A large percentage of all the other stuff amounts to nothing when you stand looking at a grave stone. We can recall a million situations, emotions, and conversations, but besides pictures and heartache, we only have their love to take with us where we go and, if we are lucky, a memento. It feels as if that isn't nearly enough.

The more distance we achieve, the greater will be the

realizations of love's worth, I hope, for today it still hurts all over. Although I can speak with my father-in-law's spirit and see him sitting next to his granddaughters in light, it is all changed, and I am not sure why God thinks it is for the better. Gratitude for those I do share with even now allows for some measure of comfort, but loss cannot all be for gratitude, learning, and love—can it? It does not seem enough.

Acceptance of a life changed, whatever that change may be, forces us to abandon the way things were, in every fashion. We are resigned to acceptance of uprooting, because to hold on is fruitless and ineffective. Letting go of all we knew, except love, is no small assignment.

> "Acknowledgment grows as we recognize the cycles of living and dying."

Acknowledgment grows as we recognize the cycles of living and dying. We try to assure ourselves that everything is in Divine timing, although we may fight it with the weapon of our horrifying feelings of present. We remember that with faith and perspective, we are exactly where we need to be at this very moment, and that when we experience discomfort we know information is right in front of us. But these lessons are of little use when this catastrophe was so intangible to our own cause and effect—a force of nature out of our control. That we feel powerless, for an indescribable reason, makes it appear more unfair.

Keeping love in loss takes reminders of how love feels when we suffer loss. In searching for any sort of relief from the anguish of death we look in every place available and are sometimes surprised by the source of support. I will take any I can get this moment. With all my questions, few answers, and shared agony within our family, we fall on the couch and surf channels in hopes of, at the very least, distraction. Who would have thought my heart healed for one given second with television caressing us as *Blood Diamond* came on, and the one sentence we hear is "A moment of love can give meaning to a life." And so it is.

PART FOUR

Sharing a Life of Love Daily

"Love your humanity as well as your Divinity. What you experience in your daily life—the challenges, feelings, and relationships—are the very things you came to learn from."

— Sanaya Roman;
Spiritual Growth: Being your Higher Self

The more you feel unconditional love, the more you can share it. The more you live a life of unconditional love every day, the more you are sharing it everywhere you go, following every thought you have. Part Four entails daily tools to heal our heart space and to learn love and living well. It guides us in experiencing our dreams every day we choose. It offers helpful implements to handle the growth periods that complement the times we have stirred up energies by creating our wanted changes. These processes and insights will assist us in moving toward our heart paths, while giving us gifts of internal focus and calm to keep our passages balanced.

We are often enlivening our journeys and quickening things all around us to an overwhelming state precisely because we are learning and experiencing so much and are growing so rapidly. This section leads the way to accomplishing our desires and development with consistency and progress through simple, manageable, daily intention.

The following chapters shine on many facets of human life, and each are important in their own strand of examination and unconditional love. These approaches will aid us in measuring growth and soothing the ruffled feathers incurred from our manifesting, powerful life energies. When we take each day's situations and imbue them with unconditional love and sharing, we can live with more ease, assurance, and grace no matter what envelopes our path to the light. All of this will help us on our way to creating and living the lives we have imagined. We *can* have it all, starting with unconditional love!

CHAPTER TWENTY-THREE

Patience or Discipline

I turned on the television the other day to catch an enlightening conversation between David Letterman and Oprah Winfrey. He is hilarious, and I adored his weekly segment, "Will it Float?" with juicy anticipation, but who besides Divinity would have thought that his observations on the compelling dynamics of child rearing would engage me so thought-provokingly as to further stimulate the study of polarities on this path we travel?

When describing his biggest dilemma in raising and guiding his son, Letterman brought up the eternal feelings of uncertainty in knowing whether to implement patience or discipline. I found this tantalizingly brilliant as I was writing about the daily habits we aspire to in reaching and sharing our dreams. His astute assessment substantiates the veracity of applying either discipline or patience in attainment of our endeavors.

The answer, which he knew and we know, is to employ both patience and discipline, but as with many areas of life, it is the degree and timing, and not the behavior, that can be the most perplexing. In our relationships, as well as our goals, we may wonder if we're doing enough, applying the correct amount of pressure, or pushing too far. When we truly know ourselves, we can move forward through conscious recognition of when exercising patience or discipline is most appropriate.

KNOW YOURSELF

There is a peaceful quality in being honest with yourself and your trials. You can establish a balanced approach in being true to your destinies and best efforts. When we know ourselves and ignore the outside voices or demands on our energy, we are able to ascertain our needs more clearly. We realize that we have been working diligently, and as other necessities of life creep in, we are wise in our understanding and allowing for time off to read, rejuvenate, and refresh our internal wellspring. We permit pride in our momentum and growth as we realize with astonishment just how far we have come. We know we are advancing in our development because we feel peaceful more often. We return love to any whom enter our space, sharing what we have gained. We feel energized as we find many reasons to get out of bed each morning.

If we are not sustaining this wonder and awe at our lives, we may need to instill new measures to affirm our path. Are we working for the wrong things, or continuing a particular course with old, outworn concepts? Are we giving into the resistance that often accompanies newness and the stretching of our limits? Do we need to persist with loving or believing in ourselves before we can consent to better changes or joyous growth?

Be a little more light and understanding toward yourself, the patterns you are releasing, and the spaces you yearn to inhabit. Note the opposites at work in your life—seasons of dedication and seasons of lassitude, times of optimism and times of pessimism. These cycles will continue throughout your life, and you can progress through them. You can find pleasure in a newfound patience by acknowledging divine timing, gently breathing yet persisting through strange or strong growth phases, and by serenely awaiting the gravity of new perceptions to set in and to set you free with unconditional love.

TOO MUCH OR TOO LITTLE?

So have you done your best today? Have you tried everything you can, or are you letting yourself off the hook by believing your lazy side, which insists that you can and should do no more? Are you actively pursuing your calling and giving might to bettering your world? Are you following your intuition, listening to guidance, and loving others at every opportunity presented? Do you feel joyful and present as you notice the beauty around you? Are you feeling grateful for your many fruits and recognizing Divinity in everyone and everything?

Or have you foregone a chance to trust your path and hope providence will lead you better tomorrow? Was an opportunity to give to another missed today because you are barely getting by with your own loads and burdens? Did you miss a chance to work joyfully on your passion because you are too tired from yesterday's wistful grasps not being completely reached? Have you let today pass with a whimper because your past is catching up to you, your head is stuck in a sorrowful time, the house is not clean, you are not sleeping well, or you regret the road you have or have not taken?

Have you dropped your head today after realizing you did not shower affection on your little ones as you had to instead pay the bills or care for a sick pet? Have you gone through your work day with stress because things are piling up as you feel like falling down?

After looking deeply into what love has done and can do for us, and after we have searched our depths with changing perspective and introspection, we now need practical tools for catching our days. This means clear steps to seize the opportunity of every day with love. A big clue is the activation of opposites. If we keep trying and unveiling new methods to help, seek, and discover, then we probably deserve a well-won break from perfection. If, on the other hand, we are couch potatoes in our efforts and approaches, protesting that we are doing everything possible, then we may be excusing or justifying our way into unsettling standstills while bewildered at our lack of progress or movement.

A BALANCE OF OPPOSITES

It is important to be excited about our growth, but also to balance it with understanding and compassion turned inward. In monumental times of flux we need to be gentle with ourselves. We need to balance growth with integration. Do not fold up if you are in a quieter processing time. Relinquish fears if you have yet to begin following your heart. Spirit knows patience is deserved and important to your overall blossoming to breathe before running again. We need action and observation, hope and relief. We all know our bodies need rest after aggressive movement, and we must allow for our lives and minds to replenish as well.

Gain momentum in your dreams with loving discipline, acting consistently, and allowing for respite and quietude. Do not place so much significance on any lull that you collapse yourself into feeling you will remain there forever. Change is constant, and you can rely on everything passing with time. Use daily routines of conscious choice toward your goals, with a lot of self-love, positivity, and flexibility about where you are, how fast things are moving, and what you are learning through your new dynamic experiences.

Keep close to your heart the sacred wisdom that our journey toward unconditional love *is* what heals us, keeps us safe, and lifts us above uncertainty. It bestows upon us Divinity itself. It *is* the essence for which we longingly search. We come to know through this journey that everything really is about love.

Be encouraged by Sarah Ban Breathnach's insights in *Simple Abundance: A Daybook of Comfort and Joy*, a book I read daily. This passage was written just for us, in the inexplicable nature of our search for love in its splendor: "Love will sustain you when passion's path takes unexpected twists and turns. Love will dissolve your fears by creating opportunities you couldn't have imagined before you began the search to discover and recover your authentic self. And when doubt, despair, and denial threaten to dismantle your dreams, love will rear up in your defense."

She goes on soothing with this reassuring vision: "The next time you feel frightened or fragile, stand very still. If you do, you might feel the tip of an angel's wing brush against your shoulder."

Employ all tools in your arsenal to contact your dreams daily. When you know you could do more, do more. If you have been pushing relentlessly, allow a break. Try new ways of sharing the love you are creating. And when you question the speed of your achievements, feel that love inside and ask for a message. You will receive an answer—notice it.

MEDITATION: SELF-ASSESSMENT

- Close your eyes and breathe calmly for several minutes.
- Think of what life area you would like information on.
- Ask to see a picture of yourself in this circumstance.

- Are you still or moving? Is the picture vivid or bleak?
- Put up a gauge for your effort, and simply believe the number it shows.
- Ask if the message is to do more, or to be patient, etc.
- Fill your heart with love from God/Goddess/Source, and sit with it as long as you can.
- Follow the message, and another will come.

CHAPTER TWENTY-FOUR

Positivity

O ur thoughts fill our mind, our mind creates our feelings, our feelings compel us toward actions, and our actions manifest our life. True optimism actually changes the energy around us. It raises our vibration, lights our aura, and softens our energy field. With lasting and instantaneous affects, it lengthens and improves our life and the lives of everyone around us. The imprint of optimism leaves positive energy on the signature of the Universe. Positivity changes our lives from the inside out.

How does one become an optimist? Is it pre-destined that we are either optimistic or pessimistic? Can it be understood, transformed, or changed at its most fundamental source, and if so, how? Though I have my moments of hope and faith, even pure delight and ecstasy, in my far-away dark recesses, I sometimes feel imminent doom, depression, and doubt. I cannot share love this way. Positivity is an experience I know I have not mastered (due to my husband's groans about my grumps), but I endeavor to love my lower feelings and myself while in them.

Can we be reconditioned? Is it nature, nurture, self-talk, chemistry? Is it final and complete? Can we pretend until we become changed and lighter? Can we turn into positive believers for a time or even forever? Can a pessimist like me ever find the answers and learn a more contented approach to life? The answer is yes. As we share positivity with the world, we are actually sharing unconditional love.

POSITIVITY QUESTIONED

Sunshine, Pollyanna, optimists . . . blech! I am not so much a pessimist as a worrier, although I have had to argue for this upgrade. Though I have great moments of joy and wonder, I am usually referred to by my husband as a cynic. I have intense foresight about what can possibly go wrong or interrupt the best-laid plans. I can imagine conflict in situations that have not come to pass, and I can play through numerous ends of circumstances not yet in existence. This is not the love we want to be sharing.

I pride myself on my forethought and my brain, which is constantly moving and figuring out everything for everyone all of the time. I tell myself this is a gift. I keep the planet held up and spinning for everyone in my sphere, and some outside—an arduous, self-induced responsibility which stems more from necessity and duty to help than from arrogance of fooling myself that I am actually doing it well. However, I have come to realize that these feelings of holding up the planet are not healthy or fun and are usually of severe detriment to the faith and joy of anyone present to my incessant calculating.

Is it the way I was raised? Is planning for and expecting the worst intrinsic in my nature? Did I witness something long ago that turned my attitude toward negative possibilities and fears instead of hope and trust? What about my basic temperament finds it so easy to believe that the Universe is unfriendly? Is it that some of us had unstable childhoods or felt misunderstood as children? What is it within our nature or around our environment? What is it in our conditioning that inhibits unconditional faith and joyousness? If it is a matter of trust and perception, can it be changed, and if so, how?

Why some are struck with continuous flashes of positive reassurance while others obsessively ponder over that which could go wrong remains an enigma. I have wrestled with and studied this quality in my life, and I still wonder why there are such opposing ways to manage living. I have done a lot to come far, and I have clear tools with which I run at fears fully armed, but I do not have an ingrained sense that all is well. What is the great secret to optimism? Is it possible to be perpetually positive? Does negativity affect all of us some of the time, or just some of us all the time?

Why do some of us approach the new as if it were something to fear or be worried about instead of an opportunity for wonderful miracles to enter our lives? Why do we not see light for all our paths? What is it that turns us toward negative or fearful states of mind, and how do we learn to change it to innate trust and security? Where is our calm living within the moments of thoughts for the future, or our okayness that it all turns out right? I want to live that way, feel that way, but I sometimes live paralyzed in trepidation. I am plagued with questions more than given answers in this dilemma, but as I continue asking, and search through my confusion, I uncover answers through my experiences.

PRACTICE POSITIVITY

I know that we get what we think about—the Law of Attraction comes into play here as well. This is often more unsettling to those of us who worry, adding an additional layer of what could go wrong—not the effect we need. I have learned a lot about how to manifest positive desires instead of walking around unconsciously and being upset when life is not fulfilling. Although years of reading, taking classes, and going within for guidance has brought more light and faith into my life, sometimes I must fight for every positive belief I utter in defiance under my breath. The irony is not lost on me, for this is my flaw, which I strive tirelessly to transform.

Optimism is as natural to some people as drumming was to me. I had vast natural talent for my musical skill, and I worked hard at it to be sure, practicing more than four hours a day to satisfy my perfectionist tendencies. For some of my students who worked hard and practiced often, it never came easily. So I am humbled as I know I do not possess natural talent for optimism. But I also know I can work through my tools and follow advice from the masters until I put one foot in front of the other toward the goal of seeing a less terrible view of tomorrow's potential.

It is tedious, and it is work, but in hindsight, I can pat myself on the back because I have made progress. The fact that it does not come easy becomes another lesson in loving myself while experiencing all facets of life and emotion. We all have our special lessons of improvement through trial and tribulation rather than only omniscient, God-given abilities. What would be the fun in that?

If you share this difficult path with me, learn to be easy on yourself and to turn consistently to our tried-and-true realizations with loyalty. What we learn through the grit of persistence becomes our primary ally. It does not need to be painstaking as we simply allow our feelings of fear, then gently push past them with appreciated words on a page or thoughts lent by another until the fear is surpassed by hope penetrating our spirits for happier daily living.

In the movie *The Saint*, Val Kilmer asks Elizabeth Shue

how she has stayed so positive, and her answer is faith. Therefore, as we practice positivity, we can build on the faith, trust, and perceptions developed in chapters Ten and Eleven.

REMAIN PRESENT

We know that "time" is of the essence because when we remain present we can be less overwhelmed by the potential of harm. One way to keep to our present is by returning to our senses (a specific meditation in Chapter Thirteen). Avoiding undue worry or fear about the future is another way to stay present. When we stop the negative fear of our internal babbling and turn to positive words we actually want, receiving what we desire is more possible.

This leads us to affirmations, which are a great way to redirect our obsessive worry. They may begin as words, but if we say, write, and feel them, we not only end the cycle of doom and gloom, but also may begin to recondition our mind's ability for broader ideas of how things can unfold. I like to say prayers or mantras with visualization for extra feeling power. Employing this single function is responsible for most of my success in becoming positive.

"Everything you worry about will not come true."

Breathing is always a great way to come back to our bodies and what is happening in our day right before us, as well as to release. When we breathe deeply and pay attention to our breath, we can better instill peace and calm. When we feel overwhelmed by the pictures we have set into motion in our heads, we can use practical steps like breaking big objectives into smaller, more manageable steps while bringing our thoughts back to earth time and reality. We must remind ourselves to be real about our mind's ability for embellishment and fearful fantasies, and we must remember to compare such thoughts to actual or sensible functions. Everything you worry about will not come true, but wasting the day or moment on worry means it is gone forever.

UPBEAT SELF-TALK

While it is important to ask for help when we need it and to communicate feelings honestly, verbalizing constant negativity can have enormous impact on how we all go through the world. Try an experiment in noticing and monitoring the way in which you choose to interact verbally with your environment and those who share it. It is important to observe and create your language as well as your inner self-talk to contain the content of what you want in your life instead of its opposite. We share and create love through positivity.

While being open and forthright helps in our connections with others, we are not talking here of ceasing useful, positive communication. By choosing words from beauty, love, or spiritual tones of peace instead of anger, pain, or glorified drama, we can change our world, our relations to others, and the very energy within and around us. Share the good.

Realizing that our inner dialogue creates our thoughts and feelings, and then words and actions, we need to carefully own the power that sound adds to our thoughts as they become spoken words, sometimes floating out of our mouth when we least expect them. One of my favorites, Ralph Waldo Emerson, says this on the subject: "If you have not slept, or if you have slept, or if you have a headache, or sciatica, or leprosy, or thunder-struck, I beseech you, by all angels, to hold your peace, and not pollute the morning."

If you cannot consciously process feelings and worries

without poisoning the field around you—and it may be a new awareness for you to care about such things—do something to change this contamination. Do not complain aloud. Do not allow the negative thought or pointless fear to bind to you with words. By resisting the temptation to express this lower, slower vibration through speech, it more easily dissipates to be replaced with golden light and positivity. In this process, we more easily notice and expand love around us. We can even achieve verbal gratitude of the potential beauty of this moment. Do whatever it takes to stop yourself from becoming a negative verbal fountain.

It is healthy to listen and be aware of both positive and negative thoughts, but deny yourself the luxury to speak every incessant doom or gloom that comes into your mind. Do not add to the insanity of the world; it needs no more. Set the complainer free and center in your divine connection, neutrality, or heart space. Watch where you speak from and learn to take your words out of your emotional center to your higher self.

Before you utter words, see if they are neutral or charged, and then diffuse their charge by releasing, either through grounding, expelling consciously via journaling, beating pillows, or bathing. You create clarity this way. You will feel differently when you positively manage what you say, and those around you will thank you for it even if they do not specifically notice the reason they further enjoy your company. You will be beautifying the environment, and you will very simply be making the world a happier place. Do not be surprised if you are happier too; as we know, our words are magnetic.

If you need to speak the anxieties creeping into your gut throughout your day because you have not released or integrated them, do so privately or consciously. Warn your friend or partner that you will be spouting all the crap you can think of for the next five minutes. When you have finished, give thanks, and meditate for a better way.

It is important to regularly take the quiet time needed in order to sort out new ways of enhancing communications. And when you get better at this, be brave and try going through one entire day without verbalizing a single grump, gripe, groan, moan, whine, kvetch, mumble, grumble, ache, worry, or fear. You might be astonished at the amount of complaining that wants to come out, even while you pride yourself on being a growing, light, and loving person.

This experiment may not be easy because our society encourages articulating every thought, especially negative, and it has capitalized on people sharing and spreading them. We can have our feelings without spreading uncontrolled negativity. We need not buy their products or play their games; we will consciously choose to heal ourselves and the spaces we inhabit. Cheerfulness goes a long way toward enjoying the life we want. Pay attention to thoughts and the words they might turn into. Strive for positivity. Use your filters and look for cheery thoughts to express. Utilize the wisdom from Thumper, of *Bambi*, "If you can't say nuffin' nice, don't say nuffin' at all." With this mindfulness we can be anything, no matter what appears so bad it must be spoken.

The Sufis advise us to speak only after our words have managed to pass through three gates. At the first gate we ask ourselves, "Are these words true?" If so, we let them pass on; if not, back they go. At the second gate we ask, "Are they necessary?" At the last gate we ask, "Are they kind?"

MEDITATION: RELEASE NEGATIVE, FILL WITH POSITIVE

- Close your eyes and get into your space.

- Imagine a grounding cord from the bottom of your spine into the center of the earth.
- With an exhale, let all your negative thoughts or feelings drop down this open tunnel to be recycled.
- Picture a giant golden sun above your head.
- Write "positivity" on the inside of it, then fill it with positivity. Watch it fill.
- Bring the sun close and pop it. Feel it fill your body and space.

We can read and study all the books written on becoming an optimist, but what we feel as innate behaviors of positivity might still seem elusive. So we turn contemplatively inward for the broader remedy. Maybe the answer—the purpose of our search for the good—is simply unconditional love. If we are in a space of eternal, encompassing unconditional love, then positivity will find us in all moments, wherever we are. If we develop love as our central temperament, our core essence and fundamental feeling, then all positive feelings—peace, fulfillment, presence, connection, goodness, happiness, joy— fall beautifully into place. This is what we want to be sharing with the world.

CHAPTER TWENTY-FIVE

Follow Your Dreams

Our dreams turn us on, light our fires, and get us up in the morning. We act on them every day, by choice. We usually know somewhere hidden inside just what we were meant to do, what we really want to do. It is that one word that catches your interest when you hear it uttered from across the room at a gathering. That one course you know you would follow if you weren't concerned about providing for your family, or moving, or failing. It is what you would do if you won the lottery jackpot today. *That* is your calling! *That* God cheers as you share.

Whether you listen to that inner voice or believe in your ability to have all you desire, your dreams are etched on your soul if you look. It is magic waiting to be unearthed, mysteries of the Universe ready to explode into the heavens. If you can, share these gifts daily and you will feel a life of love.

FIND YOUR DREAMS

If you do not recognize your dreams, then engage in stillness to ponder or explore alternatives. More commonly, we all know what we desire, but consciously acknowledging that desire is a matter of how far we have suppressed or ignored its potential in our lives. We know it by opening to our instincts and feelings. The Universe continually presents our calling in its highest truth if we listen.

We find it by noticing synchronicities we encounter and by giving them their due credence, such as the words we hear repeatedly in songs or in common conversations, the messages we see on road signs, across billboards, or around the home or office, and in the books that call to us or fall off the shelf. We know when we turn on the television and see something related to what we were just thinking about. We understand when we notice the thoughts that will not go away.

These are taps on your shoulder and very important clues. We can use these serendipitous moments as confirmations of sought-after goals, support from Divinity, and passions worthy of pursuing. This is the Universe's way of letting you know that you are on the right track, that Spirit does see you and is lifting you in your new dreams and ventures. Believe these signs, and trust that the whole Universe is conspiring to help, sustain, and nourish your deepest aspirations.

If you are not certain what your desires are, write lists of things you might like to do. Write of things you have done that satisfied you. Brainstorm feelings or conditions you want in your life no matter the outer form, such as unconditional love. Introspection, along with helpful books, such as *Callings* by Gregg Levoy, present useful ways to narrow your search, and spark your inner interest. Keep going.

KEEP DREAMS PERSONAL

Once we get the courage to begin following our dream, we come across many obstacles. Many of these obstructions can be classified in the self-sabotage category, but there is also truth in the simple advice of not sharing our seedling dreams with others just yet.

No matter how gung-ho we are in the pursuit of our passions, when we are in the vulnerable stage of our callings, we are very impressionable to the words and opinions of others. We may think we want our dream so much that nothing can stop us or stand in our way, or we may move quietly forward every day with trepidation in each shaky step. It takes time to gain courage in our chosen direction. It takes consistency, repeated glory, and steady footing. Until we are well established in our self-assurance, it is wise to keep our longings private.

I learned this lesson the hard way, delaying my passion and purpose and nearly giving up completely because of one inconsiderate incident. My vulnerable seedling, which I had finally gained pride in, was put off for numerous months until I regained perspective and hope enough to try again. When this person neglected my work, placing it aside in a sign of disregard to me, I let my power be taken because it simply touched my own self-doubts. I could eventually give a big thank you for this incident because it brought me this awareness. It opened the door to really look at my own reservations, and internal weakness.

However, I encourage each of us to progress in our own time, with our own needs, with a small push out of comfort, to build up our internal wellspring before subjecting our "work" to the carelessness of another, no matter how well-intentioned or all-knowing they might seem at the time. Such sharing could interrupt our daily progress.

Most often, others do not realize the giant impact of their single comment of misgiving. Some may even think they are protecting you or doing you a favor. We cannot hold against others the effect they have on our own thoughts or actions, but we can be knowledgeable about our limits and not place our importance outside ourselves. Even with this observation, it may remain difficult for us to believe in ourselves, our highest hopes, our best dreams.

I have mastered many skills in my lifetime, and I have halls of honor for work I have done in many areas of my life, but when we reach down deep into a real and true dream, it potentially unlocks chaos simply because of its importance. When we try something new, something we are not already great at but want to be, it is then that our soul raises questions and opportunities to glean the most valuable of experiences.

There are those lucky few who can plow ahead no matter the consequences or opposing forces. We all have certain areas where we exude these qualities—endowments evolved from childhood, single-minded focuses of accomplishment we stuck to, skills passed down within family generations or past lives, or even those unique talents in which we have unbounded natural abilities. Nevertheless, with wisdom comes growth periods where we endeavor to reach outside our grasped concepts or skills. This is a beautiful, and scary, acknowledgement of our leaps and bounds in expanding our spirits and evolving selves.

As we step into new domains and nurture new ideals and wishes, it is this very excitement of newness that both carries us forward and shakes us in our boots. These are the times to breathe and center inside. These are the moments to rely on our own gut feelings and strong intuitions. These are the places in which to be gentle with our self-created debacles of perfection or expectation, and certainly, until we have grown in confidence and strength, we need not let others be privy to either these hopes or fears.

There may be a rare friend or companion who shares unconditional love with you, but many others will play on these worries without realizing it. Some may even have their own agendas. If we could only engage in the Supreme Being's perspective for a moment to mourn all the dreams, delicious ideas, and delightful accomplishments that could have changed lives, or even our world, but never made it out, we would know how much is lost due to the doubts or dread perpetrated by another's unkind, sometimes innocent force.

If you need support, check in with Divinity or your deep internal Source, but be leery of involving another, for you may not like what they have to say about your fascinating epiphanies. And if you think you know how someone might respond to your excitement, then trust your knowing and let it be—no need to hear anything negative to block your potential greatness. Give your own approval and a big okay to keep going with wonderful self-love. Someone somewhere will get it someday. When you are ready, absolutely thrust it to the world, but beforehand know there is nothing uglier to bring a dream crashing down into pieces than a little interjection of outside doubt, misunderstanding, or even jealousy.

If you have already made the mistake of sharing with another who stomped upon your young crops, know your dream was not finished growing strong and beautiful. Get back up on that horse and—for goodness sake—continue forward. The world needs your dream today. It is easy to say others cannot stop you until you encounter a negative force, but see it for what it is—forgive the detour, brush yourself off, and keep going. Resistance gives you strength to push up the steep parts of the hills. Be true to yourself. And follow your heart . . . it always knows.

ACTING ON YOUR DREAM

When you recognize inspiration in a package delivered distinctly to you, act on it. For when you connect with energy and reflect it through your unique gifts, you also know by morphic resonance that it exists in the ether now, awaiting its form. While it will sit quietly on your doorstep hoping to be noticed, if you turn it down, even through attrition, it will seek another receiver. It will be patient while you work with it, learn and mold it into your life, in your time, and bring it to completion, but it will not be ignored to die; it will eventually pass to another to be born in a varied form.

You need not worry that you will lose your dream if you do not work quickly or constantly. Spirit knows your best intentions and is pleased with any amount of energy and faith. As stated earlier, the main problem with fulfilling our potential is not being unaware of its presence in our lives or knowing what we want, but our own lurking self-doubts. This is not aided by the interference of others.

Knowing what your dream is yet standing immobilized in your fear, unable to move forward, is to some extent the most daunting obstacle in our way, and it is usually self-induced. Once you get past yourself, realize that you do not have to accomplish a lifetime of goals all at once. We are generally overwhelmed when we see the entire picture or path before us, when we feel the burden of a whole enterprise weighing on our shoulders. Give yourself a break and remember to breathe. Meditate upon the very helpful quote by Goethe: "Only engage, and then the mind grows heated—Begin it, and then the work will be completed!" You cannot reach the end until you start at the beginning. All we have to do is *begin* the work. It is not in our power, or our best interest, to finish any big task in a single moment. Just begin one act today!

Break down your dream into doable steps and take a forward step on a consistent basis. Remember that some of these steps will be patience and faith. This is important. And if you are still overwhelmed or lost as to where and how to start, look into the Kaizen techniques employed by the Japanese. A wonderful handbook is *One Small Step Can Change Your Life, The Kaizen Way* by Robert Maurer, Ph.D. These techniques show how to proceed into any goal with steps that are so minute they are laughable. Nevertheless, what this genius uncovers is a sure way to rewire the human brain so it accepts newness and change while bypassing the normal chemical reactions of fear and being overwhelmed. Moreover, it really does work. How do you eat an elephant? One bite at a time!

BELIEVE IN YOURSELF

As you rely on these practical tools, remember to believe in yourself. Be proud of the days you do stick to your word, and work joyfully on your projects. Be pleased when you reward your life with time toward your dreams. Love every day, and your dreams reveal themselves.

"Be pleased when you reward your life with time toward your dreams."

You can have what you wish. You can be a vibrational match to your dreams; just keep at it with perseverance and love, and each moment you engage in it is successful. Redefine society's definition of success and make your own. Victory is every time we show up to forge the process of making our dreams come true. Victory is sharing our visions daily towards love. We triumph when we notice we are afraid and still build and follow those creations we know will make us happy and better the world. There can be no failure so long as we keep trying. Keep sharing all the good you come across. Failure is only in giving up, stopping, and learning nothing; everything else is success. Movement is still moving and creating no matter how small the effort or faith, so continue with your gestures of action, and the Universe will respond in kind.

We can sabotage our best efforts if we rely on a single finished product to assure our achievement. Discover that your success is going to sleep at night knowing you did what you love, you gave it your best, you worked at it when it was not easy, and you stayed the course when the going got rough.

"Failure is only in giving up, stopping, and learning nothing; everything else is success."

Whether you pile on issues of money, naysayers, or deep internal worthlessness, promise to get out of your own way and see the brightness and possibility of what you desire. Intend your creation and success. Doing what you love, following your dreams—that is the way to bring the money, quiet the cynic, and prove yourself valuable inside.

So begin without delay. One step, one declaration, one intention, one belief of support at a time, and we can move mountains, and heal the world—all because of a simple idea inside our hearts combined with boundless energy put into action daily. The world is waiting for your gift, your dream, and your creation, and no one else can fulfill your piece; it is priceless and unique. Do what you can, and the sustenance of all the celestial bodies will rise to meet you.

MEDITATION: CENTER AND MOVE FORWARD

- Get into your meditative space.
- To help hold your center, picture a bubble around you that encompasses your entire body three feet around you in every direction.
- Paint your bubble any color you like.
- This space is yours and delineates your aura boundary.

- Work this space using your energy tools, for it is all you can control in the entire world.
- Think about your dream and work the picture in your head.
- What does success look like?
- Release negativity from this picture and fill it with light. Make it feel good.
- What one step can get you closer to that bright dream today?
- Now that your energy is clear and activated, come out and act on your dream.

CHAPTER TWENTY-SIX

Sources of Inspiration

If you are not getting out of bed every day with a smile, you need more inspiration. Do not plod through your days feeling out of sorts. Consider the swift snap of inspiration—one interesting connection is all it takes to lift you. Our lives simply call to be inspired, and it does not take moving mountains to do so—it only takes an instant of clicking with your soul. What clicks for each person is unique. We only need to allow the inspiration to touch and motivate us. Find what moves you, and share it with the world to give love and receive inspiration daily.

If you cannot put your finger on what feels off in your life, or why you don't feel excited about tomorrow, maybe the solution is in simply asking. Turn to any person and ask what does it do for them. Most everyone will enjoy giving his or her tips on this subject, for it creates joy even to recall the sensation. It is like asking a beloved couple how they met or fell in love; you can see the stars return to their eyes just in the telling. Take note of what brings those stars or smiles to you, and employ them to regain any lost excitement for the days we sometimes unconsciously allow to fuse with drudgery.

Samuel Johnson writes, "Our brightest blazes of gladness are commonly kindled by unexpected sparks." Look for inspiration wherever you can. In the oddest places, we may hear an answer to a prolonged, plaguing concern, or we may rejoice upon witnessing a synchronicity. One moment of inspiration can change the course of a life, and these magical instances can occur anywhere, at any time. When it hits you, you know it, and if seized, you will never be the same. This is a blessing. Any time we are moved, we have an opportunity to experience and share the unbounded.

We can create space for these opportunities to find us as we prime the pump in any way that works. Great leaders and random folks can bring inspiration, as can speech, song, nature, or silent witnessing. Join with me in considering how inspiration strikes and stirs our imaginations as we watch favorite movies, listen to cherished songs and singers, get lost in stories, write stories of our own, and move our beautiful bodies.

MOVIES WITH MEANING

When we are bereft of inspiration, cannot make ourselves ask for help, or do not have a wise person at our disposal, we can turn to entertainment for assistance. While I have certain issues with media and chuckle at the "kill your television" stickers, I can agree it has value, part of which is its wide accessibility. While media does much to promote fear and consumption to the detriment of our society, there are movies with meaning that can give us the shift we need at just the right moment. When we are mired in struggle or have forgotten our way, these two-hour distractions offer great relief. If we know our perspective needs a tune-up but are too tired to try, we can take a break for a recommendation in hope. If we need to laugh and believe we can't, cinema can adjust our attitude.

You'll know a movie is a source of inspiration if the general effect opens your eyes to a greater truth or provides a gentle awakening. You may hear that one sentence that resonates with your spirit and gets you through the day. A scene of beauty may jump out, and you may remember it when faced with difficulties. You may feel better about your day through the struggles of another, or you might simply forget your strife long enough to catch your breath.

Movies may also provide a synchronicity or confirmation that changes or guides your life. Breaking out in laughter could be the very thing you need, as amusement is often lost in adulthood. You may come across important information of a perspective you did not know you were missing. Even if nothing magical occurs, distraction may be all you need to reset your day. One interesting thought from a character can heat up your mind and get you to the next step. Be it small or large, you can find solace in the creative brilliance of our time.

There are thousands of movies we can rely on during those days of pulling the covers over our heads or wishing for tomorrow. Typing in "spiritual film" or other search phrases online produces an endless list of great movies. I share some of my list here, and you can take my recommendations or create your own list, adding to it as you discover new two-hour increments of release. Two hours is plenty of time to forget our burdens and become enraptured in a story that can help get us back on track.

One of my very favorites is *Groundhog Day*. My great friend Andrew finds it intriguing to picture me watching this movie every February 2nd and is humored by me getting caught in its repetition, but I love its message. The film never fails to relieve tension at perceived failures and bring hope. In humorous undertones of this repetition, much like the opportunities afforded us by the Universe, Bill Murray moves from sarcasm to anarchy, then from manipulation into resignation. His growing knowledge is all that accompanies him through the monotonous days, but it is only after he is touched by love that he becomes of service, inspired to live. Out of this he manifests and shares his best life.

I also love *Oh God* for its message of a connected and caring humanity, for the premise of us being here to help one another, and for showing us that God wants us to take care of the earth and each other. It doesn't hurt that it stars George Burns, and of course, John Denver.

I benefit from the cult classics of my adolescence in *The Breakfast Club* and *Ferris Bueller's Day Off*, depicting the trials of growing up, dealing with others in the unique relationships of high school, and looking to the future.

To *Hoosiers*—which I have seen more than any other movie and even recorded on audio tape in my childhood, never having enough music to listen to—I owe a certain piece of my character. This movie has class and inspiration to me. And awesome music.

I return repeatedly to *The Secret, Mind Walk, What the Bleep*, and Dr. Wayne Dyer's specials as consistent aids in refocusing. These movies open my thoughts and gently bring me back to my own power to create. I actually watched *The Secret* every morning for most of a year to strengthen my attention on creating the life I chose, to believe in my ability to manifest, and to keep me on track. It always grounds these concepts within me and re-starts my havingness, and I use it as a foundational recurring tool to this day.

I revel in the awe, chivalry, and idealism in *First Knight*. I like the writing in movies of this time because I miss how folks used to speak and love. I find grace with Leelee Sobieski's portrayal of *Joan of Arc*, and I adore the loyalty of Chad Willett, her Jean de Metz. This story speaks to the depth of my soul and the plights of women and spiritual visionaries, lighting the way to truth with faith.

I search for movies with spiritual themes as well as re-incarnation, Divinity, and the like, and so enjoyed *White Light* and *The Shack*. I cry appreciatively at the messages in *October Sky* of reaching for dreams, being encouraged, and learning to stand up for what one knows inside.

Sense memories brought from childhood are *The Sound of Music* and *The Ten Commandments* at Easter time. My sweet childhood dog Britta even died during *The Ten Commandments*. I first fell in love with Patrick Swayze—Goddess bless his spirit—in the mini-series *North and South*. And I enjoy the character building and escapism of *Krull*, although the Cyclops gets me every time.

Because of my children, I have been lucky enough to fall in love with a few animations for their great, uplifting music. Our favorites, sung at the top of our lungs, are *Quest for Camelot, Hunchback of Notre Dame, Mulan, Anastasia*, and *The Lion King*. On a quick television note, I loved *The West Wing* for its intelligence, dialogue, and actors, and always keep *Friends* close to my heart for its humor, wit, and real life understanding with levity. My loyal daytime escape for thirty years has been *Days of our Lives*, and I am partial to John Black.

My first all-time favorite movie is *The Count of Monte Cristo*, with Jim Caviezel and Guy Pearce. The beautiful stars, language, and messages of justice and love never fail to fulfill me. I fall in love with Edmond Dantes every time we share these two hours together.

The second is my sacred collection of *The Lord of the Rings* series from cinematic genius Peter Jackson. I cannot say enough about its splendor, guidance, strength, and hope. As a family, we watch the extended version of all three many times throughout each year, and the standout messages live with grace and are the essence of breathtaking majesty. I repeat numerous sentences from these movies in my daily existence as I believe wholeheartedly that "even the smallest person can change the course of the future" and that "we may yet make it." These works of art contain countless inspiring conversations and circumstances, and nowhere else have I delighted in such wonderfully written wordage and eloquent expression.

My life has been changed and moved by hundreds of movies, and I only mention some here. Utilize any you love for your own sparks and distractions, and do not underestimate the power of these stories to light a few feet of your path. There is something for everyone and on every subject in this cinematic search.

MEDITATION: INSPIRATIONAL MOVIES

- With a piece of paper handy, close your eyes and ask what kind of help you might need today.
- Remember movies that inspired or soothed you as a child. Write them down.
- Consider what type of movies would suit your mood or need, such as motivational, spiritual, full of love, etc. Plan to research new movies soon.
- Watch one today

MUSIC

While music is deeply personal and tastes vary widely, we all have our favorites. You can tell music inspires you when it makes you feel good. If the lyrics, melodies, or rhythms stick in your head or come out of your mouth, music has moved you. One of the easiest ways to change how you feel is to turn on music. Cry, dance, or heal, and let it fill your soul.

I am inspired by all of John Denver's music and touched by *Les Miserables*—knowing every word and having seen it live six times. I am awakened by Keane, and I am uplifted singing with my family and friends to The Indigo Girls. I thoroughly enjoy Christmas music, especially the Christmas albums of Narada, Manheim Steamroller, John Denver, and (because I grew up dancing) *The Nutcracker*.

I adore Broadway hits such as *Wicked, Evita*, and *Sweeney Todd*, and even put on the soundtrack of *Hair* in my friend Linda's car, singing every stinking word of it during a band road trip to Utah. My all-time favorite is the brilliance of *The Greatest Showman*! I love my friend Tanya who also knows every word and sings them with me as loud and as often as possible. Talk about inspiring, healing, and sharing!

I used to collect volumes of bagpipe and drum music, favoring the World's compilations when they came out from the annual August contests. The musicianship in these volumes is astounding, with inspiring mentors. "By The Water's Edge" is a moving pipe melody, "Joey's Tune" sings to my soul with memories and hopes, and *Live in Ireland*'s "Journey to Skye" by The 78th Fraser Highlanders will always be my epitome of delight. Standing in the circle of a good bagpipe band and getting moved through its ensemble is an exquisite experience unmatched.

When I need soothing, I turn to albums *Fairy Ring* by Mike Rowland, *San Juan Suite* by Michael Gettel, and the soundtrack to the movie *Country* released by Windham Hill artists. I found a unique treasure in Olivia Newton-John's spiritual *Grace and Gratitude* and have childhood memories of healing with the album *Above the Tower*, the songs "We are the World," and "One More Night."

While Paul and I fell in love, we also fell in love with *Hearts of Space*, spending endless loving hours with candlelight to the more soothing and rapturous journeys. This is musical ecstasy in our relationship, as is the sweetness of John Rutter. Paul used to hold me, and conduct with my hands in his, to the entire *Requiem* sung by the Cambridge singers. I also love *Liquid Mind* to relax or rest to, and I almost never start writing without Pandora on Tim Janis.

I like many more artists such as Alanis Morissette, Journey, Air Supply, Simon and Garfunkel, The Corrs, The Cranberries, Donna Lewis, Judy Collins, Josh Groban, Alison Kraus, Wilson Phillips, as well as ballad singers like Phil Collins and Chicago, and most eighties groups. I fall back on lots of renaissance, chant, Palestrina, new age, musicals, movie soundtracks, and hair bands, and within each of these categories are implicit uses for my emotional needs. My favorite soundtracks for dancing around in my living room are *The American President*, *Forrest Gump*, and *Sense and Sensibility*, which are also great writing backdrops. And if I had it, I would add the soundtrack to *The Lord of the Rings* series.

A little of everything is my style, with long use of my trustworthy others. I am one of those who can get into a song, and listen to it on repeat for half a day straight. The hypnotic effect soothes me. Everyone recognizes themselves somewhere within music, and is so moved.

I advocate music be integrated into all parts of life, and I encourage listening as background noise during most times. Find connection between activity and emotion with specific melody or hypnotic feel. I also esteem the attachment of a soul's vibration with making music in any form. A strange feeling used to overwhelm my senses when I leapt into the space of practicing drumming for hypnotic hours. There is great reason for the energies of St. Cecilia and music being one of the seven intelligences.

MEDITATION: INSPIRING MUSIC

- Turn on a song you have liked lately, and close your eyes.
- Mindfully explore what about this music inspires your life.
- Find one beautiful melody, or seek out lyrics of whatever comes on.
- Really listen to the words, or if you feel so inspired, move your body with music.
- What sort of song would you write in this moment?
- Find a plethora of songs for your healing repertoire.
- Discover guidance within the unknown.

READING AND WRITING

While not everyone enjoys writing, maybe because of unending essays or graded creativity in school years, everyone can find a book that inspires their path. Whether romance stories draw out your passions or self-help books permit you to see yourself, the world of books enables learning and seeking and affords delight for any mood. Reading wisdom has the capacity to inspire answers to any situation. When you write, you can say anything you want, and that is an amazing connection and release. You can even write inspirational affirmations and share them. Look for passages that stir something inside you, whether a poem or a simple sentence. Post them around your space, and memorize enticing quotes.

I obviously love reading and writing so profoundly that I am an author. I believe the single greatest skill we learn as humans is the ability to both record our thoughts, ideas, and stories, and read those of others. Books transcend time and space. Reading carries us to heights and creations we may not touch or see, and they teach us anything we long to know. I am so grateful for authors who have come before me. I attempt only to add to the literature of the world with my own words written as a tablet of respect, admiration, and sacred appreciation.

Although I rarely enjoyed reading throughout school, mainly because of the choices and time constraints dictated to me, I found a great love for books later. I did find writing early, as a personal, lasting form of expression—thank goodness. The solace I experienced through writing anything, anywhere, at any time, was an unmatched sustenance that probably saved my life. Paper, pen, and privacy to unload my emotive thoughts were all I often had as a true friend, and usually all I needed.

As I grew up being painfully unique—seeing light arrays around people, explaining feelings in colors and numbers, discovering life and people through deep sensitivities—I felt misunderstood and desperately alone more than the average lost teenager. When I was distraught, writing comforted me, and saved me through my own fantasies and imagination of better places. It allowed me freedom and peace just to know that one space could be trusted with my fearful and painful thoughts.

Writing also eased my torture as a stable and safe form of release while experimenting with my private and tender insides. I could go through an entire day encountering misunderstandings and being made fun of, and it was only when I got home to my journals and poetry and books that I was in protective custody and could finally be myself. There I could be loved for who I was, unloading my heartache and loneliness in any way I deemed fit. I connected deeply with Simon and Garfunkel singing about how they had their books and poetry to protect them.

I cannot get through a handful of pages of Hemingway without a sudden opening or need to write. Passages carry me traveling to his dynamic locations, enjoying the company of his characters, hiding his real life within the lovely mystery of his words. I never read fiction until I discovered Hemingway, and now with an inexplicable connection I want always to be reading him. I seem to know him intimately, and he is a fervent spiritual writing companion.

My childhood favorite was *My Side of the Mountain* as I relished thoughts of living on my own inside a big tree in a forest with only nature for companionship and survival. And I pass on to my children the *Sara* series of early spiritual awareness, manifesting, and creating our life, even as youngsters. I re-read *Way of the Peaceful Warrior* every autumn to sharpen my mind's focus and center my desires. It supplies spiritual backup and synchronistic awakening within my daily life. I read *Spiritual Growth* by Sanaya Roman on a loop. Perhaps my favorite book of all time, at least during the last ten years, it is never far. Her entire series honors inspiration and positive spiritual information.

When Paul and I first began dating, he introduced me to Dan Millman and Richard Bach. Their books were my first experience of loving reading and finding books so great that I chose to read on my own while in school. Although my dad introduced me to *There's No Such Place as Far Away* when I was young, and I awakened with *Illusions* and *Jonathan*

Livingston Seagull, it was *The Bridge across Forever* and *One* that created a special and personally sacred bond of love between Paul and me.

I hold precious many old works of brilliance from other times and wish I could accurately appreciate them. Although John Donne takes time and concentration for me to understand fully, I welcome the challenge. I love reading Shakespeare aloud by a stream, opening to the love and rhythm of his words, and I agree with Hemingway when he called him "The Champion," though our love for *War and Peace* might put Tolstoy in the ring.

I keep one of Abbie Graham's books in a fabric-covered box because it grabs my soul. It is so potent I can only read a page of it at a time, and it remains deeply intoxicating. In addition, it is a hundred-year-old book; it took a very long journey for my husband to find it. What a priceless gift! I find Virginia Woolf potent and am certainly stimulated into thought by her observations. And my cousin Michelle, the avid reader, heralds Willa Cather.

In all my time on earth, I endeavor to elongate it only to fit in all the books I want to read and read again. Beyond Tolkien, Tolstoy, and Hemingway, I am just now being turned on to the classics. I have much yet to learn about the greats.

The last decades have been the backdrop for much introspection, spiritual observation, awareness, and healing in my life. Because Dr. Wayne W. Dyer largely promoted this approach to life, he became one of my favorite leaders in thought. His work in general, but especially *There's a Spiritual Solution to Every Problem*, has kept me upright with understanding through much turmoil. I also use Ted Andrews's work of *Animal Speak* for my own edification as with numerous reference books on dreams, writing, astrology, crystals, and more.

I read Sara Ban Breathnach's daily book *Simple Abundance* repeatedly, which for twenty-three years has been my morning companion and confidant in growth. The information it contains is always illuminating and humorous. I bought it for gifts to my sisters who had not yet discovered their love for reading, as well as for most of the women in my life. I adore the masterworks of Marianne Williamson with her astute truth and intensity towards love and light.

So many books have guided and consoled me that, as with music and movies, I can only honor the highlights here, and regretfully leave masterful repertoires unmentioned. I am currently learning and lightening through the Saint Germain series of true edification, beginning with *Unveiled Mysteries*. But the book I would rescue from fire (besides my growing collected works of Hemingway) is *Light from Many Lamps,* which seems an anomaly to find but has comforted me throughout various ordeals. I picked this up decades ago in a sidewalk sale for a going-out-of-business bookstore, and redeemed it for fifty cents. I had no idea what a treasure I had found. This faithful companion of quotes from the greats is always in my bedside table.

My shelves and table tops are filled with great works of all kinds, and I believe I could never have or read enough. Reading is a last solace of imagination, creativity, and information left to us in an ever-increasing world of technology and separation. We do well for our brains and spirits to daily read even a few pages of something uplifting and wonderful.

MEDITATION: INSPIRED READING AND WRITING

- Go somewhere beautiful with a book you like in hand, as well as a paper and pencil.
- Underline those words or sentences that touch you

as you read or flip through.

- Write a few words of how you are feeling, or journal about your day.
- Write a simple poem for someone you love, and share it.
- Or start with words that come to your mind while thinking of someone, then fill it in.
- Choose any book anywhere, open it randomly, and seek its message.

MOVEMENT AND MANEUVERS

Someone unknown once said, "I like to exercise, but it's not always possible with my hectic sleep schedule." I am partial to Robert Maynard Hutchins's humor in the statement, "Whenever I feel like exercise, I lie down until the feeling passes." Who put the word "work" in something many of us already have difficulty doing anyway? But movement is good for our bodies, and I do my best to utilize variety every day.

If you can find a form of exercise you enjoy, you are worth your weight in gold—no matter what that weight is. When I was younger, I was a dancer. My mother, two sisters, and I belonged to the dance troop/tribe Dancefusion. For more than ten years I danced many hours each night, performing on some weekends. I was young and skinny. If I had only known then to appreciate my figure. The line of my body was beautiful, my physique conditioned. I was strong, muscular, and fit to the extreme.

Point shoes gave me blisters, and on some nights I begged with an incessant teenager whine to just stay home and do nothing. But I am grateful for the skills I acquired and for those teachers who touched my life, especially Kathy Goldstein, who was my second mother by sheer hours and shared wisdoms. I wholeheartedly appreciate all that movement did for my body's awareness, exquisiteness, and optimal health. I had less gratitude at the time, taking for granted my shape and slender beauty.

I *loooved* dancing. I became pretty good and even partnered. I studied tap, jazz, and modern, but ballet was one of my first discovered avenues of true and whole expression. When one learns to move and contort his or her body by commanding every muscle, one enables the body to be a magician of expression.

I ran track most years in school, and I was forced into summer swim meets as my dad managed pools during our childhood summers. Oh how I despised that sixty-degree water in early morn. I love swimming now, and playing with kids while in the water is inspiring. But let's face it, as a teenager I was overly committed, underweight, and not very healthy. Today I am overweight and not totally healthy either, though I try.

Exercise used to feel like a chore until I approached it differently. Every time I finish any movement that makes me glow, sweat, and breathe harder, I feel great about myself. I am not sure why this payoff of loving myself and feeling proud of how I chose to spend the last hour, or ten minutes, does not do more for encouraging more movement, but like most others, I am "working" at it (which may perhaps be the problem). I'll share some activities I've enjoyed, but think about what works for you. What form of movement truly activates you into getting up?

I like forms of movement and health that I do not have to pay for, though we have paid for plenty over the years in attempts to change it up, make it exciting, keep it new, or make it easy. We have all heard numerous advertisements for equipment, and workouts that are designed for particular results. We have a table full of weights—we try to throw in some weight lifting a few times a week—a pull-up bar nicely displayed in our hall, fitness "games"—some with music and dancing—various memories of apparatus long relegated to the trash, an elliptical that has become a constant ally, and even the CD series of P90X.

I really like P90X with its muscle confusion and stimulation, as I believe that using different muscles in moving and working achieves greater results. Moreover, I have to say that Mr. Tony, who runs the program, is actually motivating and supportive in comparison to most outlets we have tried (and stopped). It is a bit serious for me in its commitment only because I do not choose to put aside sometimes an hour and a half every day. I do not work like that with great consistency, and I know my life is not designed that way. Nevertheless, we often just do as much as we can. Any amount of movement is progress. That is a good mantra to remember.

"Any amount of movement is progress."

I have found appreciation at my choice to get off the couch and just walk around, bend, twist, and move while watching television. I love doing sit-ups and push-ups while I watch television. And perhaps less television would help, too. I like taking walks and hiking, but again do not utilize it with much regularity.

My favorite, and therefore most employed, form of movement is dancing around the house to loud music, intermingling weights when I need to breathe, as well as swaying my body, engaging my core, and brushing my arms around for energy movement. When I move energy while I am doing whatever jumps or skips around the house, that time provides double use and actual pleasure. I run my arms up and down, intending that I am clearing out yucky energy, and it does not matter what my feet are doing, as long as they are moving. After this clearing, activated by accelerating my heartbeat and sweating, I feel like my energy field is clearer. It is intentional moving—that is all I do for this magical sensation of release.

Then I will do slower movements of extending my legs or walking tiptoe, incorporating balance or stretching as I reach my hands up to the heavens and picture bringing in my golden suns or beams of colored lights to fill me with the nectar of the day. I intend this all brought in from above, filling from the bottom up, securing my survival and thriving to stability of emotions, manifesting and power, to then love, peace, prosperity, divine connection, expression and on—whatever I want or need at the time. In this way, much like meditative walking and communing with nature while one's feet are moving, I access every energy I can in my creative movement, and though it may look funny out my windows, I feel released, energized, and loving when I have finished. This inspires me to maybe do it tomorrow.

I like the combination of weights, sweating aerobically, and stretching and balancing because it aids my body in wholeness. The little yoga and tai chi I know always feels great, and keeps me supple. My friend Sheresa is a qualified Pilates instructor, and I am loving the way it makes my body feel. Maybe onto something new there. My cousin Shauna also teaches fitness, so this shows us we can find many mentors.

It may be daunting to pick a workout regimen and require it in all of your days, but it is reachable to stand up and simply lunge, sway, or kick your feet for a few moments. Jumping around, stretching, or lifting a few moments is healthy for our bodies. I also pace around the house while I read, activating the physical and distracting the mental, which makes the exercise time pass quickly. I encourage you to seek and enjoy whatever movement you can, and your body's life and longevity will thank you. Invite a friend to exercise with you. Research different workout plans and try each out to see which brings you joy and consistency—try anything, but do something.

Moving however my body dictates helps me not only connect with and learn to listen to it, but as it brings my spirit more into my body, it also heals and creates energy. Moving outside adds an extra level of spirit, even if it is just riding my bike. I love my choice when I am done, and I feel better physically and emotionally. When I move by any means, I can smile at myself in the mirror and think positively about what I see. This pursuit can be fun and easy if we endeavor to change our mindset—goodness knows it is important. I have tried to "love myself thin," and meditate to change my cells to be healthy. All these are inspiring for my confidence, health, discipline, power of choice, and future. This simple act of moving limbs allows great unconditional love of self. Now that "works!"

MEDITATION: INSPIRED MOVING

- Close your eyes and think what kind of exercise would be fun today.
- Ask your body what kind of movement it needs (stretching, sweating, balancing, etc.)
- Do it gently, or with gleeful inspiration. Even twelve minutes makes a difference.
- Move around your space, waving your arms intending energy work for a double healing.

- Keep breathing and moving, engaging your core everywhere, and your body will heal.

You can find inspiration through entertainment, the quiet solace of writing and reading, and listening and moving—you can even use many of these forms together. Find what makes you smile, or what excites you enough to look forward to getting out of bed, and share it with another. That is a true form of inspiring unconditional love. We all need assistance and inspiration when we get stuck or are a bit aimless, and everyone around you can help with this search.

"We all share in our search for inspired conscious living."

Test things out, find new tricks and helpers, and bring more meaning into your life. This expands love for ourselves, which expands love to the world. If nothing is doing it for you today, find something else—there are endless resources. Enlist friends or family, or even professionals to help your enthusiasm or consistency. Inspiration moves us toward our purpose and keeps us centered in what is important for our lives. Your life is not the same as another's, but we all share in our search for inspired conscious living.

CHAPTER TWENTY-SEVEN

Develop Daily

Austrian Marie von Ebner-Eschenbach shocks us out of our indifference by telling us, "Nothing is so often irretrievably missed as a daily opportunity." Add to this haunting realization a poignant quote by Annie Dillard: "How we spend our days is, of course, how we spend our lives." We have a daunting concept hanging over our perceived shortcomings. I invite you to elevate the mundane through daily attention to breathing deeply, utilizing light, and the blessed state of surrender.

EVERY DAY

Each twenty-four-hour period as marked by our sun grants us bountiful chances to apply our dreams and insights consciously. We may shudder at the reality of these two quotes as we are shaken out of procrastination or despondency. There are endless phrases of brilliance that shine on the importance and fleeting nature of any singular day. They are meant to stir you, to get you moving. Whether you prod yourself with fear or faith, worry or hope, the truth is that we must sometimes be prodded by frightening grasps of just how short this lifetime is.

If you have children, you may know these feelings well as you put away outgrown baby clothes, acknowledging that your firstborn is now in middle or high school. You tuck your children under cozy handmade quilts with a bedtime story, and then blink as they walk down the aisle to take a new name. Sometimes these instances accompany contentment and reassurance, and sometimes they scare the living daylights out of us. Our reaction depends on whether we are accessing our best throughout our days to an end we long to know, or if we are losing days, months, or even years through attrition.

Unconscious living, albeit well-intended, may have quietly led us to a place we wake up to and realize we do not enjoy. This dawning of time's passage may bring moments of splendor as we truly revel in the magnificent beauty of this moment. However, it can also jolt us into morbid discouragement as we realize we have just spent twenty-five years working at a job we despise, or have remained in an unloving relationship to which we have grown numb. Take heart, for there is no time like the present, and if that too eludes your best efforts, hope for tomorrow and try to do one thing different. This moment is a priceless gift to be recognized and seized.

"This moment is a priceless gift to be recognized and seized."

Whatever our dream, we all need to see the path's end nearing so we are moved enough to include its work in our plans for today, each day. If we let a single day go by without digging in with our hands and hearts, we have lost an opportunity. These lost opportunities may hurt, but better to learn it now and get moving than to regret again.

We can acquire the life skills we need to implement our aspirations, and we can aim at this objective with inspiration rather than fear. We want to spend our precious moments following our calling because we love it and are energized by doing it, not because we fear we will lose. Although fear and worry may work to shift us, we all have dreams of relishing in our adventures, and fright is no feeling to live in day after day. We want to revel in our choices.

We can always choose again. We need to undertake our endeavors joyfully so we know we are adding to the world and amassing light, not because we feel a strangling sense of obligation or guilt. Although we are responsible for forging our goals into an essence that can be shared and delivered, this is not a burden. If we approach any daily deed in a negative or required fashion, it is not causing our hearts to sing, nor will it anyone else's. While it is our path to bring forth our gifts to fruition, it is not the dutiful constraints themselves that will fulfill us, but how we do them, allowing any passion to lead us to light and ecstasy. These are the viewpoints for which we seek to show ourselves to the world.

With proper perspective in creating and giving, we can figure out how to incorporate the importance of our desires into our schedules. We need to be clear that if anything feels binding or is the source of feeling trapped, then we need to venture toward building into our lives more of what we truly want. If you are walking a path that does not move your very soul, or if you are not at least going toward it, then your first step will be discovery. Note any hints you come across and build upon that list. Only when you love what you are doing and delight in the time spent acting on it will you place enough importance to ensure daily measures.

Attention to our accomplishments on a daily basis, or as close as we can redeem, makes any cause a more viable contender. It may be a leap of consciousness to do what you love and trust the money and support will follow—I know it is for me—but we must find the way that keeps us heading forward. Any way we slice it, if we are not consistent and active in pursuing our pleasures, they may fly or fade away until a day far off when we can no longer resurrect their potency. Let us not take that chance, or waste this life, or even a solitary pass of the sun.

Utilize your growing wisdom, be clear about what you seek, and have nets lined up to catch you when you slip or forget. This takes minute preparation but can salvage years of aimless energy. Look for one action, one tool that gently brings your awareness present or keeps your vision in the forefront of your decisions. Rely on this light for steadiness. Commit no less than fifteen minutes every day to get you where you are headed. When you know where you want to go, commit as much time as you can possibly make. It is important, every day.

In *No Ordinary Moments,* Dan Millman talks about the process of awakening to objective reality and cutting through the mind's illusions. "This awakening can take years of conscious effort, or can occur suddenly and quite by accident." Whatever your driving passion, focus on love every day. Share what you can every day. Unconditional love is what is important beneath every action. As we grow and come into the world, we see, hear, smell, touch, and encounter innumerable occurrences. How we perceive these depends upon our unique filtering system. Our work of learning to love everything that happens to and around us brings humor. Engage in the peaceful warrior's practice of using the issues of daily life to grow and transmute pain into wisdom.

Let us release fear and act from enthusiasm. If you want it, and you go after it, especially with love, it will be yours. You are that capable. Take solace in these comforting words from Sarah Ban Breathnach: "No matter how much time it takes for a dream to come true in the physical world, no day is ever wasted."

ELEVATE THE MUNDANE

Feel love during your day to elevate everything. Share something with another each day to make it meaningful. Today is. When you look at something right in the face it is less daunting. The beauty of this day will be missed if we are longing for our yesterdays or concerned over tomorrow. We can embrace each moment as it occurs through whatever acts of attentiveness we know work for us. Following are some faithful grasps to assist watchful daily elevation.

There is a way in every day to honor the special within the mundane. Trying first to appreciate something special encourages our strength to go further when we are able. That today I found an indefinable moment of meaning within something regular elevated my life. Moments of elevation can be discovered in life's small, surprising seconds with love and sharing, and establish something memorable out of the mundane.

To observe repetitive routines and expect a mystical monument often brings dissatisfaction. They are not so obvious, these glories, but are born of our own acknowledgment of depth. It is about how and to what extent we notice. Without bright, shining lights and bells it is up to us to consider our current experience valuable, even magical. We enrich this day by choosing to be cognizant. What we are looking for will tell us what can be seen. And that which rises only from our grace and worth will be in the hour, honored.

"What we are looking for will tell us what can be seen."

It remains deeper inside, this portal to grateful, conscious living. Power is fleeting, heaven is here unknowable, but connection in any experience to something larger than ourselves or our task, we feel with remembrance. We know only that which fits, and we see only that which we can expand to recognize. With these acknowledgements we can achieve an ability at accepting all available awesomeness.

We cannot know if transformation is possible unless we are allowing at a higher rate. We hopefully understand there is no blame if we have not been elevating everything with love just yet; our present circumstance may even be the tapestry woven in mystery by our own keeper. But we can—I know this much—create more of these awarenesses, to a joyous estimate, by our presence, and focus toward their potential. These extraordinary moments are awaiting our own uncovering of the layers; it is a simple higher calling for the moments of our days, and they glee to be seized. Notice with gratefulness, and they will not escape into attrition. There is nothing like being in a flow state with the Universe.

MEDITATION: DAILY

- Read and ponder this poem in your meditative space.

Listen, and you will hear guidance.
Follow with movement, and you will be led.
Look up, and your perspective will broaden.
Be grateful, and you will receive.
Love, and you will have love.
Look for positive qualities, and they will abound.
Enjoy this moment, and it will grow.
Appreciate with awareness, and your life will be fulfilling.

BREATHING DEEPLY

The breath of life. Take a deep breath. Breathe life into your body or space. Breathe a sigh of relief. If all else fails, and we have no control over our present moment, we can pause and breathe. Most of us do not realize that the first thing we do when we feel stress is either stop breathing briefly or breathe shallowly. We can re-balance all of our systems by simply bringing our attention back to our breath and focusing it steadily, deeply, and slowly for just a few moments.

One of the best and easiest meditations we can utilize is concentrating on our breath. When our breathing is even and full, everything else is soothed. Oxygen rejuvenates all of our systems and brings our body the very life force it requires. We may not be aware what urgent constraints our body feels, or what shock it goes into as shallow breathing activates its alarms, but long, deep breaths do more for us than we know, and that is all we need to know in order to do it. No special skills or tools—just be conscious of the breath coming in and going out, over and over. An involuntary function we might otherwise take for granted needs only a bit of attention for optimum capacity and effect.

As we place awareness on our inhalations and exhalations, we can also help rejuvenate our energy and release anxiety. Deep breaths in can bring fresh air and lighter feelings. Breathing out is an aid for letting go of pressure, energy blocks, or anything we are holding onto. Sighing is a great release.

Also, pay attention to the quality of your environment and what you are relying on to sustain your physical machine. If you work or live in a stuffy building, then you are likely experiencing negative effects from bad air. Use air filters. Get outside to clean and natural places—up in the mountains where the air is clean, or by an ocean where it is ionized and wet—and breathe as much healthy, clear air into your lungs as you possibly can. It is a simple step toward better health and communication with our own bodies. Bring in love when you breathe, and calm your breathing every day.

It is said that when we are sad and cry, we take in breath after breath but find it difficult to let go of. This shows a vulnerability or fear of releasing the breath we have in us, as if we are frightened it might not come back. When we are angry, we release and blurt breath out, and maybe scream and yell, but have difficulty taking in. We sort of hold things at bay, unwilling to draw inside or receive. Coming back to feelings of love and steady breathing can balance both.

As an asthmatic, I am all too aware of my breath, sometimes struggling for each consecutive moment of life. I have also heard that asthmatics do not fully exhale when an attack begins due to fear of release without faith it will return. Or perhaps this precipitates the beginning of the attack because of the doubt that they will get more air coming in. It is often humorous to the friends of an asthmatic (assuming it is minor and all ends well) that the instant they realize they do not have their inhaler, the breathing incident gets worse, and quickly. I find this interesting as a deeper issue of trust, and I still work on its connection to my heart chakra, which includes the lungs, and ability for unconditional love.

The lungs are the organs that process grief, and grief is one main effect of aging, deterioration, and potential vulnerability for our bodies. I find my fourth chakra work interesting as my parents relate stories of watching me, waiting for me to take each next breath as helpless parents of a seemingly helpless child. I also know my dad experienced his onset of heart problems after severe grief associated with divorce— also injury within the heart center.

The heart and lungs are the major organs of our heart

space. Simple control of our breath, or attention to our heartbeat, can make a huge difference in the energy we hold there. It is crucial that it flows, as it is key to feeling, and maintaining unconditional love. Most people only breathe from the top portion of their lungs because breathing deeply into the cavernous part energetically opens access to emotional matters. As a healee begins to relax, emotions surface, and they come out the more he or she begins to breathe. This is a wonderful way to heal. This vital chest area is also where we maintain our vision of ourselves and love within the world. The core of our hearts is where we hold our picture of self. So with management of unconditional love, respiratory and circulatory survival, and our deepest picture of ourselves, we can energize these functions through right breath.

It is vital we breathe properly and efficiently. When we feel love within our breath it fills our bodies. We can look to our sinus passages, our nose and throat area for proper breathing. Congestion can often be an issue. I have intolerable trouble with keeping my nose clear. When it is not, my mouth gets dry, my asthma gets worse, I cannot sleep or eat easily, and my chest tightens as I struggle for breath. That so many faculties are involved in optimal breathing helps us recognize its importance. It is worth quality of life to see doctors and healers in order to make sure this complicated flow of air is working deeply and with ease.

There are countless breathing exercises that can induce different states of consciousness or healing throughout the body, and they can definitely shift energy. My favorite is to breathe in through the nose and out through your mouth in extended length. Though I dislike counting breaths, when the exhale is longer than the inhale it stimulates the vagus nerve, which propels rest and relaxation.

Whether you know a lot about these many techniques or

not, we all understand, to a survival extent, the significance of our breath. So pay attention to your breath, as well as to what you are breathing. Watch it go in and out slowly and deeply, and enjoy the refreshing physical stability and healing ability you always have with this hopefully effortless power.

MEDITATION: BREATHING

- Close your eyes and take a few deep breaths.
- Breathe in through your nose, and out through your mouth.
- Release with your out breath anything you are ready to let go of.
- Breathe in love, feeling it begin in your chest.
- Expand your diaphragm and lower abdomen to take full breaths.
- Blow stuff out to release.
- At the end of your release, notice your heartbeat, and relax your body.
- Come back to normal breathing patterns by focusing on love in your heart.

LIGHT

Let there be light! You are the light of the world. The light within. You light up my life. The light that casts out the darkness. Let your light shine! Shine your light on others. Work with light every day and your life will change. Call light when you wake up each morning, and you are already doing the best thing you can to start your day. Do energy work with light and ask for the light of angels to come to you, and off your day goes in the right direction. When I cannot reach feelings of love easily, I begin with light. Once the light tingles through me and I feel it flowing, love is readily accessible each day.

MEDITATION: CALLING LIGHT

- To raise your vibration, close your eyes and breathe calmly, in through your nose, out through your mouth.
- Call to the light of the sun to come to you, no matter the time or place. Go outside if you can.
- Know that light responds immediately to your thought of it.
- Watch and feel it brighten you.
- Fill and feel with every breath.
- Repeat often.

One of the two most powerful and effective tools I have discovered in advancing my soul and spiritual quest is the value of using the light. (The other is active meditation/ energy work.) I cannot express how worthwhile working with light can be for you, but I guarantee it will change your life. Like most other mechanisms of self-development, its affects might seem subtle at first, but you will soon realize and be awed by its influence. It is simple, instinctual, and you can do it in a flash, literally. It will improve your perspective, your future situations, your visualizations, and your relationships.

Moreover, all you have to do is ask light to come to you. In *Spiritual Growth*, Sanaya Roman says to just "call the light to you." Whatever this means to you, whatever that would feel like, just call it forth, and it is immediately present. It is all around us just waiting to be activated. It is happy to be of service.

As Sanaya Roman goes on to explain in her marvelous book that is channeled by the light being Orin, there is a huge new wave of light entering our planet at this time. It is changing mass thoughts, and it is here to raise the vibration of our earth. It is partially due to this magnificent light that many beings are coming together in critical mass to help heal our world. Many others, unable to have this magnetic change, are thus choosing to leave the world temporarily. This light wave brings many changes, which some may perceive as turbulence. It is ever more imperative to be consciously choosing our path and acting from love and evolution during this time. The great light is here to help us in our transformation. Light is the visual manifestation of love. Wherever light enters, darkness dissolves.

We are dependent on our most tangible form of light, the sun, for our very existence. It creates all life on our planet, sustains our climates, permits growth, and illuminates our world. Without light, everything here would die. Although we may take it for granted, it is perhaps the most important element we know.

Think how beautiful it is to watch the dawn—the transforming of night into day. The light appears from nowhere; stretching, it reaches across the sky, soon overtaking everything with a magical pinkish glow. Just like love in our hearts, light originates from the unknown then radiates far and beyond where we can imagine, changing everything it touches. It begins as a faint bluish-white tint and within moments it is bright, pervasive, and all-expanding. You cannot see where it ends or begins, it just is. It envelopes everything unconditionally and gives to all equally. It warms us to our cores. It helps us see. Even in the dark of night, it reaches us through the moon and starlight, twinkling and pulsing.

My friend Jeff once shared with me that he arose every morning to watch the sunrise. I thought this was lovely and felt as if he knew something sacred that I only pondered. My body naturally awakens me early, which used to be a source of aggravation and tiredness. I disparaged my huge sleep problems of persistent insomnia until this conversation. Now I see the sunrise most mornings, and I feel the lovely importance of those moments throughout the day. I often write at those times and awakening light fills my words. I am then sharing love.

Right along with this enlightened stroke of genius from Jeff, I came across this romantic quote from Rumi, a Sufi poet: "The breeze at dawn has secrets to tell you, don't go back to sleep." It could not be truer.

While every day's sunrise is breathtaking and inspiring, there is something extra special about the moments just prior—the dawn. When you can see the sun, you feel fulfilled and reassured, but before its entrance, profound mystery embraces the world. Light is coming, but you cannot identify its source. There is something untouchable and wise about this. Every day that I am clever enough to be a part of the transformation from dark starry skies to the mystifying glow of dawn, I am in tune with the Universe in a way unlike anything I can plan. I feel I have a leg up on those around me because I was part of the great secrets, only tangible at that holy, blessed instant. There really is something magical to dawn's quality.

If you have never looked upon the light in these ways, then take a moment to notice it. Whether a clear blue day or a cold winter's afternoon, it is there. Whether you live at the top of the world and survive by the changing light, or near the equator of the Great Gaia and bask in its heat almost continuously, it nourishes each of us.

Now, this is just the sun—the light we can see. Imagine for a second how magnificent must be the light of the Divine. If the sunlight we can see does all this, then you can begin to believe in the truly unlimited power of the light from within and above. This power is another tremendous gift given us by our creator, with power so dazzling that it was hidden in plain sight for only a few to truly realize and appreciate. We look up and wink because we know. We look around and give thanks because we utilize its supremacy, growing unbounded with its strength.

MEDITATION: FEELING LIGHT

- Go outside and look up at the sky.
- Feel gratitude for all the sun does. Even through clouds, we can feel it.
- Step into the light and bask in it for a few moments.
- Thank the sun for its presence and feel connection to the planet.
- Get up before the sun once this week, and watch the world awaken.
- Note thoughts, messages, and feelings.

Near the completion of my certification in Feng Shui, with its accompanying vast mysticism, I was honored with my initiation into the Gayatri, one of the most powerful Sanskrit mantras. This is symbolized by ritual and a mantra prayer to the sun in which we honor its energy and capacity to bring light to the planet through our hearts as committed warriors of spreading its power. Some of the Gayatri's mysteries are hidden, but this rite and ritual moved me, altered space, and even used *vibhuti*, a sacred holy ash materialized presently by only two spiritualist prophets currently walking our earth. This ceremony of becoming an arbiter for the light shifted my life, purpose, and abilities, for which I am grateful to Mr. Mario C. Veo.

Making conscious contact with our inner light or calling to divine or solar light can quicken the rate at which we see, understand, heal, connect, and create. It speeds and grows our manifestations. Adding light to our visualizations yields greater power. Light transforms our five senses by opening our intuitive centers, healing our chakra bodies, and illuminating our auric layers. It aids in our process of evolving and healing without much knowledge of exactly how it works.

Every pain or block to which we add light is cleared and dissolved with greater ease. When we need to release, a grounding cord of light is a perfect tool. When we want to connect with the power of our Universe and planet by bringing in cosmic or earth energy, light unconditionally assists us.

As I discerned the wisdom of using all colors of light, I also learned to create faster. Even solar light is suitable. Sanaya Roman assures us that holding and radiating more light *is* enlightenment. Simple. Asking light to fill your space will bring positive results, and it cannot be overused. Getting direct sunlight onto our energy bodies can even help us heal. Ten minutes on our solar plexus, or between our shoulder blades, boosts immunity.

I enjoy an array of colors in my spiritual light work: fluorescent pinks, blues, gold, healthy greens, and even brown for calming and neutralizing. I use reds, oranges, and purples as well, and notice fun differences with changing shades. We can study a vast collection of books on color, such as *Creative Color* by Farber Birren or *Change You Aura Change Your Life* by Barbara Y. Martin, but most importantly we need to trust what the colors feel like to us. You may look into a spiritual school or seek out a competent professional if you would like further details on any of your favorites.

You can connect with and bring in light all on your own, in any place. It will come to you with no training or manipulation, and you can direct it as an unconditional force of good. Its power is unbounded. Light helped create our world and continues restoring and elevating us every day we choose to access it. Know that the light, in all its colors, awaits your utilization, to each cell, in abundance.

SURRENDER

Leave behind your blocks and fears and surrender to God, to the universal energy, to unconditional love. What is occurring is being brought because you somehow asked for it or vibrated with its opposite. We can live in a space of surrender by not fighting against anything.

"Surrender is not resignation, it is allowing."

Surrender is not resignation, it is allowing. Surrender to love. As you see something working its yin or yang, ebb or flow, recognize the message in the pusher of buttons. See your present with great clarity and wake up with the realization of why this situation is presenting itself to you in the first place. This is a karmic gift. You can then take the instant with a sigh of relief and thanks, work with the more important information within it, and both utilize and be grateful for the elevated experience of your present moment. This is not giving up. This is letting go of struggle and instead opening to the deeper, real experience. This is enlightenment.

Surrender is fighting less and looking around more. It is struggling less and understanding more. When we stop pushing against the current and cease attempts to manipulate our surroundings, and instead give our will over to the flow of the Universe, we discover that this flow is perfect as it is, and we only need enter it to live as part of its ecstasy. We surrender so we might breathe more and listen to the Divine intently so we miss nothing important. When we are coming up short, are overwhelmed toward our breaking point, or are too exhausted to care, we give over to a higher power and find clues in watching for messages that lead us to path markers. Working with this energy is then effortless. Surrender daily to live love.

If our direction or our perspectives consistently take us away from peace, surrendering to the whispers will get us back on track and in tune with our souls. We do not have to fret so much or push so hard against the immovable. If we allow to be shown the next steps or way of love, our path will be lighted and resistance will let go. When we release ego's grip, our perfectionism, and our control in needing to be right or always doing it our way, the fight will stop, the competition will cease; cooperation will rise to meet us, and providence will lead us to a better, easier way.

As we relate to others, and they are not fulfilling our needs or gratifying our wants, we surrender to unconditional love, and there we find truth. When we have this acceptance and see another through this spirit, we surrender our frail manipulations over them as well as this illusion of control, and in turn we focus on our own hearts. This is how to spend our days.

MEDITATION: SURRENDER

- Take a few breaths and clear your mind.
- Give your mind a rest from its incessant workings, figuring, and noisy demands.
- Release thoughts and beliefs about what anyone should or could be doing.
- Fill your space with loving acceptance.
- Allow everyone to be who they are, where they are.
- Accept yourself as you are.
- Breathe until you feel your pressure lighten.
- Relax your body, and feel your shoulders ease.
- Say to yourself, "Everything is divine just as it is. Follow the course of love."

Encourage growth for all by being what you most want to see, hear, feel, and experience in the world. This action of unconditional love clears the space between two spirits. Surrender pain or angst to love, and release the demands placed between you. Always being pent up is no way to get anywhere we want to go. Repeat that others are okay to be themselves, as the world is okay to be itself, and you will be beautiful for growing with love.

Change your heart to freedom. Evolve and imprison no one with verdicts. See their angelic self in this space and love their best self for living with all the light they have. See yourself the same way. Shine into this realization the feelings and warming light of unconditional love, and deep breaths will confirm that all is right and well in life. Listen and flow without struggle; this is surrender.

Accept whatever is happening, even if it seems awful. Trust the Universe, and do not place such strain on yourself or anyone else that anything has to be a certain way. Things come much easier into an open vessel than a taut wire. Follow your truth and dreams, and employ compassion over fighting. Be willing to be led gently by your heart and from calmness. Feel good. Feel peace.

Only once we have reached this space of clarity can we see clearly and know that our actions engender love. Only with our intent to see wellness will we see truth. Only when we surrender the lower will we find unconditional love and live in the higher light. Our spirits then remain within our body more easily. Then we live as Spirit. When we stop clenching and instead relax into our bodies, what is before us opens wide, and it is with this ease we will discover that unconditional love and surrender guide us right to where we wish daily.

CHAPTER TWENTY-EIGHT

Aims for Daily Love

This chapter offers final ideas to aim your daily elevating process towards love. Understanding yin and yang—how all things resonate—helps us not sweat the small stuff because we learn peace in living both sides of the coin. Balance is paramount to our daily grind if we are to share love. We look at light ups, or things that really get our goat. Working what alights us every day leads us to love more, and to share clean energy. We also look at helpful appreciations to incorporate in each day in order to expand love, like sublime sustenance and our furry companions.

YIN AND YANG

Everything in our world operates according to opposites. Our planet is fundamentally wired with polarities, and as such, everything around us works by these rules. Yin and yang dictate that both positive and negative charges must be present if energy is to flow. If we want to be in accord with our environment and function harmoniously, we must live with this in mind. When we search for love, it is because we have felt love's absence. In making choices, we may encounter pain if we cling to any one side without encompassing the whole. Resistance and attachment contain the same energy within dichotomy, yet when we perceive one as okay and allowable, and the other as bad or unwanted, we lose our power over our neutral ability to choose and have. Not every day can be all sunshine, and these too are valuable.

We limit our experience by believing things to be good or bad. If we put enough energy behind any picture we buy into in this life, history and pain may repeat themselves. Until we can acknowledge all possibilities with validation, we may get stuck reliving one aspect, or attacking its opposite until we allow the wholeness of existence. Whether we believe in this concept or are even aware of it, these polarities are in continuous motion surrounding us, and they dictate how energy works.

Most are at least vaguely familiar with the concept of yin and yang. There is a necessary magnetism to our present moment: what comes also goes, and what we push away later arrives. It is, however, our free will to choose how we react to all of this data. Such is the irony of free will, which allows for pain and mistakes just as our freedom can sometimes isolate us. We cannot have good without bad or darkness without light. Human life ebbs and flows. When we cannot control or manipulate, we remember this model and practice awareness of yin and yang. Then we live daily with more understanding, peace, and liberation.

Everything in our Universe contains the energies of yin and yang, including us. In order to create anything on this earth plane, its opposite must exist. We cannot see totality without knowing emptiness. We cannot manifest the material without spirituality. We cannot have beautiful experiences without challenges. But we can allow this process and flow through the challenging more easily when we believe each day that the great will return.

Everything contains within itself a seed of the opposite

and the eventual process of everything changes full circle. Life is yang, and at the end of this creation is the yin: death. One who yells may be expressing yang energy, but soon after may retreat to a private quarter, emptied and now yin. While making love you may climax, sweat, and be very active, and after you may lie still, resting in quiet euphoria. When someone expresses hatred, anger, or indifference, he or she is calling out for love.

Out is yang, in is yin—back and front, day and night, up and down, everything parallels this energy. Women are more yin, as are dark, cool, receptive energies and the moon. Men are more yang, as are light, hot, active energies and the sun. While this is somewhat difficult to understand in the literal sense, the essence of these ideas permeate our world.

No one forces the presence of opposites, yet we are affected by their reality each moment. When you cannot accept a particular side of a situation, or be okay with receiving differently from your preferences, the very piece you resist will be manifested within your experience. This is much like being given opportunities to cultivate patience when you desire it, or coming across the challenges of anger and loneliness when you ask for love. One contains the other; they are two parts of the same energy form. The Universe must balance itself.

The energies we perceive as positive and negative must both exist in order for energy to flow. If we stifle this movement with fear, negative judgment, or unwillingness, nothing will flow. We can, however, precede this phenomenon with grace and gratitude—feel grateful for what we have, acknowledge how far we have come, how much we have grown—then, out of pain or discomfort, we realize the magnitude of our blessings. We know we can handle and have anything in the Universe and still be a whole spirit.

We are a part of the force of nature, and the cycles we see

are a part of us, every day. In the present moment watch the creation of opposites and give acceptance to all of it. Yin and yang are also the basis of much Feng Shui as it dictates all energy interaction. While you may be tired and motionless, your child is full of power and liveliness. This is the natural state of energy's movement. After the yin of sleeping, you may be activated into the yang. Know that this effect works within everything. It is enlightening to observe this dynamic going on around all of us, and to share the balance of it illuminates the shaky base of our daily frustrations, so we can see with more clarity and inclusion.

What is present today will change tomorrow, or inevitably, what is lacking in this moment will be overflowing in the next. Unconditional love projected onto seeming unfairness will eliminate the personal attack we feel is being perpetrated, and help us see that all comes back to neutral, and simply moves.

MEDITATION: YIN AND YANG

- Run around your space for one minute, making noise and moving all your limbs.
- Now sit still, close your eyes, and breathe calmly.
- This is yin and yang, and both are valuable.
- Contemplate a situation that bothered you and see all its aspects unfolding.
- Imagine now what the opposite of that would look like.
- Notice how important balance is to every equation.
- What is something you've asked for recently? Notice its opposite may already be present, which is why

you are wanting the change. Then let the opposite go with love, and focus on what you want.

- That which you do not want attracts that which you do want.
- Appreciate the balance of our Universe, and be grateful for everything.

LIGHT UPS

Who or what aggravated you today? These situations or people that light us up, get our goat, get a rise out of us, or bring to the surface feelings of anger, judgment, anxiety, or even revenge are our daily opportunities for exploration of unconditional love. When something within us is triggered, it is a chance for us to investigate our discomfort. The interesting thing about working on a core picture of unconditional love in this lifetime is that the moment you commit to such a path, everyone and everything that challenges this practice will run into your life. Everything has its opposite.

Many in-your-face opportunities will present themselves as you seek to explore a new mindset. There will be no shortage of relationships with your main agreement being to remind you to keep working this path of love. Through these polarities we discover love for ourselves. This is a gift for you to see and work toward your desire. Through daily observation and acceptance of this truth, we find peace. If it were all coming up roses, then unconditional love would be easy and would not require attention. Growth toward it would not require incarnation into the physical. But resistance, as in weight training, makes us stronger. Light ups eventually let us love.

Having a particular preference or focus will spark its

opposite to rear up so we may truly uncover layers. This resistance we need in order to reach wholeness. Once I came in to my teachers and they said I was all lit up. I thought this was good and thanked them—always humor. But they could see I had been activated by something, was pissed, fluttered, all up in arms. Someone had triggered a charge I carry.

The moment we recognize feeling stressed or shaken it becomes an opportunity. We may eventually learn to thank those who cause us grief, for, as well-seasoned button pushers, those who light us up are enabling our capacity for growth. They are fulfilling a soul agreement to work out the karma of this experience with us. Whenever something provokes us, we can recognize immediately that we have something to look at with shifted perception, and we have a chance to expand instead of contract. We have a chance to remember our angelic friend.

MEDITATION: WHEN YOU ARE LIT UP

- Notice when you are lit up by something or someone.
- Congratulate yourself for noticing—great aware-ness!
- Take it slow, sit down, and get ahold of yourself.
- Breathe and feel that unconditional love begin in your heart.
- As the light ups flash by your consciousness, use your energy tools to inspect them.
- What are you learning from this?
- What is it you seek or want from this situation or person?

- Watch your light ups, and then release them, as much as it takes to feel good again.
- Fill in with the opposing energy.
- Be grateful for the whole of your experience, your noticing, and your healing.

You can clear whatever form of negative energy your circumstance brings by expanding love through your body. You can expand it even further into your aura and the planet. Do this every day something upsets you, and looking back you will soon notice less upsets. The appearance of light ups reminds us to come back to our path of love as we create muscle strength by being pushed against. Light ups are not evil or bad; they are a gift of daily awareness to further commit to learning and seeing love, everywhere.

SUBLIME SUSTENANCE

After all this metaphysical discussion on how to train our brains to surrender and allow, let me touch on something we can all sink our teeth into—literally. Food! Food is love. Okay, that is a terrible thing to say to those of us who are overweight and tirelessly strive for more nutritional wholeness instead of familiar emotional comfort—but it resonates nonetheless. My father-in-law, who was sparing in compliments and outward warmth or kindness, found his sublime way of nurturing through his making meals for us, sending us home with food, and sustaining our physical bodies with cuisine worthy of his own restaurant.

Now, I am no slouch in the kitchen, mostly due to necessity and creativity with little in the cupboards, but Richard elevated the creation of meals to a higher order than most. He was by far the best tangible cook in my life. His inspiration and generosity of simple provisions took shape as one of the most loving forms of devotion and support he manifested.

I find the importance he placed on nourishing bodies unique but fascinating. I am grateful that my husband inherited the foundations of this understanding as well. As I grew up, it was a hassle to prepare food, and it never touched on wholeness and fulfillment like it did for my in-laws, except during holidays.

There is something beautiful about people who have an intrinsic gift for feeding others. When someone is hungry, putting something together for their betterment is divine. It seems more like a pain to me—something I have to do to take care of my family, even if I love them unconditionally. I did not learn the natural rhythm of making food. I must prepare and plan, hope for all the necessary ingredients, and put aside time in which to accomplish this chore. I sometimes enjoy cooking, and I love feeding those I love—it does come with instant gratification and appreciation from delightful squeals—but I do not possess the desire to cook all day just because. I often do not even eat much if I am alone for the day, which probably arises from a deeper lack of worth or young poverty.

That I do not seem worth the time and inventiveness to create something delicious when I am alone has rendered much inner awareness. I know that people who live alone feel this way sometimes and relegate their nutrition to those who will make food for them, and I totally understand this. It is a treat for us to order takeout, or it feels special to go out and "sit down." But this is more an issue of money and health than about self-love.

A certain feeling of love for oneself rises to the surface when time and creativity have been spent on a meal. Even simplicity in a plate of food can be satisfying, as it has more to do with giving effort to your body than anything else. No satisfaction lies in cold leftovers straight out of the fridge or something thrown together because your stomach is empty.

I know few who possess that special skill to get up and cook something delicious just because. There is nothing in me that gets up before the sun just so I can make a breakfast that consists of sausage and bacon, egg and cheese sandwiches (on homemade bread), along with blueberry pancakes and fresh fruit. And while the yummy cheese is melting into the eggs and sausage nicely, I am not already thawing other inventions for lunch and dinner. This was a true scene at the house of my daughters' grandparents. I do very well feeding most that enter my home, but I will never quite own that gift.

Richard's love for cooking came at an easy price as he helped his mother in the kitchen feeding his eight brothers and sisters instead of laboring in their sugar beet fields of northeast Colorado. Where I make garlic bread by toasting a slice and spreading on butter, followed by a sprinkle of garlic salt and paprika, Richard put nine ingredients into his garlic bread. Nine! If I am feeling fancy, I might bake it in the oven with some added parmesan (from a bottle), but every time he made it, it was in a basket covered in cotton cloth, unveiled as scrumptiousness worthy of a king.

No matter what our jobs, our names, our talents or qualms, we all must eat. Some do it way better than others, but take note of your daily love and consuming. I would love to grow my own herbs and make more cakes from scratch, but the reality for me is just not so. Some are great gardeners, and others cannot keep a plant alive, but since the issue of food is prevalent in our daily life, and not an option, it represents a look into how we treat ourselves. How we nourish our bodies, or don't, can tell us a lot about our self-value. Certain days call for convenience of time. But take occasion to treat yourself to an appetizing and visually pleasing meal.

TIPS TO ENJOY FOOD CREATION

• Find an enticing recipe, or call a family member for a childhood favorite.

• Make yourself a simple, yet beautiful and healthy meal.

• Use lots of naturally colored fruits and vegetables for healing the chakras.

• Heal your microbiome with fermented foods.

• Use healing herbs like turmeric, ginger, garlic, pepper, and nutrient rich salt.

• Invite someone to share in this creative gift.

• Take care of that body which houses your spirit and feel love.

Someone you know has made you a meal that was tempting and interesting. Get that recipe, or call a relative who is known for their cooking expertise. Food preparation is a small form of love, self-love and selfless giving, because let's face it—after all your time and energy, your creation is devoured and gone . . . a good lesson in detachment and caring for simple matters in various ways, but your self will thank you.

I may cheat a bit on some meals, but put lots of love into others. I do the best I can, and what food I prepare is a clear consistent check to see if I am loving and caring for myself. The value of gathering each day in order to sustain our nutrition might be overlooked by feelings of thanklessness or wasting of time, but it goes a long way when we do it with love and share it. It keeps us alive, and recognized, even if quietly. It went a long way to healing us when my father-in-law would insult us during the day because he was stern, but would then send us home with the fixings for dinner already cooked and put together in separate containers.

We all show love in the ways we are comfortable with, and most everyone gives what they have in abundance. Food contains a breadth of gifts if we but delve for them: nourishment, creativity, healing, connection, unity, service, fulfillment, pleasure, comfort, stimulation, and life itself. Cook for someone special more often, cook for yourself, or truly appreciate the gift from another. For as long as I live, I will miss Richard's breakfast meals when we dropped off the girls. I will always remember that through this bag of breakfast deliciousness, he said "I love you" every time. And boy oh boy, did it always taste sublime!

FURRY COMPANIONS

My first spoken word was "goggie." My goggie is my friend, my love. He is soft, furry, warm, cuddly, beautiful, and always by my side. Every moment, he is my writing and life companion. Stunning, protective, loving, always affectionate, connecting, and ever present—we share the most excellent moments, and have the clearest conversations each day. Animals communicate through mental pictures. Though I have always entertained special connection with animals, our clairvoyant work has helped immensely with the interpretation of these pictures. The unconditional love from these beings can lead our days to living and sharing a life of love.

In my bedroom, soft purring kitties enter sporadically for love, kisses, and any adoration they can pull from lying on me (and of course, whatever I am working on). Silky, communicative, playful, snuggly, here and now, and loyal, cats are also wonderful bundles of velvet and sweet squeezing. Whether a good baby nurse, a grief counselor, or a jester, animals protect, comfort us, and fill the spaces in our lives.

In our search for unconditional love, peace, and daily enlightenment, our animals are our best living examples. Some may think they are just pets to be taken care of, let out or kept in and fed, but many of us know that the wooly creatures with strong and deep eyes were sent to us as angelic gifts. Not only do these companions consistently exhibit many of the higher qualities we yearn for, but they give their ever-loving presence without fail. Let us treasure the creatures of our earth and acknowledge daily their divine contributions and qualities as our greatest tangible models of unconditional love.

When you are enduring a difficult day or longer life phase, animals are available with their warmth. They are givers. When you have an argument with a friend or partner, animals still love and caress. They are accepting. When we have not been our best or have worked tirelessly and need only to remain still, our animals comfort and snuggle. They embody the present moment.

Animals do not fret over what needs to be done or what was forgotten. They do not care what you wear, look like, or eat, so long as they can be close to you and perhaps share in the meal. They do not keep their distance until things are resolved or forgiven, for they always love us, unconditionally. They hold the vibration of immediate forgiveness, and they can teach us this treasured gift, helping us to release our own karmic debts. They are perfectly themselves, and they allow us to play, laugh, and be silly when we have taken our thoughts too seriously. All they want is to share our love.

Those of us who are welcomed home by adoring pets know their value. They are always happy to see us with joyously wagging tails or sweet purring, only hoping to be picked up or pet. They have the remarkable ability to shift our attitudes as we throw off our days and bend down to squeeze and hug them. If only we could greet others in kind. They are glad we are home, and they always let us know it. Animals are the natural illustrations of everything unconditional and pure. You simply cannot hold anger or negativity when you share your humanity with a pet. They sense your heart, and can see the goodness within you, without any attempts at convincing.

If you were not lucky enough to grow up with animals, or even have an aversion to them, you can observe and interact with their generous Zen-like characteristics in numerous ways. Learn to appreciate the lessons they offer by noticing the actions of any animals around you. Squirrels and birdies in your yard will offer this gift if you look. You can go to a pet care facility and play with abundantly loving animals just to experience their presence. Shelters are grateful for volunteers to walk dogs or give affection, and you will leave having been the one taken care of. Sit in nature, and feel your spirit adapt as you watch butterflies. Notice if a small creature comes near you to interact. You can care for the pet of a friend when they need a sitter. Visit the zoo.

Whether or not you own and enjoy pets on a daily basis, you can find a way to discover and envelope their endless gifts of grace and pleasure. They have much peace and compassion to teach everyone who wonders about the acquiring of such effortless living. Thank the benevolent Universe for knowing that our furry companions would assure we are never alone on this planet. The foresight this limitless charity afforded us is beyond words of gratitude.

The pets we steward and choose as our own have an unmatchable capacity to pull us out of our doldrums with their here-and-now attitudes and bring us to their natural state of pure joy. If you are in their environment with negativity or sadness, they will look through your soul with that "play with me" spark, and you are brought back to this moment in a flash. Animals are our constant when everything else in life seems turbulent. They are those who we can confide in when we do not want to worry our ailing partner about how the doctor bills will be paid, or who will see us through if we are left by the one we love. They please and assist us with nothing short of unwavering, unconditional love. It is proven scientifically that sharing your life with pets will extend your longevity and boost your health and immunity.

If your life involves adoring the creatures that share your space, you know the truth and value of their company; if it does not, no one will ever be able to explain what is missing from your life or your soul. Our fuzzy friends enable our spirits to be brought through the mundane of everyday life, and they keep us focused on love, tenderness, and nurturing. When we lose one of these friends, it brings a sadness like almost no other.

My heart broke as we watched my doggie, who was important to my existence, take his last breaths. We shared fourteen years and fourteen days together, laughing, hugging, and sharing what others could not. I could only find comfort in knowing our rare bond of love transcended space and time, sobbing until I remembered we could be reunited. I know he will find me in his new little furry body, and we will immediately recognize each other by the signs only we could know. Until then, I treasure my family in their understanding of my personal great loss when a constant source of love and joy and indomitable presence is suddenly missing. My kitties are doing more than their fair share of cuddling and anchoring for my spirit. I am proud of what has been taught me by an unknowingly sacred, incredible, and untouchable union.

It is important at this time, and any time, that we remember to be open. If we compare relationships, even with animals, we may be losing the possibility to be touched by another friend. In time we will rescue a puppy and come to love her or him for their own value. It is helpful to remain willing to consider additional relationships because we never know how a new spirit will connect with or heal us. God appreciates us taking care of all his creatures. There is a special place in heaven for animal caretakers.

Give the uniqueness of each individual—furry or soft, two or four legged—a chance to awaken the best within you. It is possible that someone for whom you have longed is yet awaiting contact. May you find, through your furry friends, the lessons and reassurances you desire to find in the world. For there, in one tiny ball of fur, is everything we need.

MEDITATION: FURRY FRIENDS

- Sit on the floor or next to a loved animal and just caress them.
- Close your eyes and feel their energy.
- Notice how they react to where and how you pet them.
- See if you can see colors of energy in or around them.
- Help your animal release, and fill them with healing, loving, or safe light.
- Feel the healing and connection yourself.
- Look your pets in the eyes, smile, be kind, and be grateful.

There is common ground that kindred spirits walk, sacred moments and memories that forever bind their souls. Drummond, my first doggie love, has come back to me as Wizard. We are side by side most of each day, returned to the solace of our union. He is once again my writing companion. He makes me laugh every day with his silly antics, and he cuddles and loves me even more as we both appreciate, through our temporary separation, our even stronger bond. Our love was, and remains, omniscient. Thank you, Universe, for helping us find one another, again, and for keeping our spirits close. This is my reward of unconditional love.

CHAPTER TWENTY-NINE

What the World Needs Now

As this book concludes, ask yourself what might be your contributions to the planet. Multiple ways to employ the unconditional love you have gotten, grown, kept, and shared are listed here. Consider what will help your spirit give the love it needs to receive, and then go and do, for the good of all.

MAKE A DIFFERENCE

Giving grants, service saves. Make a difference. Without guilt, for that helps no one. It is easier than you think to make a difference in someone else's life, either locally or globally. Give what you need and remember essence over form.

"When I chose to give what I needed, I felt better."

When I might miss my husband in a late afternoon or evening, I grab and give love to Clara, my youngest. I immediately feel better, and she squeals with delight at the spontaneous affection. With cuddling and tickling, soon we are both closer and smiling. It was not that I necessarily needed Paul at that lonely moment, but I did need to connect. When I chose to give what I needed, I felt better, and so did the recipient of my unconditional love. Remember, sharing love grows love.

To share love, we can participate in community donations of time, goods, services, or money, and we can do this on any scale that works for our lives. Give blood or advice, give hugs or food, give a safe space or a warm bed. Share your gift, whatever it may be, with the world. With today's technology, we can interact with the world at large easily, and intercede on behalf of one in need with the click of a button. Millions of people and animals need help in thousands of cities, in myriad ways. With motivation and a little creativity to care for the good of the whole, we can participate in the world we share and genuinely make it a better place for all.

If you are lonely, go to a place where others might share your isolation, such as an orphanage or home for the elderly. You might be surprised how fulfilling the visit is, and you might even hear inspiring stories that lift you and encourage you to do even more. If your seclusion runs deeper, you could help a local animal shelter exercise pets on a consistent basis, or adopt a few furry friends in need of the same love you long for.

If stress is a prevalent problem in your life, you could offer to get active by walking around parks picking up trash, shoveling, or sweeping in needed lots. You could make grander gestures by helping to feed the hungry or supply medications to poorer nations using the small monies collected in your change cup. You may attend laughing workshops that not only help your mood, but also help incite the cheer of others. Or you may give thoughtful words of kindness to a child in your vicinity that needs a boost in confidence or hope.

We can be active or passive in our charity. We can find endless avenues of connecting that help us to both give and receive. We truly have so much that can be of service to others. We can roll up our sleeves and work physically to get in contact with the world and its people, or we can assist discreetly. Look into your needs, and then brainstorm on a parallel circumstance of people who could also benefit from the awareness of your own wishes.

When we give healings in our classes, our teachers let us know we are also receiving a healing; by helping someone to move their energy, we are moving ours too. Whatever you need or lack in your life, you can be sure another does as well. Maybe you are the one to recognize the empty space, and whoever you run into with your creative flash will be the one to fill it. You could very well fill the void for each other simultaneously.

You could participate with big brothers or sisters and eventually help another to understand how to fill these spaces for themselves, just as you learn it. This act can guide a lost child or teenager and shift the course of their life. You can volunteer to help a new politician who still has integrity and works for what you believe in without taking monies from special interest groups. You can buy a meal or a blanket for a homeless soul in your area and bestow them with overflowing unconditional love. Cook a meal for or send a card to a friend in need. Reach out and engage in the flow of grace.

It is tragic that as humans we cannot care for all of our humanity, but we can change this with one moment of love after another. Just as people can give blood without any long-term detriment because it replenishes naturally, we have the means to help another without losing anything ourselves. Give anything you have to give. Give what you can when a nation experiences catastrophe, and your ten dollars may save a life. If you have come into recent prosperity or see another lacking what you have in abundance, then share a little, even once.

What the world needs now is help and love. Even just a moment of prayer for our planet or a country in need will add light to our world. If you cannot reach out today, or have no time or energy to share, then be that waterfall of unconditional love so that others may drink of it when in your presence. This is a magical way to share.

As we contemplate parting ways and how to shift from reading unconditional love to living it, we near thoughts of how we will do this on our own. We integrate, and give evidence that love has found expression through our living. Our actions will expand love through us with intention. We have wellsprings of love's supplies within us. We know what to look for and think of. We recognize the need for love, and the call for it. Now we choose love, and bestow it. We smile and spread joy. We fill with and impart unconditional love, and we are replenished. We share our abundant good fortune and bounty with another. That is how we know it is nourished and carried forward. That is how we know we are living it.

If all you can muster today is a smile, then give it, and you will still be rewarded in kind. Work your way up. Begin with the shortages in your own life and within your own heart, and as you expand your reach, you will touch others, and be touched. We are so blessed in our lives when we take stock with gratitude, and often our true wealth goes unnoticed or unappreciated. But when you look at another in need of the simple means for survival, or love and kindness, and you realize just how much you have, share it, and grow your spirit in giving. When we give to any cause with unconditional love, we actually grow that muscle within our lives. We can usurp our guilt or ingratitude, and shift the lack in our lives by helping out in any way. This helping fulfills the need in another, and then fills all the space around us with giant beauty. By recognizing with a full heart that we have much to offer we begin to know our own strength and power; that our one loving gesture, and a small amount of time or thought, really can make a difference.

MY DIFFERENCE IN THE WORLD

My end-to-end thoughts over the past years of my life accumulate with this work, and its publication is how I hope to make a difference in the world. Mister Rogers, who made a huge positive difference in the world, said, "Every tiny gesture, every warm word, every shared smile matters. Every second is an opportunity to make a choice." And he reminds us simply that, "To love someone is to strive to accept that person exactly the way he or she is right here and now."

"Love is where you find it." Look for it. I have this remarkable yet unassuming poster of heart shapes found all over by Rick Ruggles. In a cloud, a leaf, in the grain of wood— it is simple evidence of love everywhere. Since receiving this ever-giving gift, my entire family takes notice of heart shapes. When we are hiking and see heart-shaped rocks, we call out, "Love is where you find it." When we see heart-shaped clouds, simple shadows, or random objects in the shape of a heart, our girls yell, "Love is where you find it." It is a bonding thread between us. May they someday know how profound is this exercise of seeking love.

In *A Return to Love*, Marianne Williamson shares her hard-won knowledge that "Love is the answer." As Saint Bernadette knew, "Love is enough." And from the Muppets *Christmas Wish* with John Denver: "If you believe in love, that will be more than enough." We are all like Charlie Brown's Christmas tree: "It just needs a little love."

Sanaya Roman channels from her guide these ending words in her phenomenal book, *Spiritual Growth*: "You don't need to change yourself, you only need to love yourself." From the Dali Lama, "Compassion and love are not mere luxuries. As the source of both inner and outer peace, they are fundamental to the continued survival of our species."

Robert P. Ocker writes in *Indigo Children*: "My vision of

the future of education is based on unconditional love. This is the essence of the new human being." Later he says, "We, the educators, must be sure to surround ourselves with colleagues who have the heart and soul to raise the children of today to be the people of tomorrow."

"During this exact shift point, what our world needs most is for those who are striving to embody love, cooperation, and oneness to realize the magnitude of this golden moment," says Barbara Marx Hubbard.

From Teilhard de Chardin, "The day will come when, after harnessing the winds, the tides and gravitation, we shall harness for God the energies of Love. And on that day, for the second time in the history of the world, man will have discovered fire."

Finally and appropriately, Mother Theresa: "It is not how much we do, but how much love we put into the doing. And it is not how much we give, but how much love we put into the giving. To God there is nothing small."

In our best and reachable potential we can envision and create a world where everyone is loved, loving, and lovable. A world where spirit envelopes our minds, where our souls are led by our opening and light hearts, and where we live the beauty of poetry each moment. I continue to follow every day this path of unconditional love.

Sometimes the journey is difficult or daunting, although only because of my resistance and confusion. I know it need not be. Other days love pours from me effortlessly because with use it becomes self-sustaining. But it is always illuminating, and ever-present in enduring edification. Awakening this process of living a life of unconditional love has afforded within each experience and every interaction an endless remembrance of substance. The magnitude of our endeavor is significant at its least and transformational at its best as it ceases to limit, judge, or constrain the best or worst in us.

We can live in a world of unconditional love because we create it. We can own our right to our best selves. As we guide our futures and realities and make the world our grandest vision, we are what matters. We feel the love, and it feels good. Then we expand it onto everything and follow every thought with it.

MY WISH FOR YOU

It is my fondest wish that we all find moments of unconditional love, that we each become one who accepts each and all as we are, for the brilliant and profoundly astonishing creatures we develop into and imagine today, and for the pure magnificence we can become tomorrow. That we all grow these qualities and recognize them in others, allowing them to be seen within ourselves and then extended, is my greatest hope for humankind. Our earth is meant to be full of light, and it is returning.

If this love was not through our youth instilled, then today it can be restored. May we strive to these ends with boundless opportunities brought by simply living and loving, from universal struggles or familiar constraints, to ease and joy. Each day, each minute that we make the choice of unconditional love over views more ordinary, we are being the difference we wish to see and pass on as legacy. Grateful and changed will be the Universe and our souls as we achieve this with effortless effort.

Be well in your sought essence of unconditional love. Find it, spread it, and become the beauty living within the heart of us all. You can do it! Angels are gifting this to us all, and the Universe is celebrating your success. Let unconditional love envelope your thoughts, speech, movements, and above all, choices. This is our highest calling.

We finally see each other, wholly, because we recognize love. I know it is possible and extraordinary, and I believe in our exquisite ability to be love! It is there; look for it, feel it, grow it, bestow it, and be it. You will want for nothing more. Blessed from the heavens and Divinity is the light together we are creating. Thank you. Your generous gift is changing the world. As we part, we remain connected, forever in love. I radiate gratitude to you for following this path of unconditional love, and I wish you very, beautiful, hearty good luck!

ABOUT THE AUTHOR

Megan Loose is a certified psychic and clairvoyant reader, energy healer, and Feng Shui consultant who heals herself and others with a focus on love. Learning from the Berkeley Psychic Institute tradition, and her master teacher from the Shaolin temple, Megan has spiritual connections in numerous avenues, and as a born empath she writes with unique perspective. She is a spiritual teacher and student, turning to personal development thirty-six years ago. As a mother of magical daughters, and wife to her eternal soulmate, love and writing come together as the forefront of her life purpose. **www.meganloose.com**

BIBLIOGRAPHY

A Center For the Practice of Zen Buddhist Meditation. *The Key*. Mountain View, CA: A Center for the Practice of Zen Buddhist Meditation, 1984.

Andrews, Ted. *Animal Speak*. St. Paul, MN: Llewellyn Publications, 1993.

Bach, Richard. *Jonathan Livingston Seagull*. New York, NY: Avon Books, 1970.

Boeding, Conrad. *The Love Disorder*. Lakewood, NY: Passages Press, 1998.

Breathnach, Sarah Ban. *Simple Abundance; A Daybook of Comfort and Joy*. New York, NY: Warner Books Inc., 1995.

Carroll, Lee and Jan Tober. *Indigo Children*. Carlsbad, CA: Hay House Inc., 1999.

Davis, Ray. "Your Most Important Decision." The Affirmation Spot. http://theaffirmationspot.wordpress.com/2008/10/20/your-most-important-decision-the-affirmation-spot-for-monday-october-20-2008

Dolfyn. *Crystal Wisdom*. Oakland, CA: Earthspirit Inc., 1989.

Dyer, Wayne. W. *The Power of Intention*. Carlsbad, CA: Hay House Inc., 2004.

Dyer, Wayne. W. *There's a Spiritual Solution to Every Problem*. New York, NY: HarperCollins Publishers Inc., 2001.

Hicks, Esther and Jerry. *Ask and It is Given*. Carlsbad, CA: Hay House Inc., 2004.

Levoy, Gregg. *Callings: Finding and Following an Authentic Life*. New York, NY: Harmony Books, 1997.

Maurer, Robert. *One Small Step Can Change Your Life: The Kaizen Way*. New York, NY: Workman Publishing Company, 2004.

Melody. *Love Is in the Earth*. Wheat Ridge, CO: Earth-Love Publishing House, 1995.

Millman, Dan. *No Ordinary Moments*. Tiburon, CA: H. J. Kramer Inc., 1992.

Millman, Dan. *Way of the Peaceful Warrior*. Tiburon, CA: H. J. Kramer Inc., 1980.

Quinn, Daniel. *Ishmael*. New York, NY: Bantam Books, 1992.

Roman, Sanaya. *Spiritual Growth: Being Your Higher Self*. Tiburon, CA: H. J. Kramer Inc., 1989.

Schucman, Helen and William Thetford. *A Course in Miracles*. Mill Valley, CA: Foundation for Inner Peace, 1976.

Tolle, Eckhart. *The Power of Now*. Novato, CA: New World Library, 1999.

Walsch, Neale Donald. *Conversations with God: An Uncommon Dialogue*. New York, NY: Hampton Roads Publishing Inc., 1995.

Walsch, Neale Donald. *The Little Soul and the Earth*. Charlottesville, VA: Hampton Roads Publishing Inc., 2005.

Walsch, Neale Donald. *The Little Soul and the Sun*. Charlottesville, VA: Hampton Roads Publishing Inc., 1998.

Williamson, Marianne. *A Return to Love: Reflections on the Principles of a Course in Miracles*. New York, NY: HarperCollins Publishing Inc., 1992.

Zukav, Gary. *The Seat of the Soul*. New York, NY: Simon & Schuster Inc., 1989.